Self-Study and Diversity III

Inclusivity and Diversity in Teacher Education

Edited by

Julian Kitchen, Linda Fitzgerald and Deborah Tidwell

BRILL

LEIDEN | BOSTON

All chapters in this book have undergone peer review.

The Library of Congress Cataloging-in-Publication Data is available online at https://catalog.loc.gov

Typeface for the Latin, Greek, and Cyrillic scripts: "Brill". See and download: brill.com/brill-typeface.

ISSN 2542-9450
ISBN 978-90-04-50519-3 (paperback)
ISBN 978-90-04-50520-9 (hardback)
ISBN 978-90-04-50521-6 (e-book)

Copyright 2022 by Koninklijke Brill NV, Leiden, The Netherlands.
Koninklijke Brill NV incorporates the imprints Brill, Brill Nijhoff, Brill Hotei, Brill Schöningh, Brill Fink, Brill mentis, Vandenhoeck & Ruprecht, Böhlau Verlag and V&R Unipress.
All rights reserved. No part of this publication may be reproduced, translated, stored in a retrieval system, or transmitted in any form or by any means, electronic, mechanical, photocopying, recording or otherwise, without prior written permission from the publisher. Requests for re-use and/or translations must be addressed to Koninklijke Brill NV via brill.com or copyright.com.

This book is printed on acid-free paper and produced in a sustainable manner.

Professional Learning

Series Editor

J. John Loughran (*Monash University, Clayton, Australia*)

Editorial Board

Anthony Clarke (*University of British Columbia, Canada*)
Renee Clift (*University of Arizona, USA*)
Donald Freeman (*University of Michigan, USA*)
Ruth Kane (*Ottawa University, Canada*)
Mieke Lunenberg (*VU University, The Netherlands*)
Mo Ching Magdalena Mok (*Hong Kong Institute of Education, Hong Kong*)
Max van Manen (*University of Alberta, Canada*)

VOLUME 23

The titles published in this series are listed at *brill.com/prof*

Self-Study and Diversity III

Contents

List of Figures VII
Notes on Contributors VIII

1. Self-Studies in Diverse Voices for Inclusive Teacher Education 1
   Linda Fitzgerald, Julian Kitchen and Deborah Tidwell

2. Drawing on Privilege to Advance Social Justice: Reflections on My Identity and Practice as a Privileged Teacher Educator 16
   Julian Kitchen

3. A Tale of Becoming and Radiance: Our Evolving Teacher Educator Identities in Post-Apartheid South Africa 44
   Anita Hiralaal and Lungile Masinga

4. Wrestling with Dilemmas, Vulnerabilities, and Hopes: Being an Immigrant Mother and a Transnational Teacher Educator 61
   Jinhee Kim

5. Reconciling Knowledge: Experiences of Teacher Educators in Teaching through Integration and Playful Pedagogies 79
   Makie Kortjass and Nosipho Mbatha

6. Examining the Ethical Implications and Emotional Entailments of Teaching Indigenous Education: An Indigenous Educator's Self-Study 103
   Jennifer Markides

7. The Freedom to Be All at Once: My Journey from Literacy to Hip Hop Literacy 122
   Shuaib J. Meacham

8. Building the Boat with Funds of Knowledge: Metaphors of a Japanese Immigrant Educator at an Icelandic Preschool 145
   Megumi Nishida

9   Developing a Dialogic Space for Moving towards Critical Multicultural Education: A Collective Self-Study   165
    Gunnhildur Óskarsdóttir and Karen Rut Gísladóttir

10 A Racialized Canadian Professor's Self Study: Teaching about Multiculturalism during the Trump Era   186
    Manu Sharma

11 Navigating Shifting Waters: Reflections from a Critical Anti-Racist Teacher Educator   210
    Leanne Taylor

    Index   237

Figures

5.1 Grass basket bowls.   87
5.2 Traditional necklaces and bracelets.   88
5.3 Preservice teachers engaged in a discussion of the traditional necklace.   89
5.4 Participants playing Korobela.   90
5.5 Participants playing ibhasi lamanesi.   91
5.6 The concept map developed by Makie.   92
5.7 The concept map developed by Nosipho.   93
5.8 The concept map depicting the consolidated themes.   94

Notes on Contributors

Linda Fitzgerald
is an emerita professor of Early Childhood Education at the University of Northern Iowa. In retirement she is an active member of the campus advisory board for the Iowa Regents' Center for Early Developmental Education at UNI. In her teaching career, she prepared preservice teachers to accept into their early childhood classroom communities a wide variety of children, with a focus on the inclusion of individuals with disabilities. She took particular delight in working with practitioners who were becoming teachers of teachers in the EdD program. She also supervised practicing teachers as they found problems in their practice to research for their master's degrees. In both programs she taught self-study methods such as those in proceedings and books she has co-edited and to which she has contributed, such as *Research Methods for the Self-Study of Practice*, *Learning Communities in Practice*, both self-study handbooks, and the *Self-Study and Diversity* series, for which this is the third volume.

Karen Rut Gísladóttir
is a professor at the School of Education at the University of Iceland. She is a former elementary teacher. Her PhD thesis was a teacher research where she explored her own practice to understand how she could base students' learning on their linguistic and cultural resources. Karen's research interest is in sociocultural and critical perspectives on language and literacy and multicultural education. Her research methodology is teacher research, qualitative and art-based research methods, and self-study. She is one of the authors of the book *Collaboration, Narrative, and Inquiry That Honor the Complexity of Teacher Education* published by Information Age Publishing.

Anita Hiralaal
is a lecturer in Accounting at the School of Education, Indumiso Campus, Durban University of Technology. She has a PhD in Teacher Development Studies from the University of KwaZulu-Natal. Anita has been involved in teacher education for many years and enjoys teaching Accounting. As part of her doctoral studies, she adopted an arts-based self-study methodological approach and used many arts-based research approaches in her study. This prompted her to incorporate the arts into her Accounting Pedagogy teaching with excellent results. She has also co-authored book chapters and has written a few journal articles on narrative self-study and arts-based self-study. Anita has some novel, exciting and non-conventional ideas to share about the arts in education.

NOTES ON CONTRIBUTORS IX

Jinhee Kim
(PhD) is an associate professor in the Department of Elementary and Early Childhood Education at Kennesaw State University, Georgia, USA. She received her PhD in early childhood education from the University of Georgia. Her intertwined research areas include immigrant children and families, children in poverty (especially, children experiencing homelessness), marginalized children's voices in the curriculum, and culturally relevant qualitative research methods. Her works have been published in several journals, such as *Qualitative Inquiry, Studying Teacher Education, Early Childhood Education Journal, Journal of Early Childhood Teacher Education, Journal of Research in Childhood Education*, and *Journal of Early Childhood Research*.

Julian Kitchen
is a professor in the faculty of education at Brock University. He is the lead editor of *International Handbook of Self-Study of Teaching and Teacher Education Practices (Second Edition)*; *Writing as a Method for the Self-Study of Practice*; *Mindful and Relational Approaches to Social Justice, Equity and Diversity in Teacher Education*; *Narrative Inquiries into Curriculum-making in Teacher Education*; *Self-Study and Diversity II*; and *Canadian Perspectives on the Self-Study of Teacher Education Practices*. In addition, he is the author of *Relational Teacher Education* and lead author of *Professionalism, Law and the Ontario Educator*. Professor Kitchen is co-editor of *Studying Teacher Education* journal and editor for Springer's Self-Study of Teaching and Teacher Education Practices series.

Makie Kortjass
is a lecturer in the Early Childhood Education discipline in the School of Education at the University of KwaZulu-Natal, South Africa. Her areas of expertise include an integrated learning approach in early childhood mathematics teacher education, arts-based self-study, and playing games for understanding mathematics. Makie's current work involves lecturing in the early childhood undergraduate programme and supervising postgraduate students. She has been instrumental in developing the Bachelor of Education Early Childhood Care and Education (B.ED. ECCE) programme at UKZN. She is also involved in nationwide programmes initiated by the Department of Higher Education and Training (DHET) in partnership with the European Union (EU), in which universities work on essential common standards and materials to prepare teachers of mathematics in primary schools.

Jennifer Markides
(PhD) is a member of the Métis Nation of Alberta and an assistant professor in the Werklund School of Education at the University of Calgary. Her research

focuses on the holistic wellbeing of youth and Indigenous education. She values community-based partnerships that prioritize ethical relationships and reciprocity. Reconciliation is at the heart of her work, where understanding colonial legacies and truths predicates readiness for responsible action-taking and respectful relationship-building towards systemic and societal change.

Lungile Masinga
is a senior lecturer in Curriculum and Education Studies and has also worked in the Gender and Education discipline at the University of KwaZulu-Natal (UKZN) in South Africa. Her academic work focuses on gender and sexuality education. Methodologically, her work has contributed to the scholarship on collaborative memory-work, oral storytelling with teachers, and self-study research inquiry. She is also a member of the Self-Reflexive Methodologies Special Interest Group of the South African Educational Research Association. She is one of the guest editors in a special issue of *Alternation* on "Narratives of Social Cohesion and Academic Identities in Higher Education."

Nosipho Mbatha
is an academic in the Creative Arts discipline at the School of Education, University of KwaZulu-Natal, South Africa. She is also a doctoral student, who is at an advanced stage of her analysis. In her doctoral project she researches the integration of playful pedagogy for learning at higher education, for teacher-educators and preservice teachers. Her research interests extend collaborative work with other emerging scholars using arts-based self-reflexive methodologies to understand themselves better as academics and improve their professional practice. She is currently a candidate in the Accelerated Academic Leadership Development Program (AALDP), which awarded her the opportunity to attend Teachers College, Columbia University as a visiting scholar.

Shuaib J. Meacham
is an associate professor of Literacy Education at the University of Northern Iowa whose work examines the intersections of Literacy, race, and popular culture, specifically the learning dynamics of Hip Hop Culture. He is the co-director and founder of Hip Hop Literacy 319, a program that uses enthusiasm for Hip Hop Culture to improve their literacy skills and to prepare them for professional work environments. Hip Hop Literacy began in the early 2000s at the University of Delaware wherein high school graduates in the program boasted a 100% college attendance rate. Dr. Meacham originates from Canton, Ohio and carries out a family legacy of educational accomplishment with his wife Dr. Soh Meacham and his children, Aisha, Karis, Sabina, and James Jr. More can be learned about Dr. Meacham and his work at www.Hiphopliteracy319.com

Megumi Nishida

is a practitioner of the Icelandic early childhood pedagogical approach *Hjallastefnan* (The Hjalli model) and PhD candidate at the University of Iceland. Originally coming from Japan, her doctoral study explores her professional identity transformation from an immigrant educator to hybrid educator though self-study of her practice. In the chapter she contributed to the *International Handbook of Self-Study of Teaching and Teacher Education Practices* (2nd ed.), Megumi investigated the latest self-study movement in Japan which positioned herself as a critical friend to Japanese educators for an educational change. With her hybridity, she connects S-STEP and Japanese teacher educators' community.

Gunnhildur Óskarsdóttir

is a professor of Education at the School of Education, University of Iceland. She was the Head of Faculty of Teacher Education from 2013–2017. She did her master's degree from Aberdeen University, Scotland and her PhD from University of Iceland. Her research interests include children's learning and concept development, classroom research and teacher education and professional development. She has presented papers and research results on these issues. In recent years her interest and research focus has been on multicultural issues in teacher eucation and on how self-study can support teacher educators to generate change in their own teaching.

Manu Sharma

is an assistant professor at Thompson Rivers University in the Faculty of Education and Social Work, where she teaches foundational courses in the Masters of Education program. Dr. Sharma has previously taught a variety of undergraduate and graduate courses and supported field placements at University of Wisconsin-River Falls, Brock University, University of Toronto, and University of Windsor; in addition, she worked for the Toronto District School Board and in international settings as a public educator. She recently published a co-authored book, *Educators for Diverse Classrooms: A Case Study Approach to Equity and Inclusion in Education* (Rowman & Littlefield, 2020).

Leanne Taylor

is an associate professor in the Faculty of Education at Brock University, Canada. Her teaching is situated in the area of social justice, equity and activism in education and spans undergraduate, teacher education, and graduate levels. Her teaching and research explore the interrelationship between pedagogy, race, and identity and offers insight into the theoretical, social, and political tensions that inform equity education in K-12 and in postsecondary contexts.

Deborah Tidwell
is an emerita professor of Literacy Education in the Department of Curriculum and Instruction at the University of Northern Iowa. Dr. Tidwell's work focuses on assessment and evaluation of literacy, the implementation of effective instructional practices and interventions, and bilingual education methods and appropriate instructional practice for English language learners. Dr. Tidwell is active in the self-study research community where she has published books and articles related to self-study research and has served as the chair for the Self-Study of Teacher Education Practices SIG of the American Educational Research Association. At the university, she has served as the coordinator for the Literacy Education Program, director of the UNI Reading Clinic, director of the Jacobson Center for Comprehensive Literacy, department head for Curriculum and Instruction, and Associate Dean for the College of Education. Dr. Tidwell has been involved in federal, state, and privately funded projects for the preparation of bilingual classroom teachers for the state of Iowa, and professional development in comprehensive literacy instruction for in-service teachers working with children with significant disabilities.

CHAPTER 1

Self-Studies in Diverse Voices for Inclusive Teacher Education

Linda Fitzgerald, Julian Kitchen and Deborah Tidwell

This third edited volume of *Self-Study and Diversity* was written during a period of world-wide racial reckoning. It is being published in the midst of a global COVID-19 pandemic that directed a floodlight on inequities between those with privilege and those without. Vaccinations will soon protect the majority of people in Western (predominantly White) nations, but the rest of the world, which will also bear the brunt of climate change, may take years to reach similar rates of protection. Within countries too, there are enormous racial disparities in health care during the pandemic. At the time of publication, it will be a year since Donald Trump was defeated in his run for a second term as president of the United States. This marks the end of four years of nativist divisive racial policies, but the populist forces that led to Trump's rise remain strong in the United States. Other countries in Europe, along with Brazil and India, have democracies threatened by authoritarian politics pitting groups of citizens against each other.

This volume, *Self-Study and Diversity III: Inclusivity and Diversity in Teacher Education*, is a hopeful offering intended to move forward the conversation toward social justice in teaching and teacher education. All the authors use self-study methodology as a means to improve teaching practices by studying their own practice in collaboration with others, using a variety of qualitative research methods, while attending to rigor and trustworthiness (Mena & Russell, 2017). We have retained the series title, *Self-Study and Diversity*, and added a subtitle focus on inclusion, to maintain continuity across the three volumes. We invite readers to continue to consult the first two volumes in the series, as the authors' voices and their topics remain timely. We leave it to future authors and to the next generation of editors to go beyond diversity, equity and inclusion to dig deeper into social justice issues.

1   The Before Times

The first volume began as a way for Castle Conference participants (Tidwell et al., 2004) who had addressed diversity issues to expand their presentations and to get wider recognition by publishing a book chapter (Tidwell & Fitzgerald, 2006). Ten years later, Julian Kitchen proposed to the two co-editors at an AERA conference that it was time for a second volume. *Self-Study and Diversity II: Inclusive Teacher Education for a Diverse World* (Kitchen, Tidwell & Fitzgerald, 2016) went beyond AERA and Castle Conference presenters to include new voices. As the co-editors became more senior scholars, we felt called to offer a third volume five years later as a way to lift up and recognize voices of the Black, Indigenous, and Scholars of Color who are taking on the task of teaching the teachers for a new and rapidly diversifying world of education.

In the second volume, the editors had traced a history of self-studies addressing issues of diversity, increasingly by scholars who represented first languages other than English, and identities other than White male or female. We lamented that "social justice is still a ways from the center of discourse in the self-study of teacher education practices" (Kitchen, Fitzgerald & Tidwell, 2016, p. 8). In the meantime, a new handbook of self-study has come out (Kitchen et al., 2020), in which one of six sections is devoted to teaching for social justice, and another section takes self-study across cultures and languages.

In the chapter in the new handbook that traces self-studies presented at the biennial conferences held at Herstmonceux Castle (Garbett et al., 2020), diversity was one of three threads that emerged from a close reading of more than 700 papers, from 1996 through 2018. The Castle Conferences are held at the Bader International Study Centre (BISC), which reflects the donor family, the Baders,' "'commitment to offering students a challenging global education infused with social justice, a thirst for knowledge, and civic responsibility.'[1] It is a vision that informs the ethos inherent at the Castle Conferences" (p. 20). And social justice is indeed a goal for many self-studies, in the sense of "enabling preservice teachers to interact with pupils of diverse cultural, ethnic, or racial backgrounds in respectful and supportive ways" (p. 34). In concluding the discussion of that thread, the authors pointed out that

> diversity within the context of self-study research contains a broad range of meanings that is difficult to contain within clearly defined parameters. Self-study researchers are focused on many aspects of diversity because understanding our students and the students they will eventually teach is crucial to building the positive relationships necessary for optimal learning. … the self-study research that has been presented at the Castle Conference over the years has been focused on understanding teacher education practice, including all of the people involved in that practice, in order to improve it. (p. 41)

While social justice may not yet be central to Castle Conference presentations, the whole section on social justice in the new handbook goes beyond diversity writ large to foreground the social justice that caused push-back against a focus on diversity as a conference theme around the beginning of the 21st century (Kitchen, Fitzgerald & Tidwell, 2016). Introducing the social justice section, Monica Taylor and Michael Diamond (2020) declared, "Our intention for this chapter is to encourage the S-STEP community to increase their explicit commitment to social justice, embrace a more political stance, and ultimately engage in self-studies that result in social action and change" (p. 512). Complementing the analysis of Castle Conference papers that contributed to the diversity theme in the Garbett et al. (2020) handbook chapter, Taylor and Diamond dug deeper to find explicit treatments of social justice in self-studies, not only at Castle Conferences, but also in the self-study journal, *Studying Teacher Education*. They also honored us with reviews of the first two volumes of *Self-Study and Diversity,* together with their own volume on gender, feminism, and queer theory (Taylor & Coia, 2014):

> How can we impact and transform pedagogy, curriculum, and school structures to be more equitable, to open spaces for and elicit the voices of those who are so often invisible and voiceless, and to use our scholarly platform as a means of partnering with those who are othered and collaboratively working toward change and transformation? (Taylor & Diamond, 2020, p. 511)

With that introduction, how could we not take up the question with which they challenged us all?

The hegemony of English-speaking academics among self-study scholars is evident in the new handbook chapter, "Who Does Self-study and Why?" by Brandon Butler and Angela Branyon (2020), who reviewed 228 articles in the journal, *Studying Teacher Education*, from its inception in 2005 to 2017. They found:

> During its history, the editors of the journal have remained firmly international, representing Australia, Canada, and the Netherlands. The editorial board is international in scope with current representation from the Netherlands, New Zealand, Spain, the United Kingdom, and the United States, while the International Advisory Board is just as diverse, with additional members representing Iceland and Israel, in addition to those countries already noted. However, through our review we found that the

> authorship within the journal represents a less internationally diverse perspective and is dominated by small numbers of individual authors and institutions. ... Five English-speaking nations (Australia, Canada, New Zealand, the United Kingdom, and the United States) account for 88.7% of authors published and 83.1% of institutions published in *Studying Teacher Education*. (p. 139)

Lynn Thomas and Hafdis Guðjónsdóttir (2020) introduced the section of the new handbook that sought to challenge the English-dominant hegemony by giving a scholarly platform to those for whom English is not a first language:

> Conceptions, views, and beliefs have linguistic distinctions and are culturally located and expressed through the common language of a society. Therefore it is important to pay attention to language and culture when considering self-study research, which has strong contextual links and is often very personal. ... to turn the focus toward an exploration [of] this experience of translating and transforming self-study to fit with local contexts, languages, and cultures. (p. 1326)

Lest diversity be seen as "less than" a dominant standard, or social justice be seen as noblesse oblige toward the less privileged, Thomas and Guðjónsdóttir (2020) brought together international scholars to enrich and grow self-study scholarship:

> Listening to the voices of how different groups of people in different contexts have overcome challenges and found ways to improve their practice as well as make the process work within their linguistic and cultural communities can help us all learn more about what makes self-study so effective. (p. 1328)

2   The Genesis of Self-Study and Diversity III

The editors of this volume were actively involved in the preparation of the *International Handbook of Self-Study of Teaching and Teacher Education Practices* (2nd ed.) (Kitchen et al., 2020) as lead editor and chapter authors. In 2018, before we began to invite authors to write chapters for *Self-Study and Diversity III*, we noticed from our preliminary reviews of the self-study literature for our handbook chapters, that there remained a dearth of Castle Conference papers and *Studying Teacher Education* articles from racialized teacher educators. We decided that we could use our influence as senior scholars, as we did in the second volume of this series, to advance diverse and emerging voices in our field. In their handbook chapter, Taylor and Diamond (2020) described them as "so often invisible and voiceless" (p. 513), while Thomas and Guðjónsdóttir (2020), in their chapter, argued that one of our objectives as a scholarly community should be to "become truly international, a perspective where connections between people of every nation are emphasized and collaboration and support can lead to improvement in teacher education across national and linguistic boundaries" (p. 1330).

In 2019, when invited authors began to write their chapters, COVID-19 had not become a pandemic, and George Floyd was still alive and unknown to the world. By the time the world began to shut down and to go into quarantine against the coronavirus disease, a number of the chapters had been completed. Those that were not complete often required extensions. In some cases, the pandemic required extra resources of energy and attention for pivoting to online or hybrid teaching, both at work and for family members at home. While this affected many authors, the challenges were particularly acute for those from racialized communities. For others, the trauma caused by racial conflicts in the Trump era made writing difficult, with the murder of George Floyd by a Minneapolis police officer being a major flashpoint in 2020. These authors had to support their own communities, speak out as scholars, and attend to their own emotions while trying to find the time and energy to write their truths for their chapters in this volume. None of the authors needed a pandemic or global racial reckoning to inspire their work – all were already recognized in self-study for diversity-related scholarship. A few, in revisions if not in their initial writing, addressed events of 2020. However, an explicit connection is not needed for every one of these chapters to serve teachers and teacher educators who seek to improve their teaching in these times.

As the coronavirus disease spread and countries shut down, Arundhati Roy (2020) issued a challenge:

> Historically, pandemics have forced humans to break with the past and imagine their world anew. This one is no different. It is a portal, a gateway between one world and the next. We can choose to walk through it, dragging the carcasses of our prejudice and hatred, our avarice, our data banks and dead ideas, our dead rivers and smoky skies behind us. Or we can walk through lightly, with little luggage, ready to imagine another world. And ready to fight for it. (p. 112)

Even more than the editors could foresee as we began to invite authors to share their wisdom about teaching for diversity, the authors of the chapters in this volume are "ready to imagine another world." And going beyond just teaching for diversity to teaching for social justice, we all – readers and writers – also need "to use our scholarly platform as a means of partnering with those who are othered and collaboratively working toward change and transformation" (Taylor & Diamond, 2020, p. 511), that is, to be ready to fight for it.

Leanne Taylor's chapter in this volume contains examples of some of the social justice responses to the murder of George Floyd while the pandemic focused attention on its coverage beyond what similar murders had commanded, such as huge increases in sales of anti-racism literature and re-evaluations by teachers and other citizens about how to address systemic inequities. However, as documented by historians (e.g., Alexander, 2010/2015), sociologists (e.g., Kendi, 2019), and others (e.g., Hannah-Jones, 2019), to name a few of those anti-racism sources so widely read in the summer and fall of 2020, each advance in social justice in the United States (Emancipation Proclamation in the 1860s Civil War, Civil Rights legislation in the 1960s) has been followed by a reaction that reinstated White supremacy (Reconstruction of the South ending with Jim Crow laws, and the New Jim Crow post-Civil Rights era). And even as the summer of 2020's wide-spread racial reckoning seemed to be bending the arc of history toward justice, to paraphrase Martin Luther King, Jr., the reaction began. First with federal agency professional development trainings, then with what teachers and state-level agencies could say about racism and sexism, as of this writing attempts are ongoing to stop anti-racist education by forbidding teaching about racism.

As final drafts of chapters arrived, and formatting to publisher specifications proceeded apace, Linda and Deborah (the two editors who reside in the state of Iowa in the United States) had to deal with the reality that their state was one of fifteen in which legislators and governors strove to have their states implement the failed policies of the defeated President Trump. To our mind, these states were approaching the pandemic portal "dragging the carcasses of our prejudice and hatred" (Roy, 2020, p. 112). Perhaps of most direct consequence to teachers, in the last months of his presidency, Donald Trump issued an Executive Order "to combat offensive and anti-American race and sex stereotyping and scapegoating" (Exec. Order No. 13950, 2020). He used anti-discrimination language to do the opposite, to maintain discrimination in favor of White privilege, and "to rally the Republican base – to push back against the recent reexaminations of the role that slavery and segregation have played in American history and the attempts to redress those historical offenses" (Harris, 2021). Even though Trump's federal level Executive Order was promptly rescinded by incoming President Joseph Biden, its power of prohibition has been shifted into the language of the bills in these fifteen states (Zinn Education Project, 2021a). And one of those bills was passed and signed into law in our state of Iowa.

As Seattle high school teacher Jesse Hagopian explained in an interview on television:

> I think that one of the greatest educators of our nation was actually the uprising that happened from the spring and summer in the wake of the killings of Breonna Taylor and George Floyd, you know, that really increased the number of teachers and inspired so many more educators to begin teaching for social justice. And I think that's really what's driving these bills across the country. They wouldn't be trying to ban the teaching of structural racism if there weren't so many teachers interested in joining the struggle and the Black Lives Matter at School movement. (Zinn Education Project, 2021b)

Putting into the context of this book the prohibitions now signed into law in the state of Iowa, co-editors Deborah and Linda (had they not recently retired) could be subjected to legal action for teaching in ways described by four Canadian authors in this volume: Julian Kitchen, Leanne Taylor, Manu Sharma, Jennifer Markides. All of them teach teachers to better serve the wide diversity of students in their future or current classrooms by exposing them to what could be experienced as uncomfortable truths. The Iowa law (not yet in state code) forbids a teacher to teach in any way:

> 7 (8) That any individual should feel discomfort, guilt,
> 8 anguish, or any other form of psychological distress on account
> 9 of that individual's race or sex. (Iowa House File 802, March 16, 2021, p. 3, ll. 7–9)

As the legislators debated the bill, the only examples they gave as a rationale for the bill were of two White male college students "hurt" by efforts of their professors to teach concepts common to multicultural education. (When you read Manu Sharma's account of an encounter with a MAGA-hat-wearing student, while a professor in the US Midwest, consider what the student might have been able to do had he been able to invoke such a law against her teaching).

As court challenges to the legality of these bills proceed, their vague wording and difficult to specify enforcement mechanisms may well lead to them being struck down. In the meantime, teachers may just self-censor and use the law to avoid having to teach hard history, or to avoid unpleasant questions if not reprimands from administrators or students' parents. On the other hand, history and social studies teachers across the USA, whether in one of the states with such legislation or not, are taking pledges to "Teach the Truth" (Wong & Richards, 2021). Those are the very classroom teachers that teacher educators who teach for social justice might hope to claim.

This extended legislative account, so specific to the United States, hopefully serves to provide more context for what is at stake in the chapters in this volume. As Taylor and Diamond (2020) declared in the introduction to the social justice section of the new international handbook, "Social justice work is challenging, emotionally taxing, and at times risky" (p. 512). While only two of our authors work in the United States, contexts of reconciliation in South Africa, or hyphenated identities of teachers in Canada and Iceland, or multicultural education taught anywhere to dominant groups can be equally risky.

3 Imagining the World Anew with Models from Our Authors

After a gestation period stretched out by the exigencies of the global pandemic, we are excited to get these brave voices a wider audience. While they each tell their stories for themselves, marking what they have learned about improving their practice, we need to honor their stories of practice by listening deeply and hearing each story for its application to ourselves (Miller et al., 2002).

We begin with Julian Kitchen's chapter, "Drawing on Privilege to Advance Social Justice." Whereas Julian wrote through his identity as a queer teacher educator in the second volume in this series (Kitchen, 2016), he writes here from his positionality as a White male. We see this chapter as an extension of the editors' perspectives as older White self-study scholars attempting to make the world a better place by educating ourselves and listening to the voices of others. And, like Julian, we attempt to do this with critical humility:

> The more I come to know about teacher education and social justice, the simpler my understanding becomes. In particular, I have come to know that the tone we set in our classes is crucial to imparting understanding. The tone that has worked for me as a relatively privileged teacher educator is one of critical humility towards both the minoritized and marginalized and to teacher candidates who need to consider and reconsider their positionality and privilege. (see Chapter 2, this volume)

Given the demographics of teacher education in the Western world, we are expecting that many if not most of our readers will be members of a White majority, as will be their students. Understanding the perspectives from Black, Indigenous, People of Color and other marginalized groups is crucial for developing empathy and understanding but, according to Wilkerson (2020):

> Empathy … commonly viewed as … imagining how you would feel [is simply] not enough in the ruptured world we live in …. Radical empathy, on the other hand, means putting in the work to educate oneself and to listen with a humble heart to understand another's experience from their perspective, not as we imagine we would feel. Radical empathy is not about you and what you think you would do in a situation you have never been in and perhaps never will. It is the kindred connection from a place of deep knowing that opens your spirit to the pain of another as they perceive it …. [And even that] is no substitute for experience itself. (p. 386)

The first two volumes of *Self-study and Diversity* were organized thematically, the first one by research methods used; the second volume had one section of critical autobiographical self-studies, another section of self-study in diverse cultural settings, and a final section more explicitly oriented to social justice. In this third volume, we have self-study chapters that use a variety of methods in ways that do not fit them neatly into one kind of method. Themes also cross chapters, a kind of intersectionality, if you will. Therefore we decided, rather than categorizing chapters into mutually exclusive sections, that we would resort to simple alphabetical order by first author's last name, a common form of organization used in many Castle Conference volumes, for the rest of the chapters. In this introductory chapter, we identify and discuss some of the themes braided through the chapters as a guide to help you pick where to go in your exploration of these diverse authors and self-study chapters.

3.1   Identity

While the hegemony of the United States is represented in APA style and Webster's Dictionary spellings, the identities of the chapter authors are much more diverse than the "older White ladies," editors Linda and Deborah, who invited contributions. Two American authors speak from racialized experiences: Meacham describing Hip Hop Literacy as an alternative to a dominant school experience that can be alienating to racialized students, and Kim sharing the effects on families of failing to partner with them or to use culturally situated and informed assessments of young dual language learners.

Four Canadian authors are deeply committed to teaching not just for diversity but in working for social justice, with hyphenated identities providing powerful, if vulnerable, models. Kitchen uses his White male privilege to respectfully build a safe environment for privileged White future teachers to remove barriers to becoming teachers for social justice, using his own minoritized status as a queer teacher educator to model vulnerability. He and Sharma served as critical friends for each other's chapters, challenging each other with differing perspectives. Sharma's positions, both racialized and an immigrant from Canada to a Midwestern US state, made her particularly vulnerable. She was hired to teach required multiculturalism courses to reluctant students in the context of virulent White supremacy rhetoric during President Trump's term in office. Her case presents a strong example of the fact that "[s]ocial justice work is challenging, emotionally taxing, and at times risky" (Taylor & Diamond, 2020, p. 512), especially so when administrators fail to support the untenured faculty of color to whom they give one of the hardest courses to teach during a resurgence of White supremacy.

Perhaps at the greatest disadvantage would be Taylor, were she not teaching in Canada rather than in one of the US states with new legal prohibitions against teaching Critical Race Theory or legal punishment for any teacher who causes discomfort or psychological distress in learners with content addressing race or gender. While tenured, unlike Sharma during her time in the Midwest, and therefore not at risk of losing her position, Taylor too, as a multiracial Black woman, could be emotionally taxed, if not sometimes physically threatened, by the resistance of White American students to addressing their privileges. Taylor and Sharma's commitment to pedagogy that furthers social justice, and not just that teaches content about diversity, empowers them to continue to fight institutional racism and inequities. Markides, as an Indigenous woman teaching Indigenous education courses that make her racialized identity even more visible to her students, is vulnerable too. She would be at risk in a US state where students would be likely to experience distress as they learn for the first time about atrocities committed in the name of assimilation to their own settler culture. Like South African professors, she serves a Truth and Reconciliation goal; like Kitchen, she works hard to do so respectfully, using relational pedagogy. She draws strength from the ethical dimensions of her teaching.

Two pairs of South African teacher educators represent post-apartheid socio-political complexities of identity development and of the needs of their students – and indeed, they themselves – who suffer still from the legacy of apartheid education. Hiralaal, neither White nor Black and raised in a tightly segregated South Asian community with a history of indentured servitude, and Masinga, growing up during a most tumultuous time of violent reaction to a demeaning Bantu Education System, helped each other to see how their identities as teachers had developed and were still evolving. Kortjass and Mbatha work for social justice by addressing the language barriers that prevent their majority Black students from fully engaging their academic challenges.

Using Indigenous arts, they make learning more accessible for early childhood teacher candidates by integrating math with familiar crafts (Kortjass) and for creative arts teacher education students by engaging them in playful pedagogy with familiar group games (Mbatha).

Two chapters are written by teachers in Iceland, one by an immigrant from Japan, Nishida, and one by Oskarsdottir and Gisladottir describing a collaboration among 5 immigrant teacher educators and 9 colleagues with Icelandic heritage. Unlike chapter authors from North America or South Africa, minorities in Iceland are free from long and violent legacies of slavery, colonialism, and segregation on that island. And yet, language barriers and cultural differences are requiring more multicultural education in teacher preparation courses there too. As with all the other chapter authors, the ones in Iceland see difference as a strength rather than a deficit, and value the contributions made by new citizens from outside of Iceland, a value they want to be sure to inculcate in future teachers.

Much in evidence across these chapters is intersectionality. In a seminal work often cited as the source of the concept, Crenshaw (1991) not only argued against looking at the effects of either race or gender in isolation, or even just race and gender together: "My focus on the intersections of race and gender only highlights the need to account for multiple grounds of identity when considering how the social world is constructed" (p. 1246). All but two chapters are written by women, and nine are also women of color. In addition, three had immigrant status at the time they were writing, amplifying challenges posed by both race and gender. Kim and Taylor each write explicitly about their intersectional identities, and Kitchen uses tensions in his own categories of identity to support the intersectional identities of his students.

3.2 *Career Stages and Teaching Backgrounds*

Besides a range of geographic and disciplinary identities, the chapter authors represent a wide variety of career stages, from doctoral students who are experienced teachers, through all the stages of academic rank up to full professors with international leadership in self-study. They bring to their teaching of future teachers and of other practicing teachers a similarly wide range of age of students with whom they have worked. Nishida, for example, is nearing the end of her doctoral studies, while working as an early childhood educator in a preschool. Others have finished their doctorates while writing these chapters and anticipate more secure teacher education positions. Sharma has returned to Canada, to a tenure-track position, where she continues her work on social justice. Some have been promoted to associate or full professor while writing their chapters. Further along the spectrum of rank, Kitchen has taken on a variety of leadership roles in the Self-Study of Teacher Education, including editing the journal *Studying Teacher Education*, through which he can encourage teaching and scholarship for social justice. And the other co-editors, Fitzgerald and Tidwell, have recently achieved the status of Emerita Professor upon retirement from teacher education careers that encompassed the founding and growth of the Self-Study of Teacher Education Practices Special Interest Group in the American Educational Research Association and the biennial Castle Conferences.

3.3 Methods Employed

No account of a collection of self-studies would be complete without attention to the variety of methods used. In describing the power of counter-narratives, Taylor and Diamond (2020) wrote, "Within the context of addressing social justice issues, opening up and expanding spaces to include diverse voices, perspectives, and narratives that disrupt and challenge the status quo is paramount" (p. 526). Narrative methods prevail in the chapters in this volume, including the autobiographical approach of Meacham, deep description of Sharma, narrative inquiry of Kitchen, and innovative "mindful walk" and metaphor construction of Nishida. Hiralaal and Masinga employ the decolonizing narrative of storywork, while Taylor and Kim specifically invoke counter-storytelling. Kitchen, Kim and Markides use a variety of methods to engage their data in addition to narrative.

Arts-based methods can overcome some of the limitations of text in a dominant language for non-native speakers, both in teaching learners from preschool through higher education faculty levels and in generating and analyzing data in self-study. Kortjass and Mbatha, in an effort to overcome language barriers for their South African teacher education students, used Indigenous crafts and games to implement integrated curriculum in math and playful pedagogy in creative arts, while having the arts also inform their collaborative study. Oskarsdottir and Gisladottir introduced sculpture and poetry as methods to generate the dialogue about improving the practice of multicultural education among 14 faculty colleagues, and they also used the created products to support their data analysis process. For Meacham, Black music provided a powerful vehicle for reinventing literacy for students and for framing his autobiographical inquiry. Film played a similar role for Markides, while metaphor was both text and art in Nishida's self-study of her hybrid identity and teaching.

4   Concluding Invitation to the Reader

The powerful accounts by the diverse set of authors in *Self-Study and Diversity III* demonstrate that diversity is a strength. We trust our readers will respond to the urgent calls in the chapters to both build back a better world on the other side of the pandemic portal and build a new world in which diversity is seen as a strength and social justice is a priority. We hope that critical humility and radical empathy will guide privileged readers to use their voices and roles in education to advocate for equity and justice. As we close our trilogy, we look forward to future volumes edited by racialized education scholars on equity, diversity, and social justice.

While we as educators are inspired by lofty visions, we conduct our work alongside small groups of colleagues and classes of students. It is in our work with them that we influence lives, a few at a time. Please take at least one practice from each chapter that you read and find a way to implement it in your own classroom. Use self-study methods to improve your use of those practices. Document your stories and share them with others in conferences and in print. These self-study accounts can help improve teaching practices for all learners, and especially for those facing the most challenges.

Note

1   https://www.queensu.ca/bisc/about-us/heritage/

References

Alexander, M. (2015). *The new Jim Crow: Mass incarceration in the age of colorblindness* [Narrated by K. Chilton]. Recorded Books. (Original work published 2010)

Butler, B. M., & Branyon, A. (2020). Who does self-study and why? In J. Kitchen, A. Berry, S. M. Bullock, A. R. Crowe, M. Taylor, H. Guðjónsdóttir, & L. Thomas (Eds.), *International handbook of self-study of teaching and teacher education practices* (2nd ed., pp. 135–176). Springer. https://doi.org/10.1007/978-981-13-6880-6-5

Crenshaw, K. W. (1991). Mapping the margins: Intersectionality, identity politics, and violence against women of color. *Stanford Law Review, 43*(6), 1241–1299.

Exec. Order No. 13950, 3 C.F.R. 60683 (2020). Retrieved June 13, 2021, from https://www.govinfo.gov/content/pkg/FR-2020-09-28/pdf/2020-21534.pdf

Garbett, D., Fitzgerald, L. M., & Thomas, L. (2020). Tracing self-study research through biennial Castle Conferences at Herstmonceux. In J. Kitchen, A. Berry, S. M. Bullock, A. R. Crowe, M. Taylor, H. Guðjónsdóttir, & L. Thomas (Eds.), *International handbook of self-study of teaching and teacher education practices* (2nd ed., pp. 15–55). Springer. https://doi.org/10.1007/978-981-13-1710-1_2-1

Hannah-Jones, N. (2019, August 18). Introduction: The 1619 project. *New York Times Magazine*, 14–26.

Harris, A. (2021). The GOP's "Critical Race Theory" obsession: How conservative politicians and pundits became fixated on an academic approach. *The Atlantic*. Retrieved June 13, 2021, from https://www.theatlantic.com/politics/archive/2021/05/gops-critical-race-theory-fixation-explained/618828/

Iowa House File 802 As amended and passed by the House March 16, 2021, p. 3, ll. 7–9. Retrieved June 12, 2021, from https://www.legis.iowa.gov/docs/publications/LGR/89/HF802.pdf

Kendi, I. X. (2019). *How to be an anti-racist*. One World.

Kitchen, J. (2016). Inside out: My identity as a queer teacher educator. In J. Kitchen, D. Tidwell, & L. Fitzgerald (Eds.), *Self-study and diversity II* (pp. 11–26). Sense.

Kitchen, J., Berry, A., Bullock, S. M., Crowe, A.R., Taylor, M., Guðjónsdóttir, M., & Thomas, L. (Eds.). (2020). *International handbook of self-study of teaching and teacher education practices* (2nd ed.). Springer.

Kitchen, J., Fitzgerald, L., & Tidwell, D. (2016). Self-Study and diversity: Looking back, looking forward. In J. Kitchen, D. Tidwell, & L. Fitzgerald (Eds.), *Self-study and diversity II: Inclusive teacher education for a diverse world* (pp. 1–10). Sense.

Kitchen, J., Tidwell, D., & Fitzgerald, L. (Eds.). (2016). *Self-study and diversity II: Inclusive teacher education for a diverse world*. Sense.

Mena, J., & Russell, T. (2017). Collaboration, multiple methods, trustworthiness: Issues arising from the 2014 International Conference on self-study of teacher education practices. *Studying Teacher Education, 13*(1), 105–122. https://doi.org/10.1080/17425964.2017.1287694

Miller, C., East, K., Fitzgerald, L., Heston, M., & Veenstra, T. (2002). Visions of self in the act of teaching: Using personal metaphors in collaborative selves study of teaching practices. *Teaching and Learning: The Journal of Natural Inquiry and Reflective Practice, 16*(3), 81–93.

Roy, A. (2020, April 3). The pandemic is a portal. *Financial Times*, 112. Retrieved June 13, 2021, from https://www.ft.com/content/10d8f5e8-74eb-11ea-95fe-fcd274e920ca#comments-anchor

Taylor, M., & Coia, L. (Eds.). (2014). *Gender, feminism, and queer theory in the self-study of teacher education practices*. Sense.

Taylor, M., & Diamond, M. (2020). The role of self-study in teaching and teacher education for social justice. In J. Kitchen, A. Berry, S. M. Bullock, A. R. Crowe, M. Taylor, H. Gudjonsdottir, & L. Thomas (Eds.), *International handbook of self-study of teaching and teacher education practices* (2nd ed., pp. 509–543). Springer. https://doi.org/10.1007/978-981-13-1710-1_16-1

Thomas, L., & Guðjónsdóttir, H. (2020). Self-study across languages and cultures. In J. Kitchen, A. Berry, S. M. Bullock, A. R. Crowe, M. Taylor, H. Guðjónsdóttir, & L. Thomas (Eds.), *International handbook of self-study of teaching and teacher education practices* (2nd ed., pp. 1325–1337). Springer. https://doi.org/10.1007/978-981-13-1710-1_44-2

Tidwell, D., & Fitzgerald, L. (Eds.). (2006). *Self-study and diversity*. Sense.

Tidwell, D., Fitzgerald, L. M., & Heston, M. (Eds.). (2004). *Journeys of hope: Risking self-study in a diverse world*. Proceedings of the Fifth International Conference on Self-Study of Teacher Education Practices, Herstmonceux Castle, East Sussex, England. University of Northern Iowa.

Wilkerson, I. (2020). *Caste: The origins of our discontents*. Random House.

Wong, A., & Richards, E. (2021, June 11). 'Children deserve to be taught': Teachers in 22 cities are planning protests over laws restricting racism lessons in schools. *USA Today*. Retrieved June 11, 2021, from https://www.usatoday.com/in-depth/news/education/2021/06/11/critical-race-theory-bills-nationwide-teacher-protests/7620025002/

Zinn Education Project. (2021a). *Bills against teaching history*. Retrieved June 10, 2021, from https://docs.google.com/document/d/1Ts5piNRFaQTLvG21tBbrppkfskHdjuxFDEKDRCC8dTY/edit#

Zinn Education Project. (2021b). *Jesse Hagopian on CBS news: Decries GOP attacks on teaching history*. Retrieved June 13, 2021, from https://www.zinnedproject.org/news/hagopian-on-cbs-news/

CHAPTER 2

Drawing on Privilege to Advance Social Justice

Reflections on My Identity and Practice as a Privileged Teacher Educator

Julian Kitchen

We live in a society in which opportunities and advantages are unevenly distributed. The term "privilege" has gained currency as a means for identifying unearned advantages conferred on particular groups. The terms "White privilege" and "male privilege," popularized through the work of Peggy McIntosh (1990), have heightened awareness of the myriad of implicit and hidden ways in which Whites and males remain advantaged in a society that professes equality under the law.

The Oxford English Dictionary defines privilege as a "special right, advantage, or immunity granted or available only to a particular person or group." It is "a built-in advantage, separate from one's level of income or effort" (Collins, 2018, p. 39) that confers greater power and resources to members of privileged groups. Those who are privileged in multiple ways are more likely to be successful in their careers and other endeavors. In the Privilege Walk,[1] a common activity in equity workshop, participants step forward or back based on their answers to questions related to privilege. Typically, able-bodied, straight, cis-gender White males from affluent families start their journey many steps ahead of, for example, inner-city African Americans.

The concept of privilege, particularly White privilege, has shed light on a fundamental underlying socio-political structure that hinders and, often, blocks the advancement of minoritized groups. McIntosh's (1990) image of "an invisible package of unearned assets" (p. 1) has raised awareness among both minority and majority members of taken-for-granted freedoms and immunities from harm. Yet the concept often meets resistance from those with relative privilege and anger from conservative groups (Pence & Fields, 1999).

In order for the relatively advantaged to understand social inequity and possible complicity in it, they need opportunities to explore the issue and reflect on their own identities, dispositions and experiences. In *The Unschooled Mind*, Howard Gardner (1991) argued that the intuitive conceptions of children are not dispelled by "the usual text-and-test setting" (p. 7) of primary and secondary education. These erroneous yet robust simplifications, stereotypes, and misconceptions need to be unlearned in order to educate for understanding.

Unschooled conceptions among teachers, especially those not educated in the social sciences and humanities, need to be engaged systematically through meaningful activities and thoughtfully reconsidered through careful critical analysis if people are to develop deeper understandings of equity, diversity and social justice. We need to appeal to their reason and humanity, rather than browbeat or dismiss them. Argument and persuasion too often shut down meaningful engagement by eliciting child-like emotions of resistance and resentment.

In my twenty years as a teacher educator, I have been very concerned with issues of social justice. I have long been aware of my identity and have written about my identity as a queer teacher educator (Kitchen, 2016a) and how my practice is informed by *relational teacher education* (e.g., Kitchen, 2005a, 2005b, 2016b). I have also reflected on how being a cis-gender, White, male professional has advantaged me, even as my sexual orientation partly undercuts masculine privilege (Kitchen, 2017). More recently, I have written about my relational approach to attending to the concerns of teacher candidates in a social justice course (Kitchen, 2020). Feedback from teacher candidates, as reported in this research, revealed that they identified the class as an open and safe space in which they could explore their privilege while increasing their awareness of social inequities in education.

In this chapter on teaching a social justice-oriented School and Society course to secondary school teacher candidates, I reflect more deeply on my own privilege and on the resistance to admitting privilege among teacher candidates. I explore how I draw on my identities to position myself as a teacher educator who can guide relatively privileged teacher candidates to unpack their advantages as an important stage in becoming respectful of diversity, understanding of the challenges faced by those who are less advantaged, and being open to applying inclusive principles and practices in their careers as teachers. At the same time, I acknowledge that I need to inquire more into how I address the needs of minoritized teacher candidates in my classes. Also, writing a handbook chapter titled "Preparing Preservice Teachers for Social Justice Teaching: Designing and Implementing Effective Interventions in Teacher Education" (Kitchen & Taylor, 2020) has helped me recognize that I could do more to challenge the White supremacy and ethnocentrism" that programs unconsciously "reinforce and reify" (Bazemore-Bertrand & Porcher, 2020, p. 73).

While I challenge the contemporary privilege discourse, I reject the complicity of "neutrality." As Freire (1995) wrote, "Washing one's hands of the conflict between the powerful and the powerless means to side with the powerful, not to be neutral" (Freire, 1995, p. 122). A stance of neutrality, as Taylor and

Diamond (2020) wrote, "naively disregards the ways in which injustice and inequity are normalized in schools and even teacher education programs" (p. 526). Teacher educators, the majority of whom are White and privileged (Kroll, 2006), need to expose teacher candidates to systemic oppression in a manner that is respectful and relational.

In order to engage teacher candidates in reflection on their positionality and privilege, it is important for teacher educators to focus on self-awareness and growth. "Our job," as Taylor and Diamond (2020) wrote, "is to offer them new ways of knowing and thinking that open potential avenues for change" (p. 528). Labelling or "imposing our political beliefs on our students does not in fact empower them" (p. 528).

1 Importance and Challenges of Teaching about Privilege

While the concept of privilege has existed for many years, the term gained currency thanks to an article by Peggy McIntosh (1990) titled, "White Privilege: Unpacking the Invisible Knapsack." This short piece, which has inspired numerous workshops on privilege, emerged from a realization that both males and White people often enjoy unacknowledged and unearned advantages thanks to invisible systems that confer advantage on particular groups. McIntosh wrote:

> I think whites are carefully taught not to recognize white privilege, as males are taught not to recognize male privilege. So I have begun in an untutored way to ask what it is like to have white privilege. I have come to see white privilege as an invisible knapsack of unearned assets that I can count on cashing in each day, but about which I was "meant" to remain oblivious. White privilege is like an invisible knapsack of special provisions, maps, passports, codebooks, visas, clothes, tools, and blank checks. (p. 1)

"Describing white privilege makes one newly accountable" and prompts the question "having described it, what will I do to lessen or end it?" (McIntosh, 1990, p. 1). While drawing attention to subconscious advantage prompts action and change among some, the reality is that changing conceptions is more complicated. In reality, by being "deeply embedded into American life," White privilege is "both unconsciously enjoyed and consciously perpetuated" (Collins, 2018, p. 39). DiAngelo (2018) employed the highly connotative terms "White supremacy" – to describe how Whites benefit from privileged access to wealth, employment, and safety – and "White fragility" – to characterize defensive responses to being labelled as privileged. The concept of privilege, according to Collins (2018), "has fallen victim to its own connotations" by engendering "discomfort among those who are not used to being defined or described by their race" and less affluent White people who have endured their own struggles (Collins, 2018, p. 39). This understandable defensiveness is reinforced by the weaponization of the term by both sides of the equity debate. For example, conservative commentator Dennis Prager (2016) argued that there "are simply too many variables other than race." Prager, who dismissed White privilege as a fallacy, began by lamenting that Whites are twice as likely as Blacks to commit suicide. He then offered examples of other privileges as a means of trivializing the concept of White privilege, before concluding by blaming inequities on "poor values or a lack of moral self-control." Progressive voices also trivialize the term privilege when, for example, they summarily dismiss the views and experiences of White, male Democratic Party candidates for president. In order to engage teacher candidates in reflection on their positionality and privilege, it is important for teacher educators to focus on self-awareness and growth, to avoid labelling them as we encourage them not to label others.

2 Methodology and Methods

The self-study of teacher education practices is a hybrid methodology that employs "various qualitative methodologies" to examine "a wide range of substantive issues" in teacher education (Zeichner & Noffke, 2001, p. 305). As self-study's ontology is grounded in respect for the "authority of experience" (Munby & Russell, 1994) and the "craft knowledge" of teachers (Grimmett & McKinnon, 1992), teacher educators are encouraged to continuously examine the role of the self in the research project and "the space between self and the practice engaged in" (Bullough & Pinnegar, 2001, p. 15).

In this self-study, I draw on the methods of narrative self-study (Clandinin & Connelly, 2004) to tell and retell stories of professional practice (Kitchen, 2009) that have helped me understand my personal practical knowledge as a teacher. I draw on my stories of identity as they relate to issues of male, White and socioeconomic privilege. This includes telling new stories based on my recent teaching concerning privilege and social justice, and retelling stories of my queer and masculine identities that have been presented previously (Kitchen, 2016a, 2017).

I also draw on a range of qualitative methods to examine my practice teaching a School and Society course over three years. The data was collected in

2016–17 (2 classes – 55 teacher candidates), 2017–18 (3 classes – 66 teacher candidates) and 2019–20 (1 class – 29 teacher candidates, with all consenting to use of their comments within the limits set forth in the consent letter approved by the university research ethics board. In order to obtain rich data and ensure trustworthiness (LaBoskey, 2004), I used several methods. First, in my teacher educator journal I reflected on the tensions between myself and my context (Bullough & Pinnegar, 2001). Second, I collected teacher candidate feedback most weeks through the use of "exit cards" (Patka et al., 2016). Third, personal reflections and reader response journals from teacher candidates were examined; these were corroborated with feedback contained in formal anonymous course evaluations. Finally, critical friend (Mishler, 1990) Manu Sharma, a South Asian woman with a rich history of studying and enacting social justice as a teacher and teacher educator, served as an external collaborator with whom I could correspond concerning my experiences and the challenges of teaching such a course to predominantly mainstream teacher candidates. These sources, in addition to providing rich data on my experience teaching a social justice course, contribute to the trustworthiness (LaBoskey, 2004) of the insights resulting from the research into self and practice.

By composing "a text that at once looks backward and forward, looks inward and outward, and situates the experiences within place" (Clandinin & Connelly, 2000, p. 140), I puzzle over the tensions I experience as a privileged teacher educator working alongside relatively privileged teacher candidates, as well as the broader tensions inherent in teaching teachers about privilege and social justice. In the sections below, I explore several themes related to privilege and positionality that arose for me as a relational teacher educator (Kitchen, 2005a) in a social justice course.

3   Teacher Educator Privilege and Critical Humility

> We often refuse to accept an idea merely because the tone of voice in which it has been expressed is unsympathetic to us. (Friedrich Nietzsche)

The more I come to know about teacher education and social justice, the simpler my understanding becomes. In particular, I have come to know that the tone we set in our classes is crucial to imparting understanding. The tone that has worked for me as a relatively privileged teacher educator is one of critical humility towards both the minoritized and marginalized and to teacher candidates who need to consider and reconsider their positionality and privilege.

As a teacher educator, I have sought to respect teacher candidate experiences, model constructivist pedagogy, and bridge theory into practice. As one always "teaches the self" (Pinar, 1980), understanding my personal and professional experiences is crucial to being a conduit for self-understanding by teacher candidates (Kitchen, 2005a). Sensoy and DiAngelo (2014) wrote:

> [W]ho a person is [as a knower] is intimately connected to that person's socialization into a matrix of group locations (including race, class, gender, and sexuality). As such, practicing seeing knowledge through the concept of positionality is a key pedagogical goal in the social justice classroom. (p. 5)

Thus, in teaching for social justice, I need to reflect deeply on how my identity and practice are informed by positionality and privilege in order to serve as a conduit for the learning of others.

3.1 *Critical Humility*

To be humble is to be modest, aware of one's own limitations, and open to alternative perspectives. The term "intellectual humility" refers to the cognitive awareness that one's personal beliefs may be fallible. Intellectual humility involves overcoming self-centered inclinations to become receptive to alternative understandings of the world around us (Leary & Banker, 2018). Ordinary people, particularly those who are privileged by race, class and/or gender, need to develop greater intellectual humility in order to move beyond their positionality and resistance to social justice. Liberal intellectual elites, who are perceived to sit in judgement of anyone who is not politically correct in every way (Barro, 2017), need to demonstrate intellectual humility towards people who may value religion, are unselfconsciously patriotic, respect the police, possess guns, and are not attentive to identity issues (such as gay rights or migrant rights), if they are to break down resistance and promote understanding and social justice.

While intellectual humility primarily relates to ideas, it can be associated with openness to the experiences of others, as embodied by humanist psychologist Carl Rogers (1961), who wrote:

> I have found that truly accepting another person and his feelings is by no means an easy thing … I find that when I can accept another person, which means specifically accepting the feelings and attitudes and beliefs that he has as a real and vital part of him, then I am assisting him to become a person: and there seems to me great value in this. (pp. 20–21)

Among social justice educators, "critical humility" is employed as a term to describe the capacity to be humble and self-critical while committing to challenging dialogue concerning social justice (European-American Collaborative Challenging Whiteness, 2012). Such humility is evident in Gary Howard's (2006) *We Can't Teach What We Don't Know: White Teachers, Multicultural Schools*, which thoughtfully and gently inspires White educators to "look deeply and critically at the necessary changes and growth we ourselves must achieve if we are to work effectively with the real issues of race, equity and social justice" (p. 5). One approach to social justice is to create spaces in universities where prejudiced comments are unwelcome. While this is a laudable goal, Boostrom (1998) cautioned that silencing discussion diminishes critical thinking and moves resistance underground. If we want the teachers we prepare to demonstrate critical humility to minoritized and marginalized students, however, we need to help privileged teacher candidates face their fears in order to release their resistance. Yet, truly accepting teacher candidates is not easy, as it requires teacher educators to demonstrate critical humility both towards those who are disadvantaged and those who may resist social justice education.

Özlem Sensoy and Robin DiAngelo enact such critical humility in their work as social justice educators and scholars. In the social justice textbook *Is Everyone Really Equal?*, Sensoy and DiAngelo (2017) humbly invited readers to move beyond their own positionality to critically examine social justice issues. By accepting and understanding readers' feelings, attitudes, beliefs and fears, Sensoy and DiAngelo made a persuasive case for releasing resistance and evoking humility towards the students and communities they will serve. DiAngelo and Sensoy (2014) also engender critical humility through classroom strategies that open the door to authentic reflection and discussion among teacher candidates. They argued that teacher educators cannot be effective in attending to privilege and promoting social justice unless we are respectful of teacher candidates and utilize effective strategies for promoting engagement, critical thinking and deep reflection.

Relational teacher education, which has guided my practice as a teacher educator, is inspired by the respectfulness and humility of Rogers. It is based on respect for adult learners and a genuine belief that each prospective teacher must construct her/his own meaning as a curriculum maker (Kitchen, 2005b, p. 201). As Dominice (2001) wrote, "Each adult learner has his or her own relationship to knowledge, and this relationship is influenced by the social and cultural characteristics of the individual's life history" (p. 83). Thus, teacher candidates "have individual frames of reference that they need to examine and interpret to become successful" (Kitchen, 2016b, p. 175). While they enter with a rich range of learning experiences, their personal practical knowledge is often juxtaposed with "radically simplified conceptions of teaching" (Scardamalia & Bereiter, 1989, p. 37) based on the thousands of hours spent in classrooms that need to be disrupted. But this disruption needs to be handled thoughtfully by teacher educators who understand teaching and learning, convey respect and empathy, and are receptive to growing alongside teacher candidates (Kitchen, 2005a).

In the first week of School and Society, the following was displayed on a slide:

> Critical intellectual humility leads to generosity to one's own and the 'other.' For me as a teacher educator, critical humility entails:
> Respecting your beliefs, values and culture;
> Inviting you to consider the experiences of those less included in society;
> Trusting you as a professional committed to all students;
> Allowing you to find ways to contribute in ways consistent with your worldview.
> (Journal, January 13, 2020)

I then attempted to demonstrate this commitment to humility through activities that open up discussion, as well as thoughtful and respectful comments on their responses to readings. I also made explicit my own grappling with issues, including my efforts to understand and respect the perspectives of conservative and religious groups.

I aim for humility in in my relationship to minoritized and marginalized voices. I invite guests into my class to share their lived experiences; for example, in 2020 workshops were conducted by homeless youth and an Indigenous educator. Increasingly, however, I find that the Internet makes available many excellent videoclips that can be employed throughout a lesson to reflect the experiences of minoritized communities This is evident from comments recorded in my journal of January, 24, 2020 concerning a lesson on discrimination and prejudice. "*The Hate U Give* videoclip put issues in context and help me learn about oppression," wrote one candidate after viewing the movie trailer and a scene in which a Black father sits his children down for "the talk" about being stopped by the police. Several students watched the movie that weekend. Another "appreciated the real-life example of the Asian man sharing his experience of online dating which provided a great insight into marginalization." Another reported that a short video featuring personal stories and clips from movies (Yi, 2016), was "really helpful to see examples related to each type and category."

Also, I am attentive in listening to the voices of academics, teacher educators and critical friends who are racialized. Finding language that does not inadvertently label people is a challenge; consistent with others in the field I generally employ the term "minoritized" and capitalize "Black" and, more recently, "White." When I expressed empathy for a resistant teacher candidate, critical friend Manu Sharma reminded me that "challenging a student's viewpoint which may be very narrow may be your ethical responsibility as an educator" (Correspondence, January 25, 2018). Later, she continued to serve as my conscience: "engaging in this discussion from [a strong justice] angle will yield greater change in systemic racism" (Correspondence, April 16, 2018). I took notice and developed a heightened awareness of the risks of slipping into privileged thinking. Manu's feedback on this manuscript was invaluable in reminding me of the limits of my perspective as a privileged educator. She questioned word selection (e.g., privilege "blocks" not just "hinders" the advancement of minoritized groups). She drew my attention to the limitations of this chapter in addressing the needs of minoritized teacher candidates in my classes.

I also recognize that minoritized teacher educators may be particularly vulnerable teaching social justice courses to teacher candidates who identify with dominant groups. Barbara McNeil's (2011) account of her experiences as a Black woman teaching such a course and living alongside White colleagues illustrates this challenge. McNeil's self-study examined her marginalization by White teacher candidates and the silence of other faculty. McNeil's vulnerability was compounded by her lack of rank as a novice tenure-track professor with no roots in the community during the first few years. On the other hand, a tenured, White, cisgender male teaching such a course "will be read by most students as not biased but instead as objective and legitimate" (Sensoy & DiAngelo, 2014, p. 5); this has been my experience even though I am openly gay. As a teacher educator with considerable earned and unearned privilege, I recognize that I need to do more to support minoritized teacher educator in "redesigning courses and disrupting teacher education" (Bazemore-Bertrand & Porcher, 2020, p. 85). In the spirit of critical humility, I try to imagine what Manu Sharma and Barbara McNeil might experience or how they might challenge my thinking and practice

3.2 *Acknowledging My Privilege as a Teacher Educator*

A professional commitment to social justice has led me to reflect on how my experiences as a gay, middle class, White, cisgender male have shaped my identity as a teacher educator. Self-study has afforded me opportunities to probe deeply into these my intersecting identities and how they are lived out in my performative self in the classroom.

In "Inside Out: My Identity as a Queer Teacher Educator," I drew on queer theory to identify key tensions for me as a teacher educator in a heteronormative world (Kitchen, 2016a,). I recognized that the tension "between needing to be accepted as gay (and accept myself) and wishing to be recognized as a complex, multi-faceted individual" (p. 19) had helped me better appreciate similar tensions and the intersectional identities of others who face greater challenges. While openly identifying as queer categorizes me as belonging to a "subordinate masculinity," I have often benefitted from norms of "hegemonic masculinity" (Connell, 2005), "the cultural ideal of masculinity that legitimizes patriarchy and the collective, institutional power of men in institutions" (Kitchen, 2017, p. 88). This is evident in the following account of an introductory class:

> I wear a grey suit with a starched white shirt and purple striped tie. The suit's muted tone conveys strength and professionalism ....
>
> I try to maintain a tension between accessibility and authority. I hide my shyness and nerves behind a mask of confidence. The thirty faces that stare back at me are predominately white, and sixty percent female.
>
> I smile and welcome them to the class. I acknowledge that *Professionalism and Law* seems like an intimidating course, yet assure them that the material is accessible and that I will do all I can to help them succeed.
>
> I introduce myself. I tell them that I have been at the university since 2006, and have been a teacher educator since 1999. I note that I wrote the textbook – i.e., I know my stuff ....
>
> I emphasize my authority by noting that I am the director of Indigenous education and the project lead in the redesign of the teacher education program. I draw attention to publications in teacher education journals and books, as well as funded research on Indigenous education in the north.
>
> Having asserted authority and caring, I then enter into a zone of discomfort. I feel a knot in my stomach and a wave of panic. My face reddens and my voice falters.
>
> I mention that my recent research on bullying and gay-straight alliances has heightened my awareness of the role teachers can play in making schools safe for all students. Having raised the issue, I then note that I have also written about queer theory and my identity as a queer teacher educator.
>
> While they absorb this disclosure, I plow ahead with my introduction to the course. (Kitchen, 2017, pp. 90–91)

Revisiting this story through the lenses of race and gender, it is evident that I offset potential subordination by emphasizing markers of hegemonic masculinity through my business suit, sense of authority, and emotional restraint. Thus, I am partly complicit in hegemonic masculinity – benefitting from the positive stereotypes of White males – even as I disrupt conventional notions. I experienced a certain degree of gender strain as I explicitly adapted to the masculine ideal of a White professional. At the same time, I attempted to model being a decent man who demonstrates a duty of care, community-mindedness, courage and healthy risk-taking as he grapples with the issues discussed in class. This is evident in comments from teacher candidates on exit cards, such as "I appreciated you explaining blurring and shifting boundaries through current and relevant examples" and "unpacking different perspectives in connection to various topics" (Journal, January 24, 2020). While deeply committed to social justice, I manage my emotions and responses (Cutri & Whiting, 2015) and trust in the capacity of teacher candidates to grow.

By acknowledging and problematizing my privileged and marginalized identities, internally and in dialogue with teacher candidates, I am better able to help teacher candidates reflect on their intersectionalities. In a lesson on teaching effectively for social justice, I echoed Gandhi's call to be the change you wish to see in the world.

4   Teacher Candidate Positionality and Privilege

> Tell all the Truth but tell it slant –
> Success in Circuit lies
> Too bright for our infirm Delight
> The Truth's superb surprise
> Emily Dickinson (1890/1961, pp. 248–249)

I have no trouble believing that White and male privilege exist. I recognize that I have benefitted from this. I recognize that, like me, most of teacher candidates in my classes are White, cisgender and relatively privileged economically. I also acknowledge that such privilege undermines equity in our society, particularly in schools where the population is increasingly diverse. Demographic evidence indicates that in many urban school districts the majority of students of color, and that in twenty years they will be the majority in North America, while the vast majority of teachers will continue to be White (e.g., Banks et al., 2005). I acknowledge that this presents challenges for White teachers of minoritized students (e.g., Howard, 2006) and that the teaching profession needs to recruit and retain vastly more teachers of color (e.g., Chubbuck & Zemblylas, 2016). As acknowledgement is insufficient, I attempt to model being a privileged educator who draws on his privilege to open the minds of relatively privileged students and support minoritized ones.

I am hesitant, however, to baldly assert this at the beginning of the School and Society course. I tell the truth about social justice but, rather than blind teacher candidates with the light, strive to create a safe and open environment in which to come to understand the need for equity, diversity and social justice in schools. As their many years of schooling are "often juxtaposed with simplified conceptions of teaching" (Kitchen, 2005b) and unexamined "delight" in their social positioning, it is important to curate their discoveries. Thus, I "tell it slant" by sharing knowledge in a relational manner that is respectful of, and empathetic to, teacher candidates. Relational teacher education, which has guided my practice for years, "is based on respect for adult learners and a genuine belief that each prospective teacher must construct her/his own meaning as a curriculum maker" (Kitchen, 2005b, p. 201). I regard privilege as a complex concept that needs to be examined, critiqued and taught in a thoughtful and respectful manner. Although many teacher candidates may possess privilege, they do not feel very privileged as they prepare to enter the workforce. In this section, I focus on how I introduce privilege to teacher candidates in a manner that is critical while demonstrating respect and empathy for them as they engage in personal reflection and in critical analysis of the society in which they will teach. In doing so, I also problematize terms related to privilege with a view to prompting thoughtful consideration of the term through critique and reflection. This includes identifying some of the complexities and limitations of the conception of privilege, particularly White and male privilege.

The genius of McIntosh's monograph is the combination of the knapsack metaphor and a long list of unearned privileges. The knapsack image powerfully evokes the additional burden experienced by marginalized individualized and groups, The list of 50 privileges, often mundane, illustrates the injustices they are spared, while disrupting tacit assumptions about merit and privilege in daily life. For example, "I can go shopping alone most of the time, pretty well assured that I will not be followed or harassed" (McIntosh, 1990) draws attention to males being spared from the injustice of sexual harassment and Whites from suspicion as potential criminals. This list, along with similar ones developed for equity workshops, draws attention to the relative privilege that is institutionalized through invisible systems of dominance (McIntosh, 1990). By being experiential rather than intellectual, McIntosh's knapsack invites personal reflection. Yet, if the pedagogical approach is polemic rather than inviting, receptivity to reflection and growth may be replaced with defensiveness and resistance.

As a relational teacher educator, I begin a new course by setting a tone that is safe, relational, critical and playful. For example, after introductory remarks outlining the School and Society course and my qualifications, I began this year's class with a Personal Identity –Inclusive Teaching activity in which teacher candidates wrote and shared, among other things, their favorite color, why they decided to become teachers, reasons for pride in ancestors, and hopes/fears for the course.[2] This was followed by a diamond ranking activity, What Matters to Me as a Teacher? Among the nine cards to rank were equity and diversity, making learning fun, subject mastery and safe learning environment. As we debriefed their top and bottom three choices, I joked with them about their selections. If they ranked fun highly, I teasingly suggested that they did not value subject mastery. I questioned off-handedly the relative placement of a safe environment and equity and diversity. In the discussion, it became apparent that all nine topics were important and that there were many ways one might legitimately connect them together. When I first employed the diamond ranking activity several years ago, I intended it as a bridge between their conceptions of education and the social justice focus of this course. Over years, I have come to realize that this activity and debriefing signaled my openness to their perspectives and acceptance of many pathways to effective teaching. Teacher candidates wrote on exit cards, "I enjoyed building the diamond with my group and learning about the priorities of other groups" and "I like the way you approach the classroom discussion; it made me feel comfortable with the class. Knowing that you can facilitate meaningful discussion with no right answer gives me peace of mind moving forward" (January 13, 2020). Common were expressions of safety alongside challenges: "while the ideas are daunting, there are small steps we can take and should take to help," and "it made me really begin to think about justice."

This set up a safe environment in which to examine challenging social justice themes. Over the years I have employed both Step into the Circle and Privilege Walk to initiate thinking and feeling about positionality and privilege. The 15–20 statements, inspired by McIntosh's knapsack items, and subsequent steps forward (or not) draw attention to their social positioning relative to others. This is especially obvious in the circle format. For example, in response to "I can walk to my car late at night without fearing for my safety," no women step forward. Only a few grew up in rental accommodation. Typically only I step forward for "I identify as queer, gay, lesbian, transgender, bisexual or two-spirited." The Privilege Walk, which I now use, the widening gap between the privileged and marginalized draws attention to relative advantage over multiple topics. The Privilege Walk lacks the circle's heightened awareness of one's response in relation to others, but individual answers are less exposed. I follow this with an activity to draw attention to the multi-faceted nature of privilege. I currently employ a Social Identity Wheel[3] that identifies multiple sources of difference (e.g., race, gender, ability) and invites participants to consider their positionality in relation to each. Few people are privileged in all areas. I also allow for variations and flexibility. For example, while recognizing Christianity as dominant, I note that one can be seen as too religious and, thus, stigmatized in educated circles as prejudiced. I also position myself as relatively privileged, even as I may be disadvantaged at times for being gay, and model understanding of others.

Zemblyas (2010) "emphasized the proactive and transformative potential of discomfort" (p. 707) in promoting social justice perspectives. I concur that discussion of privilege generates personal and political discomfort for prospective teachers and, like Zemblyas, make myself emotionally available to them as they grapple with this and related concepts. As the truth may be too bright for them to face directly, like Emily Dickinson cautioned, I prefer to "tell it slant," to keep the "Truth's superb surprise" in play without pressing them to convert to socially just teaching. Instead, I invite them to consider issues of privilege, as well as concepts such as discrimination, systemic discrimination, and oppression. I invite them on a journey through systematic reading of critical texts and by attending to the voices and stories of others over the coming weeks. I engage with their emotional reactions through intellectual rigor in class, and constructive written feedback on their critical and personal reflections on the readings, and by modelling vulnerability and empathy in both contexts. By turning down the pressure and emphasizing the complexities of identity and privilege, I have noticed diminished resistance and, consequently, greater willingness to recognize and name their privilege than is typical in the literature (e.g., Cutri & Whiting, 2015). This, of course, might be because the divisions are more nuanced and the stakes lower in Canada than the United States, but as I have also experienced teaching a course on professionalism and law, keeping the drama low can lower defenses against discomfort. As we explore important concepts in the weeks that follow, I regularly encourage receptivity and convey my respect for them as prospective teachers who can make a difference in a myriad of small ways. Through respect and empathy, I have been able to set the stage for further growth. As Whiting and Cutri (2015) found, "when opportunities are created ... to grapple with complex, personal, emotional concepts, the vast majority of students are willing and able to perform this type of reflection and analysis" (p. 13).

Privilege, particularly White and male privilege, are explored and critiqued carefully with teacher candidates as these contested terms challenge invisible yet powerful social structures of oppression. Rather than casually label people as privileged, and thus prompt defensiveness and denial, I take the time to puzzle in front of the class with the complexities of systemic dimensions of power and privilege. "Oppression," as Sensoy and DiAngelo (2017) explained in our course textbook, "occurs when one group is able to enforce its prejudice and discrimination because it controls the institutions" (p. 61). It is important to acknowledge that while many may benefit from privilege, most do not act in a prejudicial or discriminatory manner to benefit from inequity. It is equally important to invite teacher candidates to transition from passive complicity in oppression to commitment to addressing inequities in their teaching.

Also, there are multiple layers of privilege, not all of which are equally problematic. McIntosh (1990) distinguished between privileges not worth having (e.g., benefiting directly from discrimination in the workplace) from ones that are worthwhile and should be available to all in a just society (e.g., fair court proceedings). Collins (2018), for example, identified and illustrated three sources of White privilege. The Power of Normal refers to the White privilege of taking for granted that their needs will be met while the minoritized see their needs represented primarily on the margins. While "flesh-colored" band-aids and the relegation of ethnic foods to special sections of a grocery store may seem relatively minor, the sparing of White people from injustice indicates a gap "beneath the surface" (Collins, 2018, p. 40). The Power of the Benefit of the Doubt refers to the benefit of being "treated as individuals, rather than as representatives of ... a stereotypical racial identity" (Collins, 2018, p. 40). While White people conferred this benefit have done nothing wrong, they may be unjustly enriched in educational, housing and employment opportunities thanks to "racial profiling, stereotypes and lack of compassion for [others'] struggles" (Collins, 2018, p. 40). Finally, the Power of Accumulated Power means that many White people start life further ahead thanks to the assets their parents have accumulated while others were actively discriminated against over the course of the years and generations. It is important to note that such privilege is not evenly distributed, and that women, immigrants, the working poor, LGBTQ people, and others are at times marginalized. Over the first few weeks, privilege and oppression are thoughtfully examined so that relatively privileged people can appreciate "the subconscious comfort of seeing a world that serves you as normal" (Collins, 2018, p. 41) and choose to draw on (or draw down) their privilege for the benefit of others.

In "'White Privilege': A Mild Critique," philosopher Lawrence Blum (2008) problematized the term privilege and offered ways to differentiate among privileges and make the conversation more nuanced. I find that puzzling and problematizing this concept, as someone with similar experiences, both makes the term more palatable and addresses legitimate issues raised by people who object to being so labelled. Blum helpfully breaks McIntosh's privileges into two categories: "spared injustice" and "unjust enrichment." A spared injustice, such as not experiencing an arbitrary police search, harms no one and, indeed, is a right that should be extended to all. On the other hand, unjust enrichment involves benefitting from discrimination, whether by winning a job competition over a better qualified applicant from a minoritized group or being less likely to be charged for a crime in your neighborhood as resources are dispatched to areas with large minoritized populations. While it is important to note that individuals are not complicit in injustice if they do not seek a benefit, it is equally important to recognize that the Power of the Benefit of the Doubt and the Power of Accumulated Power often benefit them nonetheless. Blum also identified a category of privileges not related to injustice, such as the benefits of being a native language-speaker. These distinctions are important, Blum asserted, in order to avoid the pitfall of labelling all people with unearned privilege as engaged in "the most heinous of the three ... unjust enrichment" (Blum, 2008, p. 313). While I encourage conversations regarding privilege that are non-judgmental and nuanced, I leave little doubt that "privilege is an ongoing dynamic that is continually reproduced, negotiated, and enacted" (Sensoy & DiAngelo, 2017, pp. 81–82).

Once the concept of privilege has been introduced, it is important to situate it in the historical context of prejudice and discrimination in our societies. Teacher candidates, especially those outside the social sciences and humanities, are often unaware of the prevalence of injustice in recent history, let alone its persistence today. Rather than assume knowledge of the lynchings of Blacks in the American South or attacks on civil rights leaders in the 1960s, I attempt to disrupt the unschooled conception that our civil societies defeated racism decades ago. They need to be aware of persistent gender discrimination long after extending the franchise to women. They need to appreciate that progress on LGBTQ rights only began in the 1960s, that same-sex marriage is a recent phenomenon, and the right of trans citizens to access the washroom of their choice is still in dispute. As Blum stated, the failure to engage with such background leaves unschooled assumptions intact as the claims of academics are not connected to a structural analysis of power and privilege. Such a structural analysis, however, also needs to recognize the diversity of minority experiences, as exceptions can be used as evidence that privilege exists for some members of minoritized communities too. This includes acknowledging that in the United States African American and Indigenous peoples have suffered sustained devastation far beyond that experienced by more recent Black immigrants, Latinos and Asians (Sensoy & DiAngelo, 2017). Finally, it is important to acknowledge the importance of economic and class inequality, both for

Whites and for people of color, for whom economic disadvantage intersects with other forms of discrimination. As most teacher candidates are White, with many of them advantaged in other ways, it is important to help them examine their privilege.

I began this inquiry by focusing on the positionality and privilege of teacher candidates because it is their development that is of ultimate importance. The approach taken in the opening classes reflects my approach to relational teacher education. The welcoming, non-judgmental yet intellectually rigorous approach are consistent with respect and empathy for teacher candidates as individuals and professionals (Kitchen, 2005a). Equally important, the feedback from candidates reveals that these qualities were conveyed to them. Finally, these first steps help them face an educational problem (Kitchen, 2005b) – addressing equity and diversity – that they were aware of, even if they may have preferred to avoid it.

5   Helping Teacher Candidates Face the Challenges of Socially Just Teaching

> Although I try to anticipate many of the challenges common to preservice teachers, I recognize that each person has to reconcile her or his personal practical knowledge with classroom practice. One commitment I made … was to help them face problems and reconcile theory with practice. (Kitchen, 2005b, p. 205)

Teacher educators for social justice do challenging work. Marilyn Cochran-Smith (2010) developed a theory of teacher education for social justice that consisted of three aspects: a theory of justice, a theory of practice, and a theory of teacher preparation. All three "integrated and overlapping" aspects need to be attended to in order to provide a "coherent and intellectual approach to the preparation of teachers" that recognizes the political nature of social justice teaching and the potential for teacher education to serve as "a site for educational change" (p. 447). Her approach aligns with a rich body of work on the importance of building culturally responsive practices that prompt deep thinking about diversity and pedagogy (e.g., Banks et al., 2005) as a means to transforming teaching for social justice. While social justice has been identified as priority in teacher education, Cochran-Smith (2010), who contended that the concept was vague and undertheorized, stressed the need to build on a theory of justice that acknowledges the need for redistribution of wealth and recognition of diverse social groups, as well as address the tension between establishing a common knowledge base for all teachers and recognizing social, cultural and racial inequity. She also argued for a theory of practice that amalgamates "knowledge; interpretive frameworks; teaching strategies, methods, and skills; and, advocacy" for the purpose of "improving students' learning and enhancing their life chance" (p. 454). These, however, are insufficient without having a theory of teacher preparation for social justice that considers multiple dimensions of becoming a teacher. Similarly, teacher educators who do not grasp justice theory can only offer well-meaning but shallow understanding of the experiences of marginalized communities and structural dimensions of oppression. As a relational teacher educator committed to social justice teaching, I take the time to understand the landscape of teacher education and adapt my practice accordingly (Kitchen, 2005b). In particular, I help teacher candidates wrestle thoughtfully with social justice themes and practices (Kitchen, 2005b, 2020) so that they can understand their own positionality, the experiences of others, and ways in which they can make a difference as novice teachers.

A perennial request from teacher candidates in a course is for practical strategies for dealing with social justice issues in curriculum and classroom management. In my journal on February 11, 2020, I wrote, "Teacher candidates asked for more tips on how to teach with equity, diversity and social justice in mind. In response to this, I made an oral presentation in which I offered a list of suggestions guided by my reading of the literature, my experiences as a teacher and teacher educator, and my work on relational teacher education." "Teaching for Social Justice: A Practical Guide" is based on my notes for the presentation.

Teaching for Social Justice: A Practical Guide

Understand and Enhance Dispositions Regarding Equity, Diversity and Social Justice
The first is what we have been doing in the course thus far. With the help of the textbook, and reflections on personal experience, you have been considering their privilege, prejudices, discriminatory practices, power is White people, etc. It is only through doing this, and coming to understand the institutional structures that aid them and leave them often blind to the realities of others, that we can take the issue seriously enough to actually do something to disrupt the structures that benefit some and hurt others.

Develop a Theoretical Understanding Systems Typically Advantage Those Who Already Possess Privilege and Power
Enhancing dispositions goes hand-in-hand with developing a theoretical understanding of power, privilege, and oppression. In relational teacher education terms, this involves understanding the general landscape of education. The literature makes it clear that theoretical understandings are crucial to going beyond simple liberal niceties.

High Standards for All Students; Rejection of Deficit Theory
An issue that has been underplayed in this course is the importance of having high standards for all students. This is something that I will give increasing stress to over the course of the year, as recent reading has reminded me that otherwise deficit theory leads to low expectations for minoritized students. These low expectations in turn lead to diminished outcomes, and self-fulfilling prophecies. The myth of laziness is one manifestation of low standards and deflating expectations. I mention a teacher candidate's written reflection rejecting his supervising teacher's low expectations for students in the non-academic stream. This reminds me of my own practice teaching experiences. I taught grade 9 English and the culmination of my practicum was group seminars for eighty minutes. My supervising teacher told her department head that she was interested to see what I would do when students failed to deliver. But they did deliver, giving generally thoughtful seminars and filling the time allocated. Later when I was at the same school for history she told me that a couple of the students were now planning to transition to academic courses. She noted that she should perhaps expect more from the applied students that she was reluctantly teaching.

Cultural Competence: Draw on the Cultures in Your Classroom
It is important to get to know the cultures of the school in which one teaches, and to draw on this knowledge through curriculum and pedagogy. Last class, I shared with you data showing that Peel District School Board students were now 45% South Asian, 5% East Asian, 5% Middle Eastern, 11% Black, and 17% White. These statistics resonated with you and helped you realize that you need to know more about these cultures. For example, you might want to study Bollywood dancing, discover books and films by Asian artists, and partake in their holidays and feast days.

The federal and provincial representatives for the Ontario constituency with the largest population of Muslims were a gay man and a lesbian. They and their same-sex partners go regularly to Muslim feasts and cultural events; indeed they have several culturally appropriate sets of clothing for these occasions. They take the time to get to know the cultures and have been rewarded with higher than average votes from these groups. This both reflects on their openness and undercuts perceptions/stereotypes that Muslims are homophobic.

Diversify the Curriculum in Your Courses
To the extent it is possible, we as teachers should diversify the content of our courses. As new teachers, it is hard to move big things in the course such as novels or units. But we can add mini-lessons on current events or famous mathematicians. And we can add short stories or poems. We can also add pedagogies that are more culturally competent. Certainly we need to take a little bit of time to ask what can be done and experiment with some of these.

Professional Development: Fill in Your Cultural Gaps
When I began teaching, I taught an English course with human rights as a main theme. At a conference sponsored by the Holocaust Remembrance Committee of Toronto, I learned more about the Holocaust, met survivors, and learned about resources and strategies to use. I also met the leader of a Jewish group fighting to remove *The Merchant of Venice* from the Grade 10 English curriculum. I told her the play was on my syllabus and asked for her thoughts. She was supportive given the context. She was concerned in her community because her local school taught the play with little acknowledgement of the problematic characterization of Shylock, thus perpetuating anti-Semitism.

In this course, we get you started. But there are ample resources that can help you to adapt to particular groups of students. The Black history month resources in the course outline are one such example. Also the new teacher induction programs provide lots of opportunities for targeted professional development suited to your particular classes. Larger districts tend to have equity officers and cultural resource people available to provide support.

Care Deeply: Attend to Students Where They Are
I hope that I model this in this course. I show my attention through listening thoughtfully and asking for their input through exit cards. I recall that Mr. Fitzgerald, whom I observed during my doctoral studies, did not acknowledge the Islamic Muslim perspective when he covered the Middle Ages in his Grade 4/5 class that was 30% Muslim. After a pause to take in the aghast expressions of teacher candidates, I noted that, nevertheless,

he was a thoughtful teacher who demonstrated empathy in his relationships with all students, notably newly arrived Afghan refugees.

Convey Respect and Empathy
It is also important that this respect be conveyed. Condescension is never good and as we know minoritized students often feel that they are not respected. I think of a boy who wore a dress as a Halloween costume. When his father asked if he might be teased, he said no Mr. Fitzgerald would make sure that doesn't happen.

Model: Be the Change You Want in the World
Preaching works less well than modelling. We as teachers may be better informed and have power, so we win the argument. But do we really persuade people especially if we disrespectfully demand respect for ourselves and for others?

Address Prejudice and Discrimination Educatively
Always address prejudice and discrimination. Where possible do so privately. The purpose is to help students grow and encourage them to learn to live more harmoniously with others. At times it is necessary to call people out in public or at least to provide a public lesson in response to something that occurred earlier. We cannot be seen to have ignored and, thus tacitly accepted, prejudice and discrimination. We must be seen to be responsive but educatively and thoughtfully. The most obvious example to me is dealing with terms like "That's so gay." Act – for example, "We do not use such language." Don't overreact – for example, labelling the student as homophobic. If the issue persists then employ progressive discipline and/or address it more broadly.

Diverse Assessments: Diagnostics and Assessments of Teaching
If a student gets an A+ then they know the material. But what does a B mean? Or D? Diagnostics and checking in are crucial to understanding and then helping students to fill in gaps. Otherwise they continue to do the same things incorrectly over and over again without learning. They fall further and further behind. This is especially true if lessons are not culturally responsive or if they lack tutoring or other supports at home.

Extra Help
While teachers should be available for extra help or homework clubs, this is particularly helpful in subjects such as mathematics where skills development is cumulative. In schools serving less affluent students (who lack

resources for tutors etc.), it's a good idea to find ways to make homework clubs after school fun or culturally appropriate so that students want to come to get support.

Enrichment Activities
Enrichment activities, such as field trips, are far more common in affluent schools than others. This is because they often attract stronger academic teachers, have more community and financial resources, and aspects of day-to-day teaching are less stressful. Yet these same students are most likely to go to museums or theatres with their parents. As enrichment experiences like these can transform lives, teachers in less affluent schools need to do more to make these things happen.

Extracurricular Activities
These opportunities to are more likely in more privileged communities. Taking the time to develop these skills and offer these opportunities can be profound. The stars in a more modest school, in particular, will get breaks they otherwise would not have. As a debating and public speaking coach, I know that activities led to scholarships and transformed the lives of my students.

Collaborate with Colleagues, Families, Communities
It takes a village. This probably needs to wait until you have some experience but the needier the community, the more crucial it is for teachers to build partnerships for success.

Advocacy and Fundraising in the Larger Community
Advocacy in the form of getting speakers from the community can make a big difference. I recall dedicated teachers and principals in areas of poverty who made enormous efforts to create partnerships and build additional opportunities for their students. This included seeking food from local stores, soliciting sponsorships, and applying for community grants.

Receptivity to Growing alongside Students
Always be receptive to growing as you teach. I demonstrate this through collecting student feedback and studying my practice. Dialogue about current events or controversies in your discipline. Demonstrate engagement in lifelong learning.

"Teaching for Social Justice" started as a defense of my approach to teaching and an attempt to honor the intent of their requests for more practical strategies. Guiding my thinking was Loughran's (2006) insight that "students of teaching need to be able to see and hear the pedagogical reasoning that underpins the teaching they are experiencing" (p. 5). More than I realized at the time, this became a manifesto articulating my practice as a relational and socially just teacher educator. It began, as the course did, with coming to know oneself and understanding key concepts in order to understand the educational context and address learning needs. Examples from my teaching career from practice teaching to doctoral research in schools to my practice as a teacher educator served to illustrate that such an approach can work. The manifesto had the desired effect, as there were few requests for practical examples in subsequent feedback or the course evaluations.

Why was "Teaching for Social Justice" a successful intervention? Guided by Gandhi's axiom "Be the change you wish to see in the world," I attempted to model the practices I advocated by conveying caring, respect, empathy and responsiveness to growing as a teacher educator. I drew on the connection made between their backgrounds and mine to inspire them to go on similar journeys of discovery in order to better serve the diverse students who will be in their classrooms. The examples were modest and suggested that expertise could be developed over time through responsiveness and caring. Acknowledging my privilege and highlighting with similarities to their experiences may have encouraged them to begin to face the challenges of teaching for social justice. By acknowledging my marginalization as a gay man, I made explicit my vulnerability while, by characterizing myself as privileged, I encouraged in them cognitive empathy – "seeing the world through the eyes of others and reflecting as a means to understanding where they might be coming from" (Journal, January 20, 2020) – and the willingness to take considered risks for the sake of others. As my critical friend Manu, reminded and cautioned me in her feedback, however, "this does not work for racialized faculty, as their stories don't usually mirror the audience's life experiences."

6   Conclusion

Teacher education for social justice is emotionally challenging work for teacher educators and teacher candidates alike. The nature of the challenge varies depending on one's positionality and privilege. As a gay, White, cis-gender male from an upper-middle-class background teaching predominantly White, middle-class teacher candidates, I position myself as their guide to living and working in unfamiliar territory. In effect, I use my privilege as a basis for understanding their perspectives and winning their trust.

While I carefully burnish my pedagogical and scholarly credentials, I pay particular attention to making myself vulnerable and accessible to them. I am open about my identity as a gay man (vulnerability) and readily acknowledge the relatively privileged status I share with many of them (accessibility). Most of all, as demonstrated in the chapter, I seek to model critical humility and convey respect and empathy to them as they engage their discomfort in order to be prepared to teach in diverse classrooms and schools.

The approach I take is illustrated with examples from early lessons from a School and Society class in 2020. The truths of social justice are front and center, but the curriculum and pedagogy were designed to be accessible and inviting to teacher candidates. "Teaching for Social Justice: A Practical Guide" conveys a vision of socially just teacher education that is challenging and accessible for teaching. It also reveals the principles I attempt to model as I use my privilege to guide them towards teaching dispositions that promote equity and celebrate diversity.

In closing, I acknowledge the limitations of this account. I recognize that many instructors of social justice courses are not privileged and that teacher education classes are becoming more diverse. I recognize the dangers of being – and/or being perceived as – too understanding of privileged teacher candidates' discomfort. Nonetheless, I suggest that this relational approach to teacher education for social justice can be beneficial in many teacher preparation contexts.

Notes

1 See, e.g., https://opensource.com/open-organization/17/11/privilege-walk-exercise
2 Adapted from https://sites.lsa.umich.edu/inclusive-teaching/2017/08/16/personal-identity-wheel/
3 https://sites.lsa.umich.edu/inclusive-teaching/2017/08/16/social-identity-wheel/

References

Banks, J., Cochran-Smith, M., Moll, L., Richert, A., Zeichner, K, LePage, P., Darling-Hammond, L., & Duffy, H. (2005). Teaching diverse learners. In L. Darling-Hammond & J. Bransford (Eds.), *Preparing teachers for a changing world: What teachers should learn and be able to do* (pp. 1–39). Jossey-Bass.

Barro, J. (2017). Liberals can win again if they stop being so annoying and fix their 'hamburger problem.' *Business Insider.* Retrieved June 13, 2021, from https://www.businessinsider.com/liberals-can-win-if-they-stop-being-so-annoying-2017-7

Bazemore-Bertrand, S., & Porcher, K. (2020). Teacher educators as disruptors: Redesigning courses in teacher preparation programs to prepare white preservice teachers. *Journal of Culture and Values in Education, 3*(1), 73–88.

Blum, L. (2008). 'White privilege': A mild critique. *Theory and Research in Education, 6*(3), 309–321. https://doi.org/10.1177/1477878508095586

Boostrom, R. (1998). Safe spaces: Reflections on an educational metaphor. *Journal of Curriculum Studies, 30*(4), 397–408.

Bullough, R. V., Jr., & Pinnegar, S. (2001). Guidelines for quality in autobiographical forms of self-study research. *Educational Researcher, 30*(3), 13–21.

Chubback, S. M., & Zemblylas, M. (2016). Social justice and teacher education: Context, theory, and practice. In J. Loughran & M. L. Hamilton (Eds.), *International handbook of teacher education* (pp. 463–501). Springer. https://doi.org/1007/978-981-10-0369-1_14

Clandinin, D. J., & Connelly, F. M. (2000). *Narrative inquiry: Experience and story in qualitative research.* Jossey-Bass.

Clandinin, D. J., & Connelly, F. M. (2004). Knowledge, narrative and self-study. In J. J. Loughran, M. L. Hamilton, V. K. LaBoskey, & T. Russell (Eds.), *International handbook of self-study of teaching and teacher education practice* (pp. 575–600). Springer.

Cochran-Smith, M. (2010). Toward a theory of teacher education for social justice. In A. Hargreaves et al. (Eds.), *Second international handbook of educational change* (pp. 445–467). Springer. https://doi.org/1007/978-90-481-2660-6_27

Collins, C. (2018). What is white privilege, really? *Teaching Tolerance, 60*, 39–4. Retrieved June 13, 2021, from https://www.tolerance.org/magazine/fall-2018/what-is-white-privilege-really

Connell, R. W. (2005). *Masculinities* (2nd ed.). University of California Press.

Cutri, R. M., & Whiting, E. F. (2015). The emotional work of discomfort and vulnerability in multicultural teacher education. *Teachers and Teaching: Theory and Practice, 21*(8), 1010–1025. http://doi.org/10.1080/14540602.2015.1005869

DiAngelo, R. (2018). *White fragility: Why it's so hard for white people to talk about racism.* Beacon Press.

DiAngelo, R., & Sensoy, O. (2014). Calling in: Strategies for cultivating humility and critical thinking in antiracism education. *Understanding and Dismantling Privilege, 4*(2), 191–203.

Dickinson, E. (1961). *Final harvest: Emily Dickinson's poems.* Little, Brown and Company. (Original work published 1890)

Dominice, P. (2000). *Learning from our lives.* Jossey-Bass.

European-American Collaborative Challenging Whiteness. (2012). White on white: Communicating about race and white privilege with critical humility. *Understanding and Dismantling Privilege, 2*(1), 1–17.

Freire, P. (1995). *Pedagogy of hope: Reliving the pedagogy of the oppressed.* Continuum.

Gardner, H. (1991). *The unschooled mind: How children think and how schools should teach*. Basic Books.

Grimmett, P., & McKinnon, A. (1992). Craft knowledge and the education of teachers. In G. Grant (Ed.), *Review of research in education* (Vol. 18, pp. 385–456). American Educational Research Association.

Howard, G. R. (2006). *We can't teach what we don't know: White teachers, multiracial schools*. Teachers College Press.

Kitchen, J. (2005a). Conveying respect and empathy: Becoming a relational teacher educator. *Studying Teacher Education, 1*(2), 194–207.

Kitchen, J. (2005b). Looking backwards, moving forward: Understanding my narrative as a teacher educator. *Studying Teacher Education, 1*(1), 17–30.

Kitchen, J. (2009). Passages: Improving teacher education through narrative self-study. In D. Tidwell, M. Heston, & L. Fitzgerald (Eds.), *Methods for self-study of practice* (pp. 35–51). Springer.

Kitchen, J. (2016a). Inside out: My identity as a queer teacher educator. In J. Kitchen, D. Tidwell, & L. Fitzgerald (Eds.), *Self-study and diversity II* (pp. 11–26). Sense.

Kitchen, J. (2016b). Looking back on 15 years of relational teacher education: A narrative self-study. In J. Williams & M. Hayler (Eds.), *Professional learning through transitions and transformations: Teacher educators' journeys of becoming* (pp. 167–182). Springer.

Kitchen, J. (2017). Critically reflecting on masculinity in teacher education through narrative self-study. In R. Brandenburg, K. Glasswell, M. Jones, & J. Ryan (Eds.), *Reflective theory and practice in teacher education* (pp. 85–101). Springer Nature.

Kitchen, J. (2019). A relational approach to social justice in teacher education. In J. Kitchen & K. Ragoonaden (Eds.), *Mindful and relational approaches to social justice, equity and diversity in teacher education* (pp. 13–29). Lexington Books.

Kitchen, J. (2020). Attending to the concerns of teacher candidates in a social justice course: A self-study of a teacher educator. *Studying Teacher Education, 16*(1), 6–25. https://doi.org/10.1080/17425964.2019.1691134

Kitchen, J., & Taylor, L. (2020). Preparing preservice teachers for social justice teaching: Designing and implementing effective interventions in teacher education. In C. Mullen (Ed.), *Handbook of social justice interventions in education*. Springer. https://doi.org/10.1007/978-3-030-29553-0_70-1

Kroll, L. (2006). Learning to address issues of equity and access through inquiry in a student teaching seminar: A self-study. In D. Tidwell & L. Fitzgerald (Eds.), *Self-study and diversity* (pp. 133–151). Sense.

LaBoskey, V. (2004). The methodology of self-study and its theoretical underpinnings. In J. J. Loughran, M. Hamilton, V. LaBoskey, & T. Russell (Eds.), *International handbook of self-study of teaching and teacher education practices* (pp. 817–869). Springer. https://doi.org/10.1007/978-1-4020-6545-3_21

Leary, M. R., & Banker, C. (2018). A critical examination and reconceptualization of humility. In J. Wright (Ed.), *Humility*. Oxford University Press. http://doi.org/10.1093/oso/9780190864873.003.0004

Loughran, J. (2006). *Developing a pedagogy of teacher education: Understanding teaching and learning about teaching*. Routledge.

McIntosh, P. (1990). Unpacking the invisible knapsack. *Independent School, 49*(2).

McNeil, B. (2011). Charting a way forward: Intersections of race and space in establishing identity as an African-Canadian teacher educator. *Studying Teacher Education, 7*(2), 133–145.

Mishler, E. (1990). Validation in inquiry-guided research: The role of exemplars in narrative studies. *Harvard Education Review, 60*, 415–442.

Munby, H., & Russell, T. (1994). The authority of experience in learning to teach: Messages from a physics methods class. *Journal of Teacher Education, 45*, 86–95.

Patka, M., Wallin-Ruuschman, Wallace, T., & Robbins, C. (2016). Exit cards: Creating a dialogue for continuous evaluation. *Teaching in Higher Education, 21*(6), 659–668. https://doi.org/10.1080/13562517.2016.1167033

Pence, D. J., & Fields, J. A. (1999). Teaching about race and ethnicity: Trying to uncover white privilege for a white audience. *Teaching Sociology, 27*(2), 150–158.

Pinar, W. F. (1980). Life history and educational experience. *Journal of Curriculum Theorizing, 2*(2), 159–212.

Prager, D. (2016, February). The fallacy of 'white privilege.' *National Review*. Retrieved June 13, 2021, from https://www.nationalreview.com/2016/02/white-privilege-myth-reality/

Rogers, C. (1961). *On becoming a person*. Houghton Mifflin.

Scardamalia, M., & Bereiter, C. (1989). Conceptions of teaching and approaches to core problems. In M. C. Reynolds (Ed.), *Knowledge base for the beginning teacher* (pp. 37–46). Pergamon Press.

Sensoy, O., & DiAngelo, R. (2014). "Respecting differences"? Challenging the common guidelines in social justice education. *Democracy & Education, 22*(2), 1–10. Retrieved June 13, 2021, from https://democracyeducationjournal.org/cgi/viewcontent.cgi?article=1138&context=home

Sensoy, O., & DiAngelo, R. (2017). *Is everyone really equal? An introduction to key concepts in critical social justice education* (2nd ed.). Teachers College Press.

Taylor, M., & Diamond, M. (2020). The role of self-study in teaching and teacher education for social justice. In J. Kitchen, A. Berry, S. M. Bullock, A. R. Crowe, M. Taylor, H. Gudjonsdottir, & L. Thomas (Eds.), *International handbook of self-study of teaching and teacher education practices* (2nd ed., pp. 509–543). Springer. https://doi.org/10.1007/978-981-13-1710-1_16-1

Whiting, E. F., & Cutri, R. M. (2015). Naming a personal "unearned" privilege: What pre-service teachers identify after a critical multicultural education course. *Multicultural Perspectives, 17*(1), 13–20. http://doi.org/10.1080/15210960.2014.9847717

Yi, H. (2016). What is the definition of microagression? [Video]. *New York Times*. Retrieved June 13, 2021, from https://www.youtube.com/watch?time_continue=4&v=bjzWENcW6NQ

Zeichner, K. M., & Noffke, S. E. (2001). Practitioner research. In V. Richardson (Ed.), *Handbook of research on teaching* (4th ed., pp. 298–330). Macmillan.

Zemblylas, M. (2010). Teachers' emotional experiences of growing diversity and multiculturalism in schools and the prospects of an ethic of discomfort. *Teachers and Teaching: Theory and Practice, 16*, 703–716.

CHAPTER 3

A Tale of Becoming and Radiance

Our Evolving Teacher Educator Identities in Post-Apartheid South Africa

Anita Hiralaal and Lungile Masinga

As human beings, we are trapped in the identity of being and becoming where being is a process of stasis and becoming is an ever-flowing process. In the process of being, change is not seen as a desirable mechanism of transformation and growth but rather as something that needs to be avoided. Again, because we are human, the fear of change is attributed to our attachment to our identities. On the contrary, our characteristics and core features that give us our identities are never static, but perpetually evolving and adapting to higher levels. Living life openly and without limitations to learning, is when we will achieve the heights of radiance, a state of becoming and not being. Embracing this ideology of our identities never being static, we show in this chapter how we used storywork as a methodological approach, to show how our identities as teacher educators have evolved in relation to the diversity of our changing contexts in post-apartheid South Africa and how we reach our stage of radiance.

1   Background

"If there is one thing Africans are known for, it is the art of storytelling. Storytelling serves to keep history, culture, and the genealogies of people alive" (Smith, 2014, p. 1). For several generations, stories from Africa have traditionally been passed down by word of mouth. Often, after a hard day's work, the adults would gather the children together by moonlight, around a village fire and tell stories which in African culture is called "izinganekwane" (tales). This form of storytelling is traditionally called "Tales by Moonlight" (Ige, 2019).

In post-apartheid South Africa, storytelling has another purpose to serve, namely to heal, reconcile, and bear testimony to the experiences under apartheid. The Truth and Reconciliation Commission was a national platform for people to tell their stories. Between 1996 and 1998, the sound of victims weeping as they publicly testified about their sufferings reverberated through town halls and churches across South Africa. It was an essential model for socio-political transformation for the nation. South Africa was once a beacon of hope on the African continent. When it made the transition to a multiracial democracy in 1994 after the abolition of apartheid, South Africans were confident of a peaceful and secure future. Nelson Mandela, South Africa's first Black president, steered the new "rainbow nation" on a course of reconciliation that aimed to alleviate the wounds left by the harsh system of racial segregation under White minority rule.

Currently, South Africa remains fraught with underlying tensions that challenge real unity among citizens from different demographic backgrounds. Despite certain moments of unity that the country has experienced, these alone are not sufficient to sustain unity among peoples who have been in conflict for over 300 years. Memories of apartheid brutality have not yet died, and issues of transformation remain pressing. At the same time, there are immense challenges to overcome, including poverty and unemployment. Today's South Africa is marked by a rapidly growing gap between rich and poor – and between Black and White, despite an overall reduction in poverty. The country that was once Africa's economic powerhouse has become economically unstable and ranks as the world's most unequal country.

With the dismantling of apartheid in 1994, and the drive for a free and democratic country, came this dire quest for social reconstruction and democratisation, redress, social justice, and equity (Jansen, 1998). A central feature of this transformation was the restructuring and reorganization of the education system especially teacher education. Initial teacher preparation, often called teacher training (Gore, 1995) was in the hands of teacher training colleges. However, in the early 2000s, teacher training colleges and technikons were closed and universities of technology were created. Traditional universities and universities of technology now provide teacher education. Whilst apartheid has negatively affected the lives of all South Africans, it has been particularly devastating for the young children of the apartheid regime. They were growing up with the trauma associated with a divided society and the "childshock" caused by political unrest and a society in the throes of major social transition. The race-based inequalities that were created during apartheid, which resulted in the population being fragmented along racial lines, are still prevalent today almost two decades after the banning of apartheid.

Two such children are Lungile Masinga, now a Black teacher educator at a traditional university and Anita Hiralaal, an Indian teacher educator at a university of technology. Leslie Marmon Silko (1977) wrote, "I will tell you something about stories ... They aren't just entertainment ... They are all we have ... to fight off illness and death. You don't have anything if you don't have the stories."

Likewise, we highlight our different teacher educator experiences in storied accounts that also includes our rewards and challenges in post-apartheid

South Africa. This chapter presents our personal story pieces followed by our voices converging in a dialogue during which we reflect on our individual story pieces. Writing our personal stories about our lived experiences enabled us to engage with past histories about our families, our communities, our educational experiences, our socio-political contexts and our teacher educator experiences and how these experiences influenced our evolving identities. Using storywork in self-study, helped us to get a broader understanding of our evolving identities and to transform our understandings of the past, present and future and of ourselves in relation to our dynamic contexts.

2   Storywork as a Self-Study Method

Generally, humans are psychologically and physiologically configured to want to make sense of their lives through their personal stories (Archibald, 2008). These stories shape our identities (Iseke, 2013) because our identities and experiences are constantly shifting. Stories influence how we feel about ourselves, how we feel about others, and how we feel about the world around us. Stories and telling them gives us a purpose in life because our stories are personally meaningful. Writing your own story (past, present and future) acts as a blueprint for creating a vision for your life.

So, in this chapter, we used storywork in self-study to create and share stories about ourselves. Storywork has come to encompass the sheer breadth of ways in which storytelling serves as a historical record, as a form of teaching and learning, and as an expression of culture and identity (Archibald et al., 2019). Storywork can also be used as a research practice of "making meaning through telling stories" (Madondo et al., 2019, p. 20). Interestingly, storywork compared to empirical data have unique properties (van Manen, 2015), because they allow us to turn back to "life as lived" (p. 70), and thus we become personally involved. Hence, in this chapter, we composed our stories as a self-study method to explore how our teacher educator identities have evolved in the face of a context that is not only dynamic but incredibly diverse.

We are South African female teacher educators, born in the years of the apartheid regime and educated under its divided rule. However, we are still diverse in terms of race, culture, heritage with socio-political background. It is this very diversity that frames our unique experiences as we compile our stories. We emphasise critical episodes and specific periods in our lives and what those experiences mean to us. We learned that the overall intention of using storywork in self-study is to provide a compelling and thought-provoking rendition, which is more than a good narrative, it is "epistemologically respectable" (O'Dea, 1994, p. 161). Ashton-Warner (1963) sums this up most eloquently when she says that in stories, "there is passion and energy, brilliances and heroisms every morning ... challenging and piercing the alarmed mediocrities; generating all manner of sensational ideas that collide and explode like astral galaxies" (pp. 21–22).

This makes us believe that researchers like ourselves, when they tell their stories using self-study, put their hearts and souls into the story because stories are a "clearer connection to their beliefs and values" (Tidwell & Fitzgerald, 2004, p. 93). This is very pertinent in this chapter because it looks at what we care about, what are our rewards and struggles in post-apartheid South Africa. We learned that "to know the past is to know oneself as an individual and as a representative of a socio-historical moment in time" (Bullough & Gitlin, 1995, p. 25). Therefore, we recollected the early influences of our home, our families, and our communities. This helped us to take a step out of our academic lives and focus on where we come from. Telling stories of our personal histories, align with the work of Samaras et al. (2004) when they say that the teacher researchers also engage in critical conversations with others in their context to get other viewpoints, one of the most important characteristics of self-study research (LaBoskey, 2004). In self-study research, the "others" are known as critical friends. Samaras (2011) stated that critical friends could be colleagues or fellow researchers who engage in critical dialogue with the researcher about their research whilst offering encouragement and support as well as constructive feedback about the study. In writing this chapter, we acted as critical friends to each other. We engaged in critical dialogue about our stories, we asked each other provocative questions and critiqued each other's stories. Consequently, in the next section Lungile will provide a rendition of her story followed by Anita who will relate her story.

3   Lungile's Personal Story Piece

Being a Black teacher educator presently at a traditional university which was once a "Whites only" domain in South Africa, during apartheid, was not without its fair share of racism, classism and sexism coupled with exploitation and marginalization. On the backdrop of this context, I share my experiences in what constitutes a dynamic narrative of how these various encounters shaped and moulded me into the teacher educator that I have become.

I was born in the 70s under the apartheid regime as a Black girl child raised in a township. In South Africa, the term township and location usually refer to the often underdeveloped racially segregated urban areas that, from the late

19th century until the end of apartheid, were reserved for non-Whites, namely Indians, Africans and Coloureds. My family and my context played a huge role in the formation of what I view, as my constantly evolving identity. The first three years of experience as an early career academic truly tested my notion of self as an educated woman who was employed based on her suitability for the post. I found myself questioning my worthiness and competence to realize my contractual obligations and personal ambitions. These internalized processes of self-doubt found me engaging in reflective moments, where my identity was at the forefront of my analysis.

Owing to my background, I knew coming in to the university, I possessed a multi-layered identity of self, which I believed shaped my teacher identity with which I came into academia. This identity was constructed through my life's experiences. I am a product of the Bantu Education system that was the brainchild of the apartheid government. The Bantu Education Act, 1953 (Act No. 47 of 1953; later renamed the Black Education Act, 1953) was a South African segregation law which legalized several aspects of the apartheid system. Its major provision was enforcing racially separated educational facilities. This education system had no life expectations for me, except as a domestic or factory worker. However, in my family, a home that was controlled by a formidable grandmother who ruled with a strong fist, that was not to be my identity. Armed with visions of who I was going to become as her grandchild, she informed me that she was to be the last person in her bloodline to work in a White man's house as a domestic worker.

The social position of the country at the time of my schooling was in its own course of becoming with the reclaiming of basic human rights. The township was up in arms, fighting the existence of what it deemed as the most demeaning education system. I saw the burning of schools and destruction of property becoming the norm since they were viewed as tools of the White man to keep us down. As a Black child of that era, the narrative about school was that of horror. We began to dream less of the future and saw less of a position that schooling was supposed to hold for our lives. I believe that my grandmother understood this battle and wanted to make sure I did not succumb to this call. For my high school years, the race of the school principal played a significant role in the decision as my parents worked with the understanding that, since the principal was White, the school was the best.

While at the school, the most significant change came with the introduction of five new teachers, who were not just White, but were also soldiers dressed in brown uniforms. We were informed that they were there to teach us, and we were going to learn how to speak their language. Never in my darkest imaginations could I have foreseen that, one of these soldiers would hold a special place in my heart. It took a lot from him to gain our acceptance let alone trust. It was not just our positions on his race that he had to dismantle, but our views of schooling. He taught us to see his language as a tool that we could use to strive for anything we desired of what our lives should turn out be. I came to see the purpose of schooling and my place in it. I started to understand who that self was and what position that self, held for my life.

In my final year of school, he informed us of a college of education that was formally for Whites only, but was then accepting Black students. This is how I became the third group of Black students to be accepted in a White college. It was in this space where everything I knew and understood about myself and the history of my country and its people were tested. I spent four years in a space that in settling ways, informed me I was not needed. That questioned, in many ways, my ability to fit in and I wondered what my presence meant to the safety and future of the college. In many ways, there was a lot of unlearning that I was expected to do, even then, I was not expected to be equal. It is those years when I truly understood racism at its different levels of expression. It was also a space where I got to understand the impact of my former education and the limitations it created. I got to see the other side of the fence, as I began to see teaching and learning differently. Even though, in the beginning I was informed I had to do that in specialized classes for Black students because White students were taught in different classes, and that it was for my own good. I began to see student protest differently as we fought to be seen and included in a White campus that clearly had no interest in our Blackness, only in how it could make us to some extent "White." The internal and external struggles during those years were what shaped and reshaped my understanding of who I was and who I was to become as a practicing teacher.

Sixteen years of teaching tested all my notions of schooling as I found myself back in a reality that had not changed and bared the wounds of apartheid. I knew the key was engaging myself in continuous learning, and it was in those years that I got my PhD. This meant entering Higher Education as a teacher educator; I already held a doctoral degree with a few publications under my belt. I knew who I was and I knew the self that my experiences have produced. However, I was under no illusion of being fully cooked. Coming into academia in a discipline that spoke to my interest and which was led by women, I thought I was home. However, I met with rejection, as I was questioned about my credentials, and questioned why I was there. All experiences of doubt came back as I questioned the very thing I treasured because the acts of my fellow feminist colleagues contradicted the writings. I had to find my way, I had to build bonds that transcended disciplinary boundaries and interest to get to the teacher educator self I am.

I have formed relationships that have guided my growth in this field and have made me into a reflexive practitioner who comprehends the impact of understanding self-identity. The current challenge to my teacher educator identity now is ironically the evolving nature of the students I teach, and my positionality in that change. I am faced with students whose interest in the field of education does not extend beyond the end of monthly cheques they hope to earn. My internal struggles now, are where this positions me and my own convictions of who I am as a teacher educator. Compounding my dilemma, is the manipulation of the university systems by students to get their way exacerbated by the politicizing of the university. The struggles, poverty, geographical locations are now being used as endorsements for not working hard. This is coming across from all racial lines. This brings a new challenge to my own teacher educator identity in the current state of higher education.

4   Anita's Personal Story Piece

As an Indian person, I lived under the apartheid regime in South Africa, not as part of the White population nor as part of the Black population. So, the identity I created for myself was not one as a South African, but as an Indian. The Population Registration Act of 1950 provided the basic framework for apartheid by classifying all South Africans by race, including Bantu (Black Africans), Coloured (mixed race) and White. A fourth category, Asian (meaning Indian and Pakistani) was later added. During the ideological apartheid era from 1948 to 1994, Indians were called and often voluntarily accepted, terms that ranged from "Asians" to "Indians" (O'Malley, 2018). This led further to seeing myself as a visitor in South Africa, despite the fact that I was born here. It's only after Nelson Mandela was elected as president (in 1994) that South African Indians saw themselves as a community that is not part of some horrible subjugation in history. Indians who were citizens before 1994, and thus discriminated against by the apartheid system, are now, post-apartheid, classified as Black for the purposes of Employment Equity; that is, they are classified as having been disadvantaged under apartheid. This did nothing to make me feel welcome in my own country because I questioned this identity as a Black citizen that was forced on me. I am not Black, I am Indian but the impression that I got was that I should classify myself as Black because then I could enjoy the spoils of the country. I questioned myself, was being Indian not good enough to secure employment. I had to renounce my heritage and my identity as an Indian then I could get employment.

Throughout my life, I clung to the idea that I was complacent in my identity as a young Indian girl, but I always tried to imagine what must have been going through the minds of my forefathers, who assembled at the port in Calcutta or Madras in 1860, to embark on the journey to South Africa as indentured laborers. A country where they lost their heritage and their identities and their caste was thrown away when they crossed the ocean. So when the Indians came here, they formed a new identity that was without caste. Indians have spent many years deleting our history and wanting to be White because we thought being White was the best thing on Earth.

In my little Indian community, we tried to salvage what little we knew about our traditions and our rituals that our forefathers brought with them from India as indentured laborers. They brought their rich heritage of delicious spices, culture and art with them, but sadly lost their language and their identities. I find it very difficult to develop an identity in South Africa when I cannot speak my mother tongue which is Hindi, nor can I communicate fluently in an African language; I speak in a language borrowed from another country. It makes me wonder how I will ever reach my stage of radiance when my identities have to constantly change to suit other people because that is just the way it is. What is also very clear in my memories is a casual racist expression used during the years of apartheid. Indians in South Africa were (and sometimes still are) referred to by the racial epithet "coolie" (News24 Correspondent, 2017). A coolie is a porter who works on the train stations in India carrying travellers' heavy luggage on their heads for a few coins.

My schooling career was uneventful as were my years as a teacher of accounting in an Indian high school. Our school curriculum was developed and controlled by White people and we were taught from primary school that White people were superior and Black people were inferior but we were never taught about Indians despite attending a school for Indians, but we had to learn about Black and White people and their histories.

For my undergraduate studies, I never attended a higher education institution full time because I married at the age of 19 and had two children by the time I was 24 years old. Fortunately, my husband was a progressive Indian man and he allowed me to study through a distance learning institution as it was unheard of in my community that a married woman should attend full-time university.

I went into higher education with my identity as an Indian teacher. My identity was constructed by my involvement in the communities of practice that I belonged to which was the Indian high school with only Indian teachers and learners. Like Wenger (1998) said, the identity of teachers develop within the social, political and historical contexts in which they work, which in my case was the school environment. Hence, my identity was shaped by my context and the wider context of Indian school education, which was different from the school education of other races in South Africa.

My first appointment in teacher education was at a college of education lecturing in accounting. This transition from school to a college of education and my identity as an Indian teacher placed me initially in a very complex situation because I came into higher education with teaching beliefs, values and philosophies of an Indian schoolteacher. But this college of education was built during the apartheid era in a Black township. A township is a residential area that was designated for the Black communities during apartheid. I dressed in colorful Indian traditional clothing, with a red dot on my forehead, clanking bangles on my wrists and other colorful jewelery, which is the norm for married Indian women. I thought the more radiantly adorned I was, the better impression I would make. On the contrary, I was very embarrassed because everybody stared at me. On numerous occasions, I would hear these comments: "AmaNdiya, hamba khaya" which translates from IsiZulu as "Indian, go home." The other lecturers were either Black or White and I was the only Indian person on the staff. I felt very isolated because I was neither accepted by the White nor the Black community of lecturers.

My being there was also different for the students because they were used to being taught by Black teachers at schools where their teachers code switched between English and IsiZulu, the mother tongue of the Black population. They were also taught by Black lecturers at the college who code-switched as well. It was the first time they were being taught by an Indian person. I felt that if I wanted to belong in that environment, I had to change who I was. But I felt like a traitor to my Indian heritage especially when I began dressing in a manner that was less colorful because I felt that that was what defined me as an Indian person. On many occasions, when I got home, my family used to look at me strangely when I exclaimed in Isizulu or did something that was totally out of character. At times of introspection, I realized that my Indian identity was slowly eroding and I was actually consciously changing my identity to fit in with my teaching environment.

But soon, the government closed all teacher training colleges and merged them with other institutions and created universities of technology. The different universities that were racially divided during apartheid were also merged. Because of the reorganization of higher education, many Black female staff were appointed at our university of technology. The situation to date is still the same, with me being the only Indian female academic staff member. Once again, I was left out because the new female staff were completely at ease with the existing female staff. The fact that as females, I would have expected them to readily accept me and include me in their circle. But this was not the case and I did not blame them. These women had gone through marginalization, discrimination and many other atrocities during the apartheid times so they were fearful of a non-Black person entering their community. They felt protective of each other and safeguarded their new-found freedom. Although I was rather lonely and I felt left out when they spoke to each other in their mother tongues because I could not understand them, I was very conscious of why they behaved as they did. But secretly, I felt that apartheid was rearing its ugly head again. Colonialism was the first thing Indian families grew as part of. When indenture was abolished, there was apartheid.

Also, this move to a university was fraught with uncertainty, fear and insecurity for all the staff, both Black and White as well as the students. No professional development was provided to ensure a smooth transition for us with a college mentality to university teaching. Teacher training colleges have been associated with the preparation of a practically skilled teacher who was competent in the classroom, on the sports-field, and with cultural extra-murals. Now we were just expected to move seamlessly into teacher education, where there is a greater emphasis on the development of reflexive and critical competencies in students. In addition I had never been involved in research activities but now I had to teach and do research, publish papers and contend with this paradigm shift. I was caught in this identity conflict. I had just resigned myself to being a lecturer in a college of education, now I was expected to become a teacher educator in a university of technology just like that. Lecturers had now become teacher educators and with that title came the recurriculation of our qualifications from teaching diplomas to degrees. The Council of Higher Education (CHE) was created to which we had to submit all curriculum documents for the new degrees that were going to be offered. When we designed the curriculum of our Bachelor of Education degree, it was rejected by the CHE who also threatened to close our teacher education programme. We were petrified that we all will lose our jobs so we scrambled around and went to colleagues and friends teaching at universities to help us design our qualifications. Coupled with compounding fear of unemployment, rejection and insecurity, I was elected as the curriculum champion in the department because my colleagues felt that I had a better command of English than they had. Although, I was fully aware that I was selected for selfish reasons, I was nevertheless very glad because I felt that for the first time, I was one of "them." I no longer feel like the odd one out; I am a teacher educator and I am growing and learning with the staff and students. Maybe, in time, all South Africans will be able to live together as one not as a divided nation.

After reading our personal stories, we came to the conclusion that just talking about the stories as a way of reflecting on what we wrote, was not going to provoke the kind of responses that we desired. We desired to reflect on our stories in a way that was provocative, a way that will leave us clamoring and thirsty for more. To our surprise, we found this way back with Dewey (1938) whose timeless ideas and suggestions presented us with the idea of dialogue as a way of reflecting on our stories. We also agreed with Bakhtin (1984) that our stories are

> eminently practical in that they are about our lives; at the same time they reflect our deepest desires, identities, and questions, i.e., our theories. To live means to participate in dialogue: to ask questions, to heed, to respond, to agree, and so forth. (p. 293)

Madondo et al. (2019) found that using dialogue led to researcher "reciprocal, mutually respectful learning from sharing their personal story pieces with each other" (p. 24). Thus, the short exchange that we term our reflective dialogue, is presented next.

5 Our Reflective Dialogue

Anita: Lungile, how do you understand your teacher educator identity after writing your storypiece and reflecting on it?

Lungile: I am learning that my identity is in a constantly changing mode and developing, and as it evolves it does not leave behind who I have been. Every new way of being that I am becoming is entangled to the old self. It has not introduced a new me. What I found is that my teacher educator identity is very much linked to every aspect of the life that I have lived and has led to who I am now as a teacher educator. I learned that I cannot separate my historical experiences, my cultural experiences everything that has moulded me. I draw my ideas and my ideologies that influences how I teach and what I think teaching is comes from that background,that is what I realized. The people that I have interacted with in that process, my grandmother, my high school teacher, all of them have influenced my concept of what is education and how to teach others to be educators. It is all entangled in that. That is what I've realized.

Anita: I always saw myself as not as belonging, I saw myself as an Indian person, I found all kinds of excuses for my Indianness. Everything happened because I am an Indian, for example my non-acceptance at the campus when

I initially started teaching there. But when I did the self-study, I sat down and thought about it. I realized that people were not going to accommodate my Indianess, but I had to change. I changed my identity to suit my environment. I actually read some literature that said that your identity is constantly evolving and how when you are placed in a different context from the one you have been used to, then your identity will change to suit your environment. In my home environment, I was taught to be submissive and not voice my opinion especially because I was a female. I realized that his could be why I took things as they were when I first got into the university. Then I realized I had to change, then probably I will find my identity, I will see myself as a teacher educator at the university. Also, if I constantly maintained that I am an Indian, and I don't belong with other people, I will not fit in at this predominantly Black institution. I had to change my views, I had to fit into my context and then my identity will change. Because right from the start, I went in to the campus not with the thought I was a teacher educator, but I went in with the thought that I was an Indian.

Lungile: So, it got you to look at the space and the people in it differently.

Anita: Yes, The first time when I wore my Indian clothes, they said *"AmaNdiya, hamba khaya"* I thought they were being offensive. When I got a little more familiar with them, I asked them why they said that and they responded "No, because you were different, we were never taught by an Indian person before, we were actually scared of you that is why we said that. We have never had anything against you because you are an Indian"

Lungile: You see now how our stories connect. They were coming from where I was coming from, where you are suspicious of the new, because the new for you always represented being rejected, not accepted, deemed less than the other. So when the new enters your life, the tendency is to react to it first before it turns out to be the worst thing to happen to you. Remember with my story, with my teacher who represented everything that was apartheid for me. He was White, English speaking and a soldier. The immediate reaction was rejection and for you, you were that soldier to them.

Anita: I never saw it that way before and at that time I thought they didn't want me there because I was an Indian. You are right, at that time I was actually a threat to them, as you saw the soldier, they saw me. In doing my self-study and reflecting on what happened to me, then I realized it wasn't like that. I believe now, it was their fear that made them react that way and I shouldn't have taken it personally.

Lungile: That means that in hindsight, we are all victims of the system of apartheid.

Anita: Absolutely.

Lungile: It created this division in our minds that we expect less from each other and we expect every person to reflect what we have been told who they are and that is how we react to each other. So when you enter into a new space, and you find these individuals that you have been told about, your reaction to them is aligned to what has been said about them. You come in already having a set mind as to who they are and how they will react to you. Looking at the connections in our stories, I see in a way that we are victims of a system truly designed to be dividing. I believe they achieved that because they did not just physically divide us but they also divided us in our minds as well.

Anita: Yes, the fact that after apartheid I went to an institution long after it was dismantled, I still thought of myself as a South African Indian. After apartheid, I shouldn't have been thinking that way. It is those kinds of thoughts that continue to divide us. Even now, in this present day we still maintain that I am Indian, you are Black, she's a Coloured and he is White. But I also read the article by Vahed (Vahed & Desai, 2010) that he wrote in 2010, that post-apartheid is a chance for us to develop our own identities whilst we come together as a united country.

Lungile: What also came through as well is when we look at the students we have now, we want to see ourselves in them. We want to see how we saw the opportunity to be in a university. We saw it as something that was going to make us be somebody and valued it because we fought for it. That is what we want to see in our students. So when we think about our task as teacher educators, we want to instill in our students, whether it's content or just the idea of professionalism and who is a teacher. Whatever it is that we say to them emanates from this. I realized that I judge my students on the basis of who I believe they should be. When I teach them, I am teaching them on the basis of who I believe they should become, because it is based on how I see the profession and my role in it as a teacher educator. All of it stems from that. When I see the lack of appreciation of the privileges that they have, the sense of entitlement that they have, it rubs me the wrong way because we earned our positions at the university. We worked hard to have it under very bad circumstances, and my story was not unique. Yet they have it differently, but it seems like the more the playing field has been leveled for them, the more they don't seem to appreciate. It affects my identity, and makes me wonder if I am still the right fit as I try to reconcile this new way of looking at my role as a teacher educator.

Anita: Do you think their home environment and communities have an effect on the way they behave? The political influences, that are saying you are entitled, and you need not work for what you need, but it must come to you.

Lungile: Yes, post-apartheid, there was an expectation and a sense that now we are going to get, we should be given because we are deserving. There was that sense that now it is my turn, now give me, do for me. Then we came up with many systems that our people needed, such as grants and housing. However, in a way it turned people into receivers. This is what the students that we have now come expecting it. Their understanding of the profession has changed.

Anita: It has something to do with the fact that a teacher's degree comes with full funding and they now enter the profession as a last resort because of money. Sadly, teaching is no longer a noble profession but a means to an end.

6 What Did We Learn about Ourselves and Diversity in Post-Apartheid South Africa?

In our reflective dialogue, we both agreed that our identities are constantly evolving. It is evident that personal histories, socio-political backgrounds and educational experiences influenced our identities and who we are as teacher educators. As Olsen (2012) commented, a person's identity is formed by their religious beliefs, race, ethnic considerations, language, class and gender. In Lungile's home, her grandmother was adamant that history will never repeat itself in Lungile becoming a domestic. What emerged is that her grandmother was the driving force behind her expectations of herself. Unlike Anita, whose home environment was completely different from Lungile's in that in her home she was taught to be submissive and not voice her opinion. However, both of us had to change our identities to suit our contexts. Lungile's background, where she was subjected to the violence and the upheaval of the apartheid struggle had molded her into an angry young person who saw no value in going to school. But the irony of the situation was the person that was the very epitome of apartheid, the White soldier, believed in her and influenced her to change her ideas about schooling and made her accept that she could be whomever she wanted to be. This became apparent when he encouraged her to apply to a previously White institution. Anita, on the other hand had never been exposed to the atrocities committed by apartheid or the accompanying violence because she was sheltered in her home and her tight knit community. Politics were never discussed in her home and she was not exposed to other racial groups so she did not experience the wrath and anger of the Black people who were subjected to such unjust and harsh treatment by apartheid.

Anita and Lungile came in to higher education with preconceived notions that had molded and shaped their identities but their different experiences dramatically led to them recreating their identities. As a teenager, growing up in the township, Lungile avoided the political actions taken by the township youth because sometimes she did not quite understand their actions but when she experienced racism in all its might at the college of education, she began to see student protest in a different light. Her identity changed because she came to this college with intentions of studying and not getting involved in politics but her treatment at the college forced her identity to change. In contrast, Anita was a mother and never attended a university as a full-time student. So she came into education with the identity of a married Indian woman and a mother. However, when she was exposed to the realities of her context at the college of education, she felt she was being marginalized because she was Indian. She had a narrow view of the world but when she realized it had nothing to do with the fact that she was Indian, she changed her attitude and with that attitude change, her identity changed as well. She accepted that she was a teacher educator in a previously Black institution. This is in line with the broad understanding from the literature that teacher educators have to transform their identities from teachers to teachers of teachers and to become researchers of teaching and teacher education (Sweenen, Jones & Volman, 2010). Anita agrees with Vahed and Desai (2010) when they stated that post-apartheid gave all South Africans the opportunity to recreate themselves and their identities within "particular cultural, racial, and ethnic milieus, and to be brought together as equals in celebration of unity through diversity in a non-racial state" (p. 2).

We agree that as teacher educators in different institutions, our situations are at present very similar in many respects. The entry requirements to study teaching are not as stringent as other qualifications so after being rejected entry into other disciplines, students see teaching as the last resort. We both have expectations of our students as future teachers but the attitude of our students who have a sense of entitlement and feel they do not have to work to achieve but they must be given everything, is altering our identities. From being dedicated and enthusiastic teacher educators, the attitude of the students is forcing us to relook at our identities as teacher educators.

7   Conclusion

Self-study fostered an understanding of our identity development as we traversed through our life journeys. We reconstructed and reorganized our identities as we moved from one environment, community of practice or context to the other. This self-study disrupted our thinking that teacher educator identity development and formation were dependent only on our interactions as teacher educators in our academic contexts. But we have come to the understanding that our identity development and formation are not fixed stagnant processes but multi-dimensional, impacted by our cultural histories, environments and experiences as well as the people with whom we interact on a personal, social and professional level.

We see our identity formation as a ball of sticky tape always moving. Sometimes, something will stick to our ball and sometimes other things will just fall off. Some will stick for a short while and when it does, it changes the appearance and the shape of our ball but when some other object sticks to our sticky tape ball, the shape and appearance is different. This is likened to our identities, the context we find ourselves, the people and situations we interact with changes how we see ourselves and this is a never ending process. Although we all live in the same world where many of our experiences overlap, the reason why we are all unique is because we ultimately choose what does or does not impact us in a crucial or unimportant way. It is through the addition of the myriad parts of our lives that come together to create our identity. So, we believe that our identities are in a constant state of becoming and keeping ourselves open to all possibilities, that's when we achieve radiance.

References

Archibald, J. (2008). *An Indigenous storywork methodology*. Sage.
Archibald, J., Lee-Morgan, J. B. J., & Santolo, J. D. (2019). *Decolonizing research: Indigenous storywork as methodology*. Seagull Books.
Ashton-Warner, S. (1963). *Teacher*. Simon & Schuster.
Bakhtin, M. (1984). *The dialogical principle*. Manchester University Press.
Bullough, R. V., Jr., & Gitlin, A. (1995). *Becoming a student of teaching: Methodologies for exploring self and school context*. Garland.
Bullough, R. V., Jr., & Pinnegar, S. E. (2001). Guidelines for quality in autobiographical forms of self-study research. *Educational Researcher, 30*(3), 13–22.
Dewey, J. (1938). *Experience and education*. Macmillan.
Gore, J. (1995). *Emerging issues in teacher education*. Innovative Links Project.
Ige, S. (2019). *African folktales*. Retrieved May 20, 2021, from https://anikefoundation.org/african-folktales
Iseke, J. (2013). Indigenous storytelling as research. *International Review of Qualitative Research, 6*(4), 559–577.
Jansen, J. D. (1998). Curriculum reform in South Africa: A critical analysis of outcomes-based education. *Cambridge Journal of Education, 28*, 321–331. https://doi.org/10.1080/0305764980280305

LaBoskey, V. K. (2004). The methodology of self-study and its theoretical underpinnings. In J. J. Loughran, M. L. Hamilton, V. K. LaBoskey & T. Russell (Eds.), *International handbook of self-study of teaching and teacher education practices* (pp. 817–870). Springer.

Madondo, S., Mkhize, N., & Pithouse-Morgan, K. (2019). "I recognised that I needed to look searchingly at my own teaching": Storywork as a self-study method for educational research for social change. *Educational Research for Social Change, 8*(2), 14–28.

News24 Correspondent. (2017). *2017: News24's year in review* [Press release]. Retrieved May 20, 2021, from https://www.news24.com/news24/southafrica/news/2017-news24s-year-in-review-20171231

O'Dea, J. W. (1994). Pursuing truths in narrative research. *Journal of Philosophy of Education, 28*(2), 161–172. https://doi.org/10.1111/j.1467-9752.1994.tb00323

Olsen, B. (2012). *Identity theory, teacher education, and diversity*. Paradigm.

O'Malley, P. (2018). Migration and conflict. *New England Journal of Public Policy, 30*(2). Retrieved May 20, 2021, from https://scholarworks.umb.edu/nejpp/vol30/iss2/

Samaras, A. (2011). *Self-study teacher research: Improving your practice through collaborative inquiry*. Sage.

Samaras, A. P., Hicks, M. A., & Berger, J. G. (2004). Self-study through personal history. In J. J. Loughran, M. L. Hamilton, V. K. LaBoskey, & T. Russell (Eds.), *International handbook of self-study of teaching and teacher education practice.* (pp. 905–942). Springer.

Silko, L. M. (1977). *Ceremony*. Penguin Books.

Smith, J. (2014). *The power of arts 1 – Telling the South African story through storytelling*. Retrieved May 20, 2021, from http://www.sabceducation.co.za/kweek/heritage-arts-culture/item/social-cohesion-through-arts-heritage-and-culture

Sweenen, A., Jones, K., & Volman, M. (2010). Teacher educators: Their identities, sub-identities and implications for professional development. *Professional Development in Education, 36*(1), 131–148.

Tidwell, D., & Fitzgerald, L. (2004). Self-study as teaching. In J. J. Loughran, M. L. Hamilton, V. K. LaBoskey, & T. Russell (Eds.), *International handbook of self-study of teaching and teacher education practices* (pp. 69–102). Springer.

Vahed, G., & Desai, A. (2010). Identity and belonging in post-apartheid South Africa: The case of Indian South Africans. *Journal of Social Sciences, 25*(1–3), 1–12. https://doi.org/10.1080/09718923.2010.11892861

Van Manen, M. (2015). *Researching lived experience: Human science for an action sensitive pedagogy*. Routledge.

Wenger, E. (1998). *Communities of practice: Learning, meaning, and identity*. Cambridge University Press.

CHAPTER 4

Wrestling with Dilemmas, Vulnerabilities, and Hopes

Being an Immigrant Mother and a Transnational Teacher Educator

Jinhee Kim

> Reporter: This is not a story about ESOL classes being evil. A lot of kids do benefit from ESOL classes and language services. This is a story about the screening process [to identify English Language Learners], and some parents have been taken aback by that process …. Lisa Garcia Bedolla is an education professor at the University of California at Berkeley. She researched the ESOL screening process for kindergartners in California …. Bedolla argues, in some cases, schools make assumptions based on a child's heritage – or answers parents give on the Home Language Survey.
>
> Dr. Bedolla: I did this study because it happened to me. My daughter got classified as an English learner. I'm a native speaker of English. So is my husband. I'm a professor of education at [University of California] Berkeley. I thought that would matter. It didn't. (Dalton, 2016, August 24)

One day, as I was heading home in my car, I turned on the radio. After some advertisements, a reporter began to discuss parents' concerns about the English Language Learner (ELL) screening process in the state where I live. Instinctively, I pushed the record button on my cell phone so that I would be able to thoroughly listen to the segment again later. This radio segment reminded me of my own concerns about a notice regarding the English Language Service (ELS) program at the school that Chloe, my daughter, attended (the names of the child and teachers in this chapter are pseudonyms). As a native speaker of Korean in a home where both Korean and English are used, I had received a letter from Chloe's school stating that she had been identified as an ELL. She was scheduled to have a test a few weeks before she began kindergarten to determine whether she would be placed in the ELS program; the day of the test was the first day that Chloe and I had visited the school since I registered her for kindergarten in May. At that time, Chloe and I did not even know who her kindergarten teacher and her classmates would be. As we entered the school,

Chloe was asked to follow a teacher into the building. Chloe seemed nervous because this school was unfamiliar to her and she had to leave her mother in order to follow the teacher. However, Chloe was somewhat prepared, as I had told her before I brought her to the school that some teachers would ask her some questions. When Chloe was first enrolled in kindergarten, I had felt excited and nervous – typical emotions among parents whose children are just starting elementary school. Soon, however, those positive feelings became contaminated by doubts, worries, and concerns after I received the notice regarding Chloe's ELL status. At the same time, I could not help but analyze the experience through my intersectional positions as a transnational teacher educator and as an immigrant mother.

In this chapter, I explore how my positions as a teacher educator and an immigrant mother interact with each other through the analysis of the firsthand experience of raising my child and in my teaching practices in teacher education. Drawing on the methodology of self-study in teacher education practices (S-STEP) (Bullough & Pinnegar, 2004; LaBoskey, 2004; Samaras & Freese, 2009), I illustrate the dilemmas and tensions that arise between "personal and professional phenomena" (Dinkelman, 2011, p. 309). This chapter introduces the perspective of an immigrant mother with professional knowledge in teacher education, a voice that has rarely appeared in the existing literature. In particular, this self-study highlights the tensions between maintaining one's heritage language and the dominant discourses and practices that affect both ELLs' language use and assessment. Despite debates regarding its definition (Polinsky & Kagan, 2007), a heritage language is commonly understood to be a minority language other than English used at home (Valdés, 2000, 2001), and it is often viewed as a deficit rather than an asset in schools (García, 2005; García et al., 2008; Sayer, 2013). With counter-storytelling (Solórzano & Yosso, 2002) from my experiences as a mother of an emergent bilingual child who uses Korean as a heritage language as well as English at home, this chapter discusses language use and assessment for emergent bilinguals who are often considered ELLs. In addition, the observations on language use and assessment in my child's schooling have made me raise several questions about my pedagogical practices in advocating for bilingualism and related assessments in teacher education. The following research questions guide this study:

1. What were the dilemmas and tensions that I, as an immigrant mother with professional knowledge, experienced while my child was in the ELS program at her school?
2. How did these dilemmas and tensions challenge and help me as a transnational teacher educator teaching teacher candidates?

1   Unheard Stories: Transnational Teacher Educators in Self-Study

Self-study is a research methodology that enables teacher educators to employ a critical tool for understanding themselves and others and for investigating teaching practices "in concert with maintaining a distance from practice to see what is happening while it is happening" (Loughran, 2006, p. 35). Self-study has been utilized in teacher education to examine teacher educators' intersectional roles (e.g., Ates, et al., 2015; Hernandez et al., 2015) and evolving and fluid professional identities (e.g., Pinnegar, 2005; Williams et al., 2012), thereby allowing for reflection upon teaching practices and providing implications for the field (Berry, 2004, 2007; Peercy et al., 2019). Although there exist studies incorporating S-STEP, there is a paucity of studies reflecting transnational teacher educators' voices "between public and private, theory and practice, research and pedagogy, self and other" (LaBoskey, 2004, p. 818). As Kitchen and his colleagues (2016) stated, transnational teacher educators have been engaged in limited self-study; there are relatively few studies that analyze the intersectional positions through which transnational teacher educators construct their teaching practices (e.g., Cortez-Castro, 2016; Han, 2016; Kim et al., 2018; Liao & Maddamsetti, 2019; Souto-Manning, 2006). Furthermore, paralleling Peercy and Sharkey's (2018) observation of the lack of self-studies in language and literacy teacher education, there are few self-studies in language and literacy among transnational educators.

Many studies related to ELLs tend to be conducted by educational researchers who are situated in contexts different from those of ELLs and their families. While I must acknowledge the significant contributions of those studies, I assert that self-study by transnational teacher educators can broaden and strengthen the understudied areas in teacher education; the inherently multilayered positions of these educators, when examined, can provide critical perspectives on teacher education. In particular, transnational teacher educators with children in the school system are in a unique position to access students' complex and private domains, which may not be available to educational researchers from outside the family context. By continuously negotiating different roles between parents and teacher educators, transnational teacher educators can strike the balance between "the intersection of self and other" (Bullough & Pinnegar, 2001, p. 15) as well as strengthening "ecological validity" (Carpenter, 1997, p. 396) in transnational contexts. In the background, this chapter unfolds the counter-storytelling on language use and assessment related to ELLs that a transnational teacher educator with an emergent bilingual child experienced.

2 Methodology

2.1 *Data Collection*

The data used in the chapter were gathered from 2015 to 2017 and included (a) several of my personal journals; (b) audio and video recordings including those featuring Chloe's verbal and non-verbal communications in contexts outside school, such as at home, in the car, and at the park; and (c) materials related to school, such as school newsletters, artifacts created by Chloe at school and sent to my home, and school information on websites. This chapter focuses on the tensions between language use and relevant assessments, centering the data collected from the period from when Chloe began pre-kindergarten to the conclusion of her year in the first grade.

2.2 *Data Analysis*

Data were analyzed through a thematic approach and according to grounded theory (Charmaz, 2014; Emerson et al., 1995). First, I conducted an initial coding process through reading and rereading each piece of data line by line "to see actions in each segment of data rather than applying pre-existing categories to the data" (Charmaz, 2014, p. 116). After reviewing each material, I saw that several initial codes emerged. The next step was to identify focused codes by constantly comparing and contrasting themes and patterns in and across the data. Through iterative readings of the data, it became clear that several focused codes were centered on language use and assessment.

Charmaz (2014) maintained that focused coding mainly occurs after the initial coding, but the process is not always linear. In this study, after identifying sixteen focused codes under the theme of language use and assessment, I kept comparing and contrasting the focused codes to see if they sufficiently narrowed and synthesized the initial codes. Through this process, seven focused codes were finalized: "school practices on language," "language practices at home," "Chloe's voices," "assessment of language and literacy," "culturally responsive assessment," "conflicts between reality and professional knowledge," and "vulnerability in teaching."

To increase the validity of this self-study beyond triangulation through multiple data sources, I tried to parallel my experiences as an immigrant mother and a transnational teacher educator with interpretations of the relevant existing literature through frequent memos. For example, related to "vulnerability in teaching" as a focused code, I reviewed the existing self-studies (e.g., Berry, 2007; Tidwell et al., 2006) and analyzed how I was situated similarly to and different from other researchers in terms of vulnerability in teaching.

3   Wrestling with Professional Knowledge on Emergent Bilinguals

Since Chloe was born, I have made efforts to maintain an environment in which Chloe can grow up as a bilingual, according to my knowledge of multilingualism in the existing literature. In particular, I have provided various opportunities such as reading storybooks in both English and Korean language, watching animated movies, and sending her to Korean heritage language school to learn Korean culture and language. Indeed, many studies have documented that maintaining a heritage language provides advantages to bilingual children's development in many ways, including socio-emotional development, such as healthy cultural identity (Phinney et al., 2001; Wright & Taylor, 1995), cognitive development (Bialystok, 2001; Bialystok et al., 2009), and higher academic achievement (Lee, 2002). Unfortunately, it has been reported that heritage languages are rapidly lost once children enter the school system (Fishman, 2001; López, 1996; Wong-Fillmore, 2000). Maintaining heritage languages has also been considered the responsibility of families rather than school systems (Cunningham, 2019; Lee & Oxelson, 2006; Weekly, 2018).

Despite my professional knowledge of the existing literature, I had consistently doubted my efforts to support bilingualism for Chloe. Was I doing the right things for my daughter? How could I help her to balance her use of different languages? To what extent should I encourage her to speak Korean at home? Was it still worth the travel for her to go to the heritage language school every Saturday if this meant sacrificing other possible activities on weekends? Similar to the dilemmas and experiences that other immigrant/transnational parents documented in the literature (e.g., Kim, 2011; Kwon, 2017; Winterbottom, 2013), I had been swayed by both advocacy for bilingualism (e.g., Bialystok et al., 2009; Phinney et al., 2001) and the negative discourses toward ELLs/emergent bilinguals (e.g., Mellom et al., 2018; Sugimoto et al., 2017), and my ambivalent attitude accelerated when Chloe was identified as an ELL in her kindergarten year. She had attended English-speaking day care since the age of five months, and when she was in preschool, I did not hear about any problems or concerns regarding her English proficiency from her teachers. Her preschool teachers assessed her cognitive, social-emotional, physical, language, and literacy development and shared the information from assessments with me. Chloe's English proficiency was not an issue at all until she was enrolled in a kindergarten class at a public school.

When she began kindergarten, I was asked to fill out the Heritage Language Survey (HLS) regarding Chloe's primary language at home. The HLS is an initial step to identify students who should receive services for ELLs under Title III of the No Child Left Behind Act of 2001 (NCLB). However, there is no standard survey across the US; there are different questionnaires among the states and among different school districts in the same states (Bailey & Kelly, 2013). Several scholars have expressed concerns about the validity of the HLS (Abedi, 2008; Bailey & Kelly, 2013; Littlejohn, 1998). In particular, Bailey and Kelly (2013) pointed out:

> (a) some HLS have ambiguous wording and (b) some HLS may have too few items to be meaningful for decision-making purposes, particularly if the questions do not focus on current language dominance and degree of English exposure information. (p. 792)

Paralleling Bailey and Kelly's arguments, when I was asked to fill out the HSL, I felt confused about how to answer some ambiguous questions. For example, I was required to choose only one language for the first question: "Which language does your child most frequently speak at home?" I could not immediately determine what Chloe most frequently spoke at home; she had used a mix of English and Korean before age three and had since tended to speak in English most often at home. Regardless, I needed to choose either English or Korean. Scratching my head, I decided to write "Korean." There was another question that made me hesitate: "Which language do adults in your home most frequently use when speaking with your child?" At home, I used to speak to Chloe in both English and Korean; particularly, when she was a toddler, I tried to balance the use of both languages. Once she went to preschool, I felt that she tended to use English more than Korean at home. I was worried about her losing her heritage language and encouraged her to speak in Korean at home. For this reason, I intentionally spoke more of the heritage language at home at that time. Doubting my interpretation of the survey question, I filled in "Korean" as the most frequently used language at home. While I experienced some concern about how accurately I was reporting Chloe's and my language use, I answered all the questions on the HLS.

As I completed the survey, I began to infer that speaking a language other than English seemed to be considered a barrier to English proficiency. The questionnaire appeared to force parents to select a single language for their answers when the household linguistic situation was far more complex. The HLS seemed to give parents the impression that maintaining one's heritage language or speaking a language other than English would negatively affect kindergarten readiness. The radio segment that I mentioned in my introduction made me recall the overwhelming and pervasive uncertainty that I felt as I filled out the HLS.

Based on my responses to the survey, Chloe was scheduled for an initial screening test for ELS a few weeks before beginning her kindergarten year. It was decided that she was placed in the ELS program. Fortunately, when Chloe was at the end of the first grade, she received another letter from her school that she would no longer receive English language services in the second grade.

While I read the letter with a deep sigh, I could not help but recall my endless self-doubt and the daily juggling that I had to implement to support Chloe as a bilingual at home.

4   Equity in School Assessments for Emergent Bilinguals

Several scholars argue that culturally responsive assessment should be emphasized in the curriculum (Hood, 1998; Montenegro & Jankowski, 2017; Sleeter & Carmona, 2017). Rooted in culturally relevant pedagogy (Gay, 2018), culturally responsive assessment "involves assuring that the assessment process – beginning with student learning outcome statements and ending with improvements in student learning – is mindful of student differences and employs assessment methods appropriate for different student groups" (Montenegro & Jankowski, 2017, p. 9). To ensure equitability of assessments, at every step before, during, and after assessment, the assessment items, tasks, and relevant criteria should be carefully addressed with different needs of learners and the process should be shared with learners (Hood, 1998; Montenegro & Jankowski, 2017; Sleeter & Carmona, 2017). However, scholars criticize the high-stakes tests designed for ELLs as persistently inequitable (Gottlieb & Ernst-Slavit, 2019; Lee, 2018; Poza et al., 2016). For example, Lee (2018) examined how English Language Proficiency (ELP) Standards [e.g., World-Class Instructional Design and Assessment (WIDA), English Language Development (ELD) Standards, and the English Language Proficiency Assessment for the 21st Century (ELPA21) Standards] are aligned with content areas and are related to cognitive expectations across proficiency levels. She found that the ELP standards tend not to reflect disciplinary practices appropriately across content areas and fail to maintain grade-level cognitive expectations for ELLs. Gottlieb and Ernst-Slavit (2019), describing testing for ELLs as "discriminatory practices in high-stakes test preparation" (p. 131), also claimed that ELLs are treated differently from the mainstream English-proficient students in the assessment process:

> The ELLs have not had any test preparation as they were receiving language support services during that time; they also don't know why they have been shuffled to a strange place .... Additionally, some of the ELLs have learning disabilities and need additional personalized accommodations in addition to the ones allowed for all ELLs during testing. (p. 130)

Similar to the typical testing scenario for ELLs that Gottlieb and Ernst-Slavit (2019) illustrated, I could observe Chloe experiencing a similarly inequitable assessment process:

> One day when I picked up Chloe from her school, she complained that she spent some time having a test, which she had not been aware of. "Mommy, I was so tired. I went to a computer lab to have a test this afternoon." Immediately, I began asking myself if I missed any information relevant to school district assessments or other planned school assessments. I asked, "What test?" Chloe answered, "I don't know. Mrs. Frank brought some of us to the computer lab and we took it." I probed, "What did she say about it?" Chloe replied, "She said they wanted to know if we are good at English." I asked again, "Who are they?" She did not say anything. Instead, there was silence for a few seconds. She said, "Mommy, don't ask me anymore, I'm tired." (Personal journal, May 2017)

While I was listening to Chloe, I thought the test must have been the Assessing Comprehension and Communication in English State-to-State (ACCESS) for ELLs as an English language proficiency assessment. I was aware that Chloe would take the test during the second semester of that academic year but did not have more detailed information. I was wondering how I missed the notice about the information of this assessment. As soon as I arrived home, I immediately checked newsletters and notes that Chloe had brought from her school, and I searched the school website, but I could not find any information related to the assessment. I began to search for all assessment dates on the school district website. I was right. The school district had scheduled the test for that week. I felt incompetent as a parent that I had not provided Chloe a more healthful breakfast that morning or asked her to go to bed earlier the previous night; had I known about the date of the test, I would have better prepared Chloe.

Often, I have noticed that school assessment discourses and practices operate differently between high-stakes tests, such as school district assessments for all students and ELP assessments, such as ACCESS for ELLs, in terms of sharing assessment information. The different school assessment approaches "can be viewed as a divining practice, a subtle, nearly invisible way of producing power relations among groups of people" (Bloome, 2009, p. XII). When a school has school district and state assessments, parents often receive messages from the school about supporting assessment environments: "no lunch visitors during the assessment period," "eat a healthy or balanced breakfast," and "sleep well." When I have supervised student teachers in elementary schools, I have also noticed signs such as "Please be quiet; testing in progress" in a hallway or on the door of a computer lab during school district or state assessment periods. Unfortunately, I had not received any message from the school when Chloe took ACCESS for ELLs, and I had no information about the test at all until I searched for the information on the school district webpage. Similarly, Chloe did not know about the test until Mrs. Frank pulled her out of her classroom and took her to the computer lab on the day of the test. When I checked with some parents whose children had been identified as ELLs in her school, they did not know either. These subtle school assessment discourses and practices made me as a mother feel powerless, marginalized, and silenced. As Montenegro and Jankowski (2017) argued, "Assessment approaches and processes can help reinforce a sense of belonging or add to students' belief that they do not belong because their learning or experiences are not deemed as valid or important" (p. 10). When students and their families are given enough information and guidance for assessments related to English language services, the learning progress of ELLs can be accurately assessed, and the students can be empowered.

Furthermore, the experiences through Chloe's schooling had nibbled away at my advocacy of bilingualism and led me to experience endless self-doubt about maintaining Chloe's heritage language. The lack of information and communication from Chloe's school regarding her English proficiency progress made me feel anxious and concerned. When Chloe was identified as an ELL upon her enrollment in kindergarten, I had several questions regarding the ELS program, but I did not receive enough information despite my efforts. For example, when I went to the open house event at Chloe's school to meet her kindergarten teacher, I asked the teacher several questions, such as whether Chloe would be pulled out of the classroom to receive English language services. She informed me that only Mrs. Frank, the ESOL teacher, could provide more specific information. However, neither teacher ultimately offered me the information that I was seeking. Later, I learned through conversations with Chloe that she had not been pulled out of her classroom for the ELS program. Only after I personally searched for information about the ELS program around the end of the second semester of the kindergarten year did I learn that there was an English Learner Proficiency Plan (ELPP). I wanted to discuss an ELPP for Chloe with Mrs. Frank, and so I sent my questions to her. Mrs. Frank kindly informed me that the ELPP plans were usually developed about a month after the school year began and that she would be happy to meet with me to discuss the plan after it was completed in the fall of Chloe's first grade year. Although I appreciated Mrs. Frank's responses, I still felt that I was not sufficiently informed about the ELS program, and I was not informed in a timely manner. When Chloe was in the first grade, I also learned that she had remained in her classroom with her first-grade teacher Mrs. Hade, who had an ESOL certificate, instead of being pulled out of her classroom for the ELS program. When I had a parent–teacher conference with Mrs. Hade, I expressed my questions and concerns regarding Chloe's language proficiency, and she told me that she was differentiating instruction for Chloe. Mrs. Hade displayed empathy as we spoke, saying that some native English speakers in the same grade level might experience difficulty in passing the WIDA test.

Even though Mrs. Hade and Mrs. Frank patiently and readily responded to my questions, I felt that there should have been more detailed information provided earlier in the academic year to parents of ELLs. With respect to Chloe's experiences, I felt powerless to engage in my child's schoolwork regardless of my privileged position as an individual with professional knowledge and experience in teacher education. At the same time, I could not help but think of what I have taught in my courses about equity in assessment. Ironically, since Chloe was identified as an ELL, I have taught a course about how to select, develop, administer, and interpret different types of assessments and the ethical considerations related to assessment practices for teacher candidates. I have encouraged teacher candidates to consider critically how assessment information should be shared with students and parents in appropriate ways. As scholars (Poza et al., 2016; Shohamy, 2001) claim, I have taught that students, parents, and school staff should share clear understandings and that schools should provide enough information on relevant assessment information and policies to support equitable assessment practices. However, I could observe that Chloe's case did not reflect what I have taught in the course.

In addition, the teacher candidates in my course are often asked to interview their mentor teachers about how aspects of culturally responsive assessments have been utilized in classrooms. While I have heard my students praise and demonstrate their respect for their mentor teachers, I often hear discouraging responses such as, "My mentor teacher said that she does not have enough time to use culturally responsive assessment in her classroom." The teacher candidates and I were sometimes frustrated that we could not observe what they have learned in my class. Although schools are pressured to maintain accountability, more attention should be paid to "tailor[ing] assessment processes and materials to have the greatest impact for their [students'] learning" (Montenegro & Jankowski, 2017, p. 10) in the classroom.

5 Wrestling with Vulnerability as a Transnational Teacher Educator

Given Shohamy's (2001) argument, "in the testing literature test takers are often kept silent; their personal experiences are not heard or shared" (p. 7), Chloe's counter-storytelling can provide meaningful insights on how a school can further support emergent bilinguals. Because I am a transnational teacher educator who teaches an assessment course emphasizing culturally responsive assessment for teacher candidates, the dilemmas and the tension that I experienced regarding Chloe's stories can serve as useful resources for understanding aspects of both emergent bilinguals and school assessments. I also acknowledge that Chloe's stories are helpful for teacher candidates to broaden their taken-for-granted perspectives on ELLs. However, I was often reluctant and hesitant to share my personal stories in my courses because of the fear that my personal stories, especially my negative experiences in the school system, would cause teacher candidates to view me as a "presumed incompetent" female faculty of color (Harris & González, 2012). I have been juggling my personal stories in my courses, and there is always "a tension between exposing one's vulnerability as a teacher educator and maintaining prospective teachers' confidence in the teacher educator as a competent leader" (Berry, 2007, p. 36). Furthermore, several scholars (Hernandez et al., 2015; Lazos, 2012; Stanley, 2006) have documented that students tend to show negative attitudes toward faculty of color. Lazos (2012) found that students tend to evaluate female faculty of color more harshly than they evaluate male and white counterparts in teaching evaluations. I was worried that sharing my personal struggles as a parent could intensify students' negative attitudes toward me as a female faculty of color and thus have an impact on my teaching evaluations.

Nevertheless, I felt I should not be silent about the tensions and dilemmas that emergent bilinguals, including Chloe, experienced in the school system. I found that I cannot clearly separate my teaching from who I am; there is an ineradicable link between the personal and the professional. As a transnational teacher educator and a mother, I noticed the gaps between what I learned in higher education, what I was teaching in the teacher education program where I worked, and what my students observed firsthand in their teaching practice. Someday, teacher candidates whom I have taught could be my child's teachers. For these reasons, I cannot overlook the challenges and tensions that children from different backgrounds may face in the classroom. Even as an informed educator, I struggled with the systematic process that categorized my daughter as an ELL, and I realized how powerful my own experiences with my daughter's school assessments can be, not only for my own understanding of the system and its impact on parents and families, but for my students in seeing how and why equitable assessment matters. This self-study can provide a different lens on parents who are in vulnerable positions, such as immigrants or native speakers of other languages. This self-study has helped me to understand how important it is for me to advocate for those who are in similar situations.

When I was preparing teaching materials and resources on culturally responsive assessment for a class session, I made the decision to share my personal experience. In the course, I had taught five keys to classroom assessment quality: clear purpose, clear targets, sound design, student engagement, and effective communication (Chappuis et al., 2011). Because I had sought appropriate and real examples for teacher candidates, the content for that session immediately reminded me of Chloe's experiences as an ELL. At first, I was thinking of sharing Chloe's case regarding culturally responsive assessment, but then, I felt hesitant to share it with my teacher candidates. After weighing the appropriateness of using my vulnerable position as a teaching material, I resolved to introduce Chloe's story as an example of efforts to maintain a child's heritage language and to consider assessment aspects for ELLs. I also referred to Lee and Oxelson's (2006) study: the researchers found that K-12 teachers tended to show indifference towards the heritage languages of students from linguistic minority groups, faced difficulty allotting the time to address these issues, and did not know how to support these students.

After I shared Chloe's story, Aria, a Latina teacher candidate, raised her hand and volunteered to openly share her experiences. I was somewhat surprised at Aria's decision to share with the entire classroom; Aria was born in the US but identified as an ELL until the fifth grade. Her heritage language was Spanish, the language her mother indicated on the HLS. Aria recounted that she read different books in the ELS program, which pulled her out of her normal classroom. She also shared her frustrations about her experiences in the ELS program due to her ELL identification. Most surprisingly, Aria's story of vulnerability deepened the session's topic and prompted other students to reexamine their views on invisible challenges for ELLs and equity in assessment. All teacher candidates began to share critical reflections on their own observations from their field placements, in which they worked at schools with predominantly linguistic minority students. Due to the role that sharing vulnerable stories played in creating a successful class discussion, my concerns that I could be seen as an incompetent teacher educator or immigrant mother whose child had struggled were partially relieved. However, my intersectional position as a transnational teacher and an immigrant mother have provided me with those vulnerabilities that, while complex and stressful, enable me to further understand current educational practices from different angles that help me to advocate for social justice.

6   Closing Thoughts

In this chapter, I explored the interplay between my positions as an immigrant mother and as a transnational teacher educator, focusing on the firsthand experiences of raising my child in a school system. The dilemmas and tensions that I, as an immigrant mother, have experienced might resonate among other immigrant parents, regardless of the different degrees of tensions and challenges that they might experience. I hope that this self-study can promote conversations about ELLs as emergent bilinguals (García et al., 2008) from an asset rather than deficit perspective. The asset perspective on ELLs should inform discussion on many school practices for ELLs, including assessments. In particular, from initial screening for ELS program placement to exiting out of the program, more sensitive and equitable attention to emergent bilinguals is needed. Indeed, Dr. Bedolla, in the radio segment that I introduced earlier, suggested alternative HLS questions (e.g., "Did your child go to preschool?", "Do you have books in the home?", "How much literacy was available to your child during those first four years before he or she started school?") instead of limited questions such as "Which language do adults in your home most frequently use when speaking with your child?" For emergent bilinguals, there should be more conversations to develop helpful HLS questions, which can create a more valid and equitable assessment process. Furthermore, besides the standardized assessments such as WIDA or ACCESS, more diversified assessments such as formative assessments (assessment for learning) in the classroom can be tools to determine ELL status and to assess ELLs' learning progress. The formative assessments emphasizing ongoing student growth and improvement (Chappuis & Stiggins, 2020) can help educators to better understand emergent bilinguals' English learning process. In particular, I am writing this chapter under the global pandemic due to COVID-19, which is significantly impacting teaching and assessments. I cannot help but think about the challenges of teaching and assessments for ELLs. I hope that this chapter can help teachers, teacher educators, and policymakers to consider how current assessments in ELS programs can better support emergent bilinguals and provide more flexible spaces to discuss the learning progress of ELLs.

Finally, upon sharing my personal stories in my courses, I exposed my vulnerability; I knew that I might be considered as an immigrant mother facing challenges and barriers rather than as a teacher educator with professional knowledge and experience in teacher education. I am in another vulnerable situation through sharing my counter-story telling with whoever is reading this chapter now. However, I have learned that my intersectional positions as both a transnational teacher educator and an immigrant mother ultimately strengthen my teaching practices. Reflecting on Skachkova's (2007) analysis of transnational female teacher educators, this self-study has helped me to realize the strength of my particular intersectional positions: I can aid aspiring teachers and other teacher educators to "examine more deeply the immigrant parents' perspectives and carefully develop our instructional resources and methods so that our students as future teachers can learn to interact sensitively with immigrant children and families" (Kim et al., 2018, p. 13). My hope is that more teacher educators, including transnational teacher educators, can engage in S-STEP to enrich their teaching practices and promote social justice in teacher education. These educators may identify their own vulnerability through S-STEP, but this is a necessary part of the process that will strengthen teaching practices in the long run.

References

Abedi, J. (2008). Classification systems for English language learners: Issues and recommendations. *Educational Measurement: Issues and Practice, 27*(3), 17–31. https://doi.org/10.1111/j.1745-3992.2008.00125.x

Ates, B., Kim, S., & Grigsby, Y. (2015). Cultural narratives in TESOL classrooms: A collaborative reflective team analysis. *Reflective Practice, 16*(3), 297–311. https://doi.org/10.1080/14623943.2015.1023277

Bailey, A. L., & Kelly, K. R. (2013). Home language survey practices in the initial identification of English learners in the United States. *Educational Policy, 27*(5), 770–804. https://doi.org/10.1177/0895904811432137

Berry, A. (2004). Self-study in teaching about teaching. In J. J. Loughran, M. L. Hamilton, V. K. LaBoskey, & T. Russell (Eds.), *International handbook of self-study of teaching and teacher education practices* (pp. 1295–1332). Springer.

Berry, A. (2007). *Tensions in teaching about teaching: Understanding practice as a teacher educator.* Springer.

Bialystok, E. (2001). *Bilingualism in development: Language, literacy, and cognition.* Cambridge University Press.

Bialystok, E., Craik, F. I. M., Green, D. W., & Gollan, T. H. (2009). Bilingual minds. *Psychological Science in the Public Interest, 10*(3), 89–129. https://doi.org/10.1177/1529100610387084

Bloome, D. (2009). Foreword: 3/5 of a language? In J. C. Scott, D. Y. Straker, & L. Katz (Eds.), *Affirming students' right to their own language: Bridging language policies and pedagogical practices* (pp. xi–xv). The National Council of Teachers of English & Routledge.

Bullough, R. V., Jr., & Pinnegar, S. (2001). Guidelines for quality in autobiographical forms of self-study research. *Educational Researcher, 30*(3), 13–21. https://doi.org/10.3102/0013189X030003013

Bullough, R. V., Jr., & Pinnegar, S. (2004). Thinking about the thinking about self-study: An analysis of eight chapters. In J. J. Loughran, M. L. Hamilton, V. K. LaBoskey, & T. Russell (Eds.), *International handbook of self-study of teaching and teacher education practices* (Vol. 1, pp. 313–342). Springer.

Carpenter, B. (1997). Empowering parents: The use of the parent as researcher paradigm in early intervention. *Journal of Child and Family Studies, 6*(4), 391–398.

Chappuis J., & Stiggins, R. J. (2020). *Classroom assessment for student learning: Doing it right, using it well* (3rd ed.). Pearson.

Chappuis, J., Stiggins, R. J., Chappuis, S., & Arter, J. A. (2011). *Classroom assessment for student learning: Doing it right, using it well* (2nd ed.). Assessment Training Institute.

Charmaz, K. (2014). *Constructing grounded theory* (2nd ed.). Sage.

Cunningham, C. (2019). When 'home languages' become 'holiday languages': Teachers' discourses about responsibility for maintaining languages beyond English. *Language, Culture and Curriculum, 33*(5), 1–15. https://doi.org/10.1080/07908318.2019.1619751

Cortez-Castro, D. H. (2016). Vivencias (lived experiences) of a feminist Chicana as praxis: A testimonio of straddling between multiple worlds. In J. Kitchen, D. Tidwell, & L. Fitzgerald (Eds.), *Self-study and diversity II: Inclusive teacher education for a diverse world* (pp. 39–53). Sense.

Dalton, M. (2016, August 24). Some metro Atlanta parents concerned about ESOL screening process [Radio broadcast]. WABE90.1. Retrieved May 24, 2021, from http://cp.wabe.org/post/some-metro-atlanta-parents-concerned-about-esol-screening-process

Dinkelman, T. (2011). Forming a teacher educator identity: Uncertain standards, practice and relationships. *Journal of Education for Teaching, 37*(3), 309–323. https://doi.org/10.1080/02607476.2011.588020

Emerson, R., Fretz, R., & Shaw, L. (1995). *Writing ethnographic fieldnotes*. University of Chicago Press.

Fishman, J. (Ed.). (2001). *Can threatened languages be saved? Reversing language shift, revisited: A 21st century perspective*. Multilingual Matters.

García, O. (2005). Positioning heritage languages in the United States. *The Modern Language Journal, 89*(4), 601–605. https://www.jstor.org/stable/3588631

García, O., Kleifgen, J. A., & Falchi, L. (2008). From English language learners to emergent bilinguals: Equity matters. Research Review No. 1. *Campaign for Educational Equity*. Teachers College, Columbia University.

Gay, G. (2018). *Culturally responsive teaching: Theory, research, and practice*. Teachers College Press.

Gottlieb, M., & Ernst-Slavit, G. (2019). Promoting educational equity in assessment practices. In L. C. Oliveira (Ed.), *The handbook of TESOL in K-12* (pp. 129–148). John Wiley & Sons.

Han, S. (2016). Teaching diversity: A reflexive learning opportunity for a teacher educator. *Teaching Education, 27*(4), 410–426. https://doi.org/10.1080/10476210.2016.1192115

Harris, A., & Gonzalez, C. (2012). Introduction. In G. Gutierrez y Muhs, Y. Niemann, C. Gonzalez, & A. Harris (Eds.), *Presumed incompetent: The intersections of race and class for women in academia* (pp. 1–14). University of Colorado Press.

Hernandez, K. C., Ngunjiri, F. W., & Chang, H. (2015). Exploiting the margins in higher education: A collaborative autoethnography of three foreign-born female faculty of color. *International Journal of Qualitative Studies in Education, 28*(5), 533–551. https://doi.org/10.1080/09518398.2014.933910

Hood, S. (1998). Culturally responsive performance-based assessment: Conceptual and psychometric considerations. *Journal of Negro Education, 67*(3), 187–196. https://doi.org/10.2307/2668188

Kim, J. (2011). Korean immigrant mothers' perspectives: The meanings of a Korean heritage language school for their children's American early schooling experiences. *Early Childhood Education Journal, 39*(2), 133–141. https://doi.org/10.1007/s10643-011-0453-1

Kim, J., Wee, S. J., & Kim, K. J. (2018). Walking the roads as immigrant mothers and teacher educators: A collaborative self-study of three Korean immigrant early childhood educators. *Studying Teacher Education, 14*(1), 22–38. https://doi.org/10.1080/17425964.2017.1411255

Kitchen, J., Fitzgerald, L., & Tidwell, D. (2016). Self-study and diversity: Looking back, looking forward. In J. Kitchen, D. Tidwell, & L. Fitzgerald (Eds.), *Self-study and diversity II: Inclusive teacher education for a diverse world* (pp. 1–10). Sense.

Kwon, J. (2017). Immigrant mothers' beliefs and transnational strategies for their children's heritage language maintenance. *Language and Education, 31*(6), 495–508. https://doi.org/10.1080/09500782.2017.1349137

LaBoskey, V. K. (2004). The methodology of self-study and its theoretical underpinnings. In J. J. Loughran, M. L. Hamilton, V. K. LaBoskey, & T. Russell (Eds.), *International handbook of self-study of teaching and teacher education practices* (pp. 817–869). Springer.

Lazos, S. R. (2012). Are student teaching evaluations holding back women and minorities?: The perils of "doing" gender and race in the classroom. In G. Gutierrez y Muhs, Y. Niemann, C. González, & A. Harris (Eds.), *Presumed incompetent: The intersections of race and class for women in academia* (pp. 164–185). University Press of Colorado.

Lee, J. S., & Oxelson, E. (2006). "It's not my job": K-12 teacher attitudes toward students' heritage language maintenance. *Bilingual Research Journal, 30*(2), 453–477. https://doi.org/10.1080/15235882.2006.10162885

Lee, O. (2018). English language proficiency standards aligned with content standards. *Educational Researcher, 47*(5), 317–327. https://doi.org/10.3102/0013189X18763775

Lee, S. K. (2002). The significance of language and cultural education on secondary achievement: A survey of Chinese-American and Korean-American students. *Bilingual Research Journal, 26*(2), 327–338. https://doi.org/10.1080/15235882.2002.10668714

Liao, W., & Maddamsetti, J. (2019). Transnationality and teacher educator identity development: A collaborative autoethnographic study. *Action in Teacher Education, 41*(4), 287–306. https://doi.org/10.1080/01626620.2019.1604275

Littlejohn, J. (1998). *Federal control out of control: The office for Civil Rights' hidden policies on bilingual education* (ED426598). ERIC. Retrieved May 24, 2021, from https://files.eric.ed.gov/fulltext/ED426598.pdf

López, D. (1996). Language: Diversity and assimilation. In R. Waldinger & M. Bozormeyr (Eds.), *Ethnic Los Angeles* (pp. 139–163). Russell Sage Foundation.

Loughran, J. J. (2006). *Developing a pedagogy of teacher education: Understanding teaching and learning about teaching*. Routledge.

Mellom, P. J., Straubhaar, R., Balderas, C., Ariail, M., & Portes, P. R. (2018). "They come with nothing": How professional development in a culturally responsive pedagogy shapes teacher attitudes towards Latino/a English language learners. *Teaching and Teacher Education, 71*, 98–107. https://doi.org/10.1016/j.tate.2017.12.013

Montenegro, E., & Jankowski, N. (2017). *Equity and assessment: Moving toward culturally responsive assessment*. Occasional Paper, 29, National Institute for Learning Outcomes Assessment. Retrieved January 24, 2021, from
https://www.learningoutcomesassessment.org/?s=Montenegro%2C+E.%2C+%26+Jankowski%2C+N.+%282017%29.+Equity+and+assessment%3A+Moving+toward+culturally+responsive+assessment.+Occasional+Paper%2C+29

Peercy, M. M., & Sharkey, J. (2018). Missing a S-STEP? How self-study of teacher education practice can support the language teacher education knowledge base. *Language Teaching Research, 24*(1), 105–115. https://doi.org/10.1177/1362168818777526

Peercy, M. M., Sharkey, J., Baecher, L., Motha, S., & Varghese, M. (2019). Exploring TESOL teacher educators as learners and reflective scholars: A shared narrative inquiry. *TESOL Journal, 10*(4), 1–16. https://doi.org/10.1002/tesj.482

Phinney, J. S., Romero, I., Nava, M., & Huang, D. (2001). The role of language, parents, and peers in ethnic identity among adolescents in immigrant families. *Journal of Youth and Adolescence, 30*(2), 135–153. https://doi.org/10.1023/A:1010389607319

Pinnegar, S. (2005). Identity development, moral authority, and the teacher educator. In G. Hoban (Ed.), *The missing links in teacher education design* (pp. 257–279). Springer.

Polinsky, M., & Kagan, O. (2007). Heritage languages: In the 'wild' and in the classroom. *Language and Linguistics Compass, 1*(5), 368–395. https://doi.org/10.1111/j.1749-818X.2007.00022.x

Poza, L. E., Valdés, G., Shohamy, E., Or, I., & May, S. (2016). Assessing English language proficiency in the United States. In E. Shohamy & N. Hornberger (Eds.), *Language testing and assessment: Encyclopedia of language and education* (pp. 1–14). Springer.

Samaras, A. P., & Freese, A. R. (2009). Looking back and looking forward: An historical overview of the self-study school. In C. A. Lassonde, S. Galman, & C. M. Kosnik (Eds.), *Self-study research methodologies for teacher educators* (pp. 1–19). Sense.

Sayer, P. (2013). Translanguaging, TexMex, and bilingual pedagogy: Emergent bilinguals learning through the vernacular. *TESOL Quarterly, 47*(1), 63–88. https://doi.org/10.1002/tesq.53

Shohamy, E. (2001). *The power of tests: A critical perspective on the uses of language tests*. Routledge.

Skachkova, P. (2007). Academic careers of immigrant women professors in the US. *Higher Education, 53*(6), 697–738. https://doi.org/10.1007/s10734-005-1976-4

Sleeter, C., & Carmona, J. F. (2017). *Un-standardizing curriculum: Multicultural teaching in the standards-based classroom*. Teachers College Press.

Solórzano, D. G., & Yosso, T. J. (2002). Critical race methodology: Counter-storytelling as an analytical framework for education research. *Qualitative Inquiry, 8*(1), 23–44. https://doi.org/10.1177/107780040200800103

Souto-Manning, M. (2006). A critical look at bilingualism discourse in public schools: Autoethnographic reflections of a vulnerable observer. *Bilingual Research Journal, 30*(2), 559–577. https://doi.org/10.1080/15235882.2006.10162890

Stanley, C. A. (2006). Coloring the academic landscape: Faculty of color breaking the silence in predominantly White colleges and universities. *American Educational Research Journal, 43*(4), 701–736. https://doi.org/10.3102/00028312043004701

Sugimoto, A. T., Carter, K., & Stoehr, K. J. (2017). Teaching "in their best interest": Preservice teachers' narratives regarding English Learners. *Teaching and Teacher Education, 67*, 179–188. https://doi.org/10.1016/j.tate.2017.06.010

Tidwell, D., Allender, J., Pinnegar, S., Manke, M., & Hamilton, M. L. (2006). Contexts for using illustrative nodal moments in self-study. In L. Fitzgerald, M. Heston, & D. Tidwell (Eds.), *Collaboration and community: Pushing boundaries through self-study*. Proceedings of the sixth international conference on self-study of teacher education practices, Herstmonceux Castle, East Sussex, England (pp. 257–262). University of Northern Iowa.

Valdés, G. (2000). Teaching heritage languages: An introduction for Slavic-language-teaching professionals. In O. Kagan & B. Rifkin (Eds.), *Learning and teaching of Slavic languages and cultures* (pp. 375–403). Slavica.

Valdés, G. (2001). Heritage languages students: Profiles and possibilities. In J. K. Peyton, D. A. Ranard, & S. McGinnis (Eds.), *Heritage languages in America: Preserving a national resource* (pp. 37–77). Center for Applied Linguistics/Delta Systems.

Weekly, R. (2018). Attitudes, beliefs and responsibility for heritage language maintenance in the UK. *Current Issues in Language Planning, 21*(1), 45–66. https://doi.org/10.1080/14664208.2018.1554324

Williams, J., Ritter, J., & Bullock, S. M. (2012). Understanding the complexities of becoming a teacher educator: Experience, belonging and practice within a professional learning community. *Studying Teacher Education, 8*(3), 245–260. https://doi.org/10.1080/17425964.2012.719130

Winterbottom, C. (2013). Voices of the minority: Japanese immigrant mothers' perceptions of preschools in the United States. *Early Childhood Educational Journal, 41*(3), 219–225. https://doi.org/10.1007/s10643-012-0542-9

Wong-Fillmore, L. (2000). Loss of family languages: Should educators be concerned? *Theory into Practice, 39*(4), 203–210. https://doi.org/10.1207/s15430421tip3904_3

Wright, S. C., & Taylor, D. M. (1995). Identity and the language of the classroom: Investigating the impact of heritage versus second language instruction on personal and collective self-esteem. *Journal of Educational Psychology, 87*(2), 241–252. https://doi.org/10.1037/0022-0663.87.2.241

CHAPTER 5

Reconciling Knowledge

Experiences of Teacher Educators in Teaching through Integration and Playful Pedagogies

Makie Kortjass and Nosipho Mbatha

When entering university, most students face challenges with language and teaching methods as they differ from high school. Language has been identified as one of the barriers in accessing knowledge, and teaching methods commonly used tend to alienate students posing issues of social justice. This chapter describes two teacher educators' collaborated attempt in an arts-based self-study approach by implementing integration and playful pedagogies at a South African university. This study aimed to use an integrated learning approach and playful pedagogy to promote teacher education knowledge reconciliation. We were also interested in learning about our roles as we facilitated the learning. The studies were conducted with preservice teachers in one Bachelor of Education (B.Ed.) class and one Post-Graduate Certificate in Education (PGCE) class in a teacher education campus. Using a sociocultural perspective as a lens, we reflect on how we employed these pedagogies considering preservice teachers' cultural backgrounds and lived experiences. We audio-recorded lessons. Preservice teachers in the early mathematics module presented and discussed various cultural artifacts to enhance their understanding of curriculum integration and make connections between mathematics and the real world. The creative arts preservice teachers used indigenous games from their childhood to develop relevant learner activities to introduce to their learners. Overall, we found that using these pedagogies was beneficial and allowed them to engage with knowledge through a technique they saw as unconventional for teaching. These approaches also enabled us to facilitate the reconciliation of social and cultural knowledge into the classroom. Teacher educators may consider affirming students' cultures to address social justice issues, breaking the barriers that often hinder students' knowledge acquisition.

1   Introduction

Makie and Nosipho are females, African teacher educators, in the school of education at a South African university. We are also at different stages of our doctoral research, using a reflexive methodology – self-study (Berry, 2009; LaBoskey, 2004; Samaras, 2002, 2011). Self-study is one of the commonalities we share in our research. We are also using arts-based methods for our doctoral research – Nosipho uses indigenous games and Makie cultural artifacts. Our research explores teaching approaches, integrated learning approach (Makie) and playful pedagogy (Nosipho) in university classrooms with preservice teachers. Makie worked with the preservice teachers enrolled for the B.Ed. in Foundation Phase (Grades R-3). Nosipho worked with student teachers enrolled for the PGCE in Senior Phase (Grades 7–9). As teacher educators before our doctoral research commencement, our teaching experiences and observations played a significant role in deciding the methodology and focus area in our research. This chapter highlights our doctoral research and shares some of our discoveries.

The university we teach in has a student demographic of 78% Black (UKZN, 2018), and our school of education has a majority of Black students, which we estimate to be over 90% (anecdotal from our class registers). With South Africa having 80.7% of the Black population (StatsSA, 2019), having such high numbers of African students is justified. However, the increasing number of students enrolling for a post-school qualification has also put various strains on tertiary institutions, staff, and structures. Universities face challenges of accommodating students from various socioeconomic backgrounds and preparing them for the professional working environment. As teacher educators, we are responsible for welcoming and capacitating preservice teachers with the necessary skills for professional teaching to be competent and responsible teachers.

Language, a multi-faceted phenomenon (Garcia, 1993), plays a significant role in teaching and learning (Chinn, 2007). Without the proficiency and adequate grasping of the teaching and learning language, other epistemic challenges emerge (Lea, 1999). Many of the students who come into university have common academic challenges, particularly academic language, which hinder them from optimally accessing knowledge. This puts students in academic distress as they are given content materials they struggle to understand because of the language register used (Cummins & Yee-Fun, 2007). University teaching approaches can also be sophisticated and add to the challenge of epistemic dissemination (Liebowitz, 2009). Having identified this challenge in our classes, we have incorporated an integrated learning approach and playful pedagogy teaching approaches that help break down knowledge for the students, engage them in a relatable way in their learning and take leadership of their learning. For this study, we asked this question: *How does using an integrated learning approach and playful pedagogy promote the reconciliation of knowledge in teacher education?*

2 Academic Language in Higher Education

Teaching is a complex activity premised upon the "acquisition, integration and application of different types of knowledge practices or learning" (Department of Higher Education, 2015, p. 9). Learning is an even more complex activity as a student has to enrol for various modules taught by different academics, demanding multiple assessment tasks during the semester. This demand is not impossible; however, it can prove overwhelming to a student who struggles to grasp fundamental concepts due to academic language in which she is not proficient. Academic language has been an ongoing international concern where scholars from various international countries have documented academic language and learning (Ahmad, 2019; Ai & Wang, 2017; Cook, 2006; Lindholm-Leary, 2012). Academic language is also a term commonly used in higher learning. However, it is not easily defined. Bailey (2007) explained academic language as knowing and proficient in using content-specific, specialized vocabulary required for relevant discourse. Cummins and Yee-Fun (2007) described reading, writing, and listening as the core language skills that determine one's proficiency. Scarcella (2003) referred to three important components necessary for gauging the register and proficiency of academic language: linguistic, cognitive and sociocultural/psychological competencies. Looking at these components, through anecdotal evidence from being teacher educators in our school, we identified that many of our students struggled with them, which could be a consequential result of the under-resourced schools and under-developed communities they come from, often in the peripheries of the province. This means that the educational background may be inadequate to cope with higher learning demands, as academic language is shaped by home and school factors (Zwiers, 2007).

Chanock (2007) advocated for the improvement of teaching and learning in universities by improving students' experience and competence in their ability to manage the transition from school to university. To some students, this transition and their ability to manage it confidently can even take them their entire university stay as they grapple with the multiple attempts in adjusting to student life. Higher learning institutions also provide students with accommodative methods for the students they enrol, such as writing centres and computer training. As teacher educators, we have identified academic language as one of the transitional challenges. We have decided to address it through our teaching approaches to accommodate our students by giving them an integrated yet relatable experience of higher learning.

As one of the academic mediators between students and knowledge, we aimed to incorporate student-friendly activities and methods to introduce and disseminate knowledge. We understand that our students enrol in university with some knowledge, and it becomes our responsibility to meet them at their point of knowing, where we can then push them to that point of not-knowing – drawing from Vygotsky's (1978) Zone of Proximal Development and scaffolding. Mackey-Smith (2019) advocated for reconciliation of knowledge for students by explaining the learning experience as an act that brings together what is and what might be. The teacher-educator plays a significant role in bringing the two worlds together for the student to partake in a learning experience that draws knowledge of the past and the future.

2.1 An Integrated Learning Approach

The term integrated learning approach has different meanings. Adamu (2003) defined it as an approach that combines the teaching of subject areas by making connections within a discipline and other disciplines. As Adamu (2003) put it, the aim of curriculum integration is for teachers to teach through connections, as he believes that individuals learn by "connection-making" (p. 13). Likewise, Mwakapenda's (2008) view is that such an integrated approach offers educators to realize that mathematics can be presented as a discipline that has linkages within itself and other disciplines. For example, the engagement of preservice teachers in measurement activities provides a gateway into the mathematical concepts and the opportunity to understand the social and everyday contexts that are not familiar to them (Mwakapenda, 2008). Thus, preservice teachers need to see the interconnectedness of mathematics lessons with language and life skills learning areas (subjects in the Foundation Phase) to teach their prospective learners.

Although the fundamental intent of teacher education programmes is to prepare preservice teachers with content and pedagogical knowledge, we argue that this should be done to make knowledge accessible by using varied approaches. This sentiment is reflected by Berry (2009), who stated that "it is not only what we teach but how we teach that matters" (p. 160). Makie thus introduced the integrated learning approach in the early childhood mathematics module using cultural artifacts. Nicol (2011) argued for the importance of increasing preservice teachers' awareness of various methods to think about when teaching mathematics. Applying the integrated learning approach, Makie wanted the preservice teachers to gain confidence in mathematics, to find mathematics understandable and connected to their lives. Her objective was to show and model different ways of teaching mathematics by applying this approach. Presmeg (2006) offered an illustration of implementing such an approach, stating that when teachers focus on a particular mathematical concept, for example, they can look for a basis in learners' everyday habits in making some connections to understand a concept.

2.2   *Playful Pedagogy*

Playful pedagogy or pedagogy of play is a teaching approach that adopts and incorporates creative teaching strategies that include an element of play in them (Cutter-Mackenzie et al., 2014). It is a systematic approach to the practice of playful learning and teaching (Mardell et al., 2016) that makes provision for play and playful approaches to learning and teaching (Wood, 2008). Over the years, there have been classic studies (Garvey, 1991; Göncü & Gaskins, 2007; Göncü et al., 2007; Vygotsky, 1978) in the field of play and its benefits to learning and as an extension to that research, researchers leading in the field of play (Paley, 1984; Whitebread & O'Sullivan, 2012; Wood, 2013) have advocated for the integration of play into teaching and learning. Wood and Attfield (2005) highlighted that there has been a more conceptual focus on promoting this pedagogy for learning, whereas more empirical research is needed to indicate its practical use in teaching.

In a South African study conducted by Smit (2015) about teachers' implementation of learning through play in their classrooms, the teacher participants mentioned that one of the reasons they struggle to use play as a teaching strategy in the classroom was, they were not exposed to it during their teacher training. Therefore, they found themselves limited on how to use play in the classroom. Having discovered this through literature and identified the challenge in my classroom, Nosipho was interested in integrating playful pedagogy through childhood games to teach preservice teachers and explore the possibilities for the students and my development. However, through conversation with preservice teachers, indigenous games emerged as everyone had played them. This led to indigenous games chosen to be integrated into our teaching and learning. Games were suitable for us, as the subject encourages physical and practical teaching methods in Creative Arts.

3   A Theoretical Perspective

Using a sociocultural perspective as a lens, we reflect on how we employed these pedagogies considering preservice teachers' cultural backgrounds and lived experiences. In Bourdieu and Passeron's (1990) classical text on theory, culture and society, they positioned classrooms as reproducers of social structures often with cultural, social and linguistic capital. Such capital may enrich the teaching and learning experience in the classroom. Our teaching approaches are relatable to our students, thus making the knowledge being shared easier to access. Fielding and Pearson (1994) suggested that teacher-directed instruction strategies are fundamental components for student development in learning for academic success. This places the teacher-educator responsible for developing strategies and activities that will help the student assimilate and comprehend their learning. The approach of teaching is at the core of the student's academic success.

We aimed to explore how, as teacher-educators, we could make knowledge accessible in our teaching. Our collaboration focused on addressing the challenge we identified in our classrooms using approaches that hinder knowledge acquisition. As self-reflexive researchers, we are compelled to change our teaching approach to help us become better teacher-educators who are interested in enriching our students' learning experience. Understanding our students' academic difficulty, we re-examined our teaching approach, aligning it to students' needs. Our modified teaching approaches aimed to address the aspects of social justice identified in our lessons.

Understanding the concept of social justice, we drew from Hlalele and Alexander (2012), who explained it as a supportive process built on respect, care, recognition and empathy. We also extended our understanding of Ubuntu principles. Ubuntu is an "intangible cultural heritage" (UNESCO, 2003) that promotes unity and *doing* earnestly for one another as a community. The current debates in South Africa concerning decolonisation of the curriculum (Mazrui, 2002; Mbembe, 2016; Ndlovu-Gatsheni, 2018) have propelled universities to review their policies, curricula, teaching and learning approaches, and begin conversations interrogating the assumptions that underpin the prioritisation of Eurocentric knowledge systems. Our university has also developed a language policy (UKZN, 2014) aligned with the national language policy (DHET, 2002) for higher education, promoting multilingualism, specifically native languages, for teaching and learning. The university teaching and learning policy (UKZN, 2008) promotes the African scholarship and teaching approaches relevant to students. Our teaching approaches have also considered these policies and incorporated the use of bilingual teaching and learning in our lessons.

4   Methodology and Methods

The self-study methodology is generally qualitative, focusing on researchers' experiences (LaBoskey, 2004; Samaras, 2011). It is an approach that includes a set of practices, processes and self-study methods that are useful to those who specialize in a discipline (Samaras & Freese, 2006). In this study, we adopted the self-study approach to explore our classroom teaching practices utilizing arts-based methods.

4.1 Arts-Based Methods

Arts-based research methods present practical and unconventional teaching methods for teacher-educators. According to Samaras and Freese (2006), arts-based self-study is a method that "promotes and provokes self-reflection, critical analysis and dialogue about improving one's teaching through the arts" (p. 73). Self-studies in arts-based methods show a need to express further social, cultural, and contextual meanings from which experiences and engagement are adopted (Tidwell & Jónsdóttir, 2020). Samaras and Freese (2006) argued that self-study arts-based methods promote a deeper connection for the researcher and their practice. These methods help the self-study researcher elicit insights about their teaching and thinking about ways of improving practice. This self-study utilized cultural artifacts, indigenous games, and concept maps to examine our practice.

4.2 Participants

As two self-study researchers who are teacher-educators at a South African university, we each engaged as primary participants in the work carried out in our classrooms. Hamilton, Hutchinson, and Pinnegar (2020) asserted that to remain present in our research as both a researcher and participant, we need to attend to personal and relational connections between and within experiences. The secondary participants were the preservice teachers enrolled in the B.Ed. and PGCE programmes. In the B.Ed. Foundation phase programme, Makie worked with 56 preservice teachers in the early childhood mathematics module. Nosipho worked with 13 preservice teachers in the Creative Arts module. All the students in this study were Black.

4.3 Ethical Considerations

Ensuring quality and trustworthiness is fundamental in qualitative research. We both received ethical clearances from our institution to conduct our doctoral studies. All our participants signed consent letters and participated willingly. We explained to them that their anonymity was protected and they could withdraw at any time. This is in keeping with Schalkwyk (2010), who asserted that researchers have to assure participants that their identifying details will not be disclosed when reporting on a research project.

In our research process, we considered the issue of trustworthiness by engaging with critical friends. Pinnegar and Hamilton (2009) claimed that teacher educators' knowledge from their studies needs to have "enough trustworthiness" to guide them in their practice and "be useful to others who wanted to understand and improve their practice" (p. 53). We presented our work individually to critical friends, who are part of our institution's self-reflexive research support group. This group comprises colleagues from different disciplines who come together once a month to share their work and learn from each other. Samaras (2011) described critical friends' role as provoking new understandings, questioning researchers' assumptions, and providing different viewpoints. With these critical friends' support, we understood and made better sense of the data. This helped us to gain different perspectives on how to improve our practice and develop as self-study researchers.

5   Data Generation

The study utilized a range of data sources, including transcriptions of audio-recorded lessons, transcriptions of preservice teachers' artifact presentations, photographs, and transcriptions of critical friends' comments and suggestions. The data were generated over five months (a semester).

5.1   *Cultural Artifacts*

Educational researchers explore object inquiry to make sense of their everyday environment (Mitchell, 2011). The use of objects in social science research has gained momentum due to a "post-social" turn in the social sciences (Pillay, Pithouse-Morgan, & Naicker, 2019, p. VIII). The works of Riggins (1994), Datson (2007), and Mitchell (2011), to name a few, have demonstrated the benefits of providing opportunities for working with objects and artifacts in social research. Pithouse-Morgan and van Laren (2012) described an artifact as "an object that has cultural and/or historical significance" (p. 418). In early childhood mathematics, manipulation of objects aids in facilitating learning and understanding of concepts. Utilizing cultural artifacts could provide possibilities to integrate preservice teachers' existing knowledge with the new mathematics knowledge. Van Laren (2014) argued that preservice teachers will be utilizing integrative structures when they teach their future learners. The possibility of integrating mathematics with everyday knowledge could be done through the use of cultural artifacts. Considering the social and cultural contexts of my students, Makie engaged them in a cultural artifact activity. She divided 56 preservice teachers into six groups to present various cultural artifacts that they had selected and brought to class to show the integration of mathematics. The study focused on the two types of cultural artifacts presented by the students, namely, grass basket bowls and traditional necklaces and bracelets.

5.1.1 Grass Basket Bowls

The preservice teachers presented the grass basket bowl as an artifact made by hand, using indigenous grass called *ilala*. They explained it was traditionally used for gathering and carrying grain. In the modern-day, the grass basket bowls are commonly used as a fruit bowl and for decoration. The preservice teachers made links with mathematics highlighting circular shapes, patterns and colors. They stated that when learners describe the pattern, they see the logic of how the pattern is made. Integrating the life skills learning area in a mathematics lesson is represented by acquiring skills in constructing this artifact. Laridon et al. (2005) explained that the techniques followed in making grass basket bowls are learned informally. However, the students felt that learners could be taught these as part of their craft-work activities and preserve the art of grass weaving. The students further explained that learning about cultural artifacts will help learners gain more vocabulary, knowledge on the types of grass, the different artifacts and the ability to describe them in their home language.

FIGURE 5.1
Grass basket bowls

5.1.2 Traditional Necklaces and Bracelets

The preservice teachers were excited when they presented traditional necklaces and bracelets. They described them as handcrafted with countless tiny beads in various colors. The necklace set in a traditional pattern with a set of beads hangs from the choker part designed to sit comfortably above the breast. The bracelets are made with the same color beads to match the necklace. Students indicated that these necklaces and bracelets are worn in traditional ceremonies and Heritage Day, but nowadays, people wear them as everyday necklaces. The students made connections to jewellery mathematics regarding the content areas: shapes, measurement and patterns. They highlighted that learners could recognize and describe shapes and patterns in the necklace with the objects in their environment that resemble these. The learners develop measurement by working practically with these objects, learning the properties of shapes, length and mass. They may also be involved in the activity of creating small bracelets. This could enhance their fine motor skills and eye-hand coordination. The beauty associated with these artifacts makes us appreciate the beauty and elegance of mathematics.

FIGURE 5.2
Traditional necklaces and bracelets

RECONCILING KNOWLEDGE 89

FIGURE 5.3   Preservice teachers engaged in a discussion of the traditional necklace

In the beginning, the students were hesitant to present their artifacts. Makie encouraged and stimulated them as she moved around the groups. In Figure 5.3, the preservice teachers discussed the traditional necklace, an artifact that they had selected. One student is talking as she points to the necklace. The other one is a scribe, taking notes of what was discussed, and the others were listening attentively. Through interaction, students get opportunities to talk in class, write or be engaged in activities that enable them to acquire new knowledge and skills (Brüssow & Wilkinson, 2010). This resonates with the sociocultural theoretical perspective we are employing in this study.

5.2   *Indigenous Games*
In the PGCE sessions, we engaged in a discussion about our childhood games. Inadvertently, indigenous games that were played by all of us dominated the discussion. The emergence of indigenous games led them to be part of our activities. There were six games chosen; however, I have chosen two to use in

FIGURE 5.4   Participants playing Korobela

this chapter. Stewart (2018) explained the word indigenous as a "notion of a place-based human ethnic culture that has not migrated from its homeland" (p. 740). We referred to our childhood games as indigenous because of the cultural context as Göncü et al. (2007) and Awopegba et al. (2013) premised play as a cultural activity. The games played were *ibhasi lamanesi* and *Korobela*.

5.2.1   Korobela

Korobela is a game played by a group of willing participants. As illustrated in the picture, participants stand opposite each other in pairs with their hands up, holding hands and fingers locked onto each other. Each pair stands next to the other, creating a train structure with their bodies. They begin to sing a song, and each pair walks under the structure from one end to the other end and joins into the structure, creating a continuous structure. *Korobela* – the song – *Shm korobela* (onomatopoeic sound, sung repeatedly in the rhythmic melody).

5.2.2   Playing ibhasi lamanesi

A group of willing individuals get together in a circle holding hands, swinging their hands inwards and forwards while singing the song and remain standing. Led by the song, when they get to onomatopoeic sounds, they rotate in a circle to one side, repeating the onomatopoeic sounds twice. All individuals are to freeze when they get to the end of the song in whatever position they are in and remain frozen. One random individual will either count or say the alphabets while everyone is frozen. If anyone moves or laughs during this time, they are out of the game.

Song: *Ibhasi lamanesi, lawela emgodini, saliphusha, saliphusha, basincisha obanana*. (The nurses' bus fell in a hole, we pushed it and pushed it, they

FIGURE 5.5　Participants playing ibhasi lamanesi

didn't give us bananas) *Asasadododo, asasarerere* (onomatopoeic sound, sung repeatedly in the rhythmic melody).

To document our activities, Makie used photography to capture cultural artifacts. Nosipho used photography and video recording of the indigenous games played. Heinonen et al. (2019) explained a photograph as a tool used to record and capture a moment that may be later shared with others who may or may not have been present during the captured moment. Photographs are used in research to capture moments of data generation, conversations, lived experience that may be useful to the research conducted. A photograph gives the reader a peek or snippet view of the captured event, highlighting the notable moment. It serves as evidence and helps the writer tell the story giving a pictorial view of the captured moment. Video and photography also help the researcher reflect vividly on the captured moments, providing an opportunity to relive the moments in the viewers' minds through video and photography.

6   Data Analysis and Discussion

Samaras (2011) described data analysis as a long process that requires the researcher to put in the time and effort to understand what happens in the classroom. Bullock and Sator (2018) described their analysis methods as coding and thematic analysis. We started to make sense of our data by engaging in the coding process individually. We coded the transcripts of our lessons and the discussion with critical friends. Thereafter, we met to discuss the various codes we had created and establish common themes and understand data that

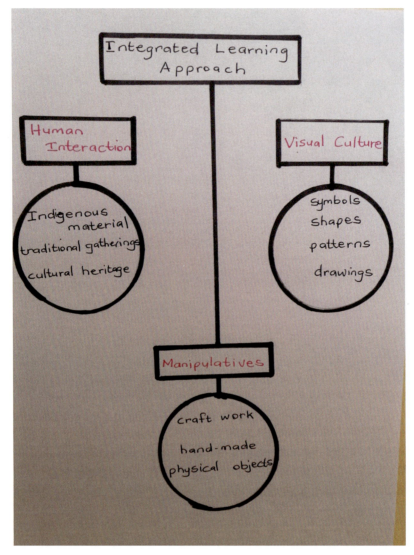

FIGURE 5.6   The concept map developed by Makie

emerged from this process (Tidwell & Jónsdóttir, 2020). We created concept maps of the coded words and phrases and categorized them into different themes. Butler-Kisber and Poldma (2010) described concept maps as illustrations used to conceptualize emergent ideas, assisting researchers in representing the ideas that emerge from the data analysed visually. Figures 5.6 and 5.7 show the concept maps that we initially developed individually.

Engaging in the process of concept mapping allowed us to take a step back and move away from "the textual analysis, and visually document the

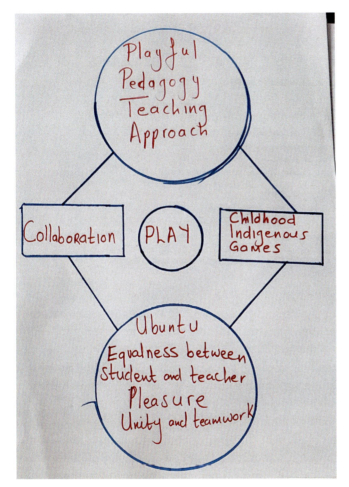

FIGURE 5.7   The concept map developed by Nosipho

relations between the interpretations of the relational concepts" by developing the diagrams "of ideas that demonstrate the links among these concepts" (Butler-Kisber & Poldma, 2010, p. 13). Subsequently, we met to consolidate the themes and discuss our discoveries. The consolidated themes are shown in Figure 5.8.

6.1   *The Role of Culture in Teaching*

Using these integrated learning approaches and playful pedagogy, cultural artifacts and indigenous games for teaching, we have found that culture played a positive role in the students' learning experience. Drawing from the sociocultural theory that situates in a cultural framework (Bourdieu & Passeron, 1977), we discovered that a students' cultural experience and integration of elements

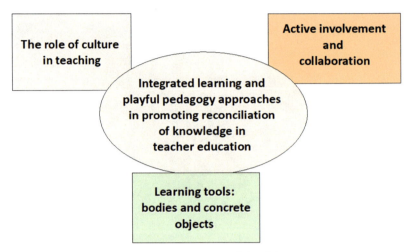

FIGURE 5.8   The concept map depicting the consolidated themes

relating to or drawn from their cultural context has a positive impact on the learning experience of the students (Chinn, 2007). When a teacher educator shows awareness or an attempt in understanding or even integrating students' cultural elements into the learning, this indicates inclusivity and recognition of the students' culture from the teacher-educator. Integrating this with Ubuntu principles (Xulu, 2010) was the most significant discovery we made in our learning.

In presenting the cultural artifacts, students make and find hands-on connections to the mathematics curriculum through their own cultural and historical backgrounds (Brandt & Chernoff, 2015, p. 34). In the playing of indigenous games, the preservice teachers, through conversations of the games, made Ubuntu principles and how they emerged through the indigenous games' playing. Alderton (2008) contended that culture is more than just an essential aspect of learning; it is a central tool through which learning develops. We view the sociocultural perspective as an imperative stance that we take in our classroom settings to address social justice issues. As teacher educators, we need to consider the cultural backgrounds and prior experiences of our students by using approaches that allow for epistemic access.

6.2   *Active Involvement and Collaboration*

As teacher educators who teach Mathematics at the Foundation phase level and Creative Arts at the Senior phase level, we have discovered that it is fundamental to be constant in our students' engagement. Nosipho, as a Creative Arts teacher educator, has learnt that demonstration is also a vital teaching method in her module as she has been encouraging her students to use demonstration during their teaching practice. During the playing of indigenous games, Nosipho participated by explaining and showing some of the moves of the game to those who did not know the game or remembered it differently. Nosipho realized that though she encouraged demonstration as a tool to teach for preservice teachers in their teaching practice, she does not use it in her teaching, and this self-discovery has led her to be more aware of what she says to students and what she does when she teaches. She has learnt to be intentional in her modelling.

Makie has learnt that she has to practice what she preaches. Through active involvement, she learned that her students understand better when she tells them and shows them what they need to do. When she moved around the groups, she noticed good interaction and students voicing their opinions and asking each other questions. Through modelling, Makie not only told the students what to do, but she showed them by involving them actively. She was pleasantly surprised when some students presented in both English and IsiZulu. This was a highlight for Makie as she was agitated when some groups were reluctant to present their artifacts. However, upon reflection, she realized that she needed to be more sensitive towards the students and understand their struggles.

She has also gained insights on how she could challenge her student teachers by providing opportunities to "demonstrate competence with mathematical tools, methods and content at the primary level" (McGlynn-Stewart, 2020, p. 177). She did this by engaging her student teachers in a cultural artifact activity to explore mathematics in context. Her challenge is to help preservice teachers create their knowledge of teaching mathematics and to support them in their learning.

6.3 *Learning Tools: Bodies and Concrete Objects*

The use of concrete objects (manipulatives) has many benefits. Research shows that using manipulatives in teaching mathematics helps learners understand abstract concepts (McNeil & Jarvin, 2007). Manipulatives serve as tools for educators to link learners' experiences with the objects (prior knowledge) to the abstract mathematical concepts (new knowledge) that the artifacts represent (Niranjan, 2013). Using manipulatives as a learning tool, Makie found their use beneficial as the cultural artifacts gave the student confidence to engage in and to share their understanding using existing knowledge. As a physically orientated subject, Creative Arts has many physical activities that require students to do them together. In engaging in the indigenous games, participants mentioned the importance of being aware of each other's bodies and taking care entrusted to you to catch, lean on, or hold during a game. This is so no one is hurt physically, and it is also an expression of care to encourage trust in one another, which promotes unity and a good rapport in the group. Therefore, Nosipho has discovered that care, unity, and trust are important elements that contribute to teamwork (Bennett, Wood, & Rogers, 1997), which are Ubuntu principles (Letseka, 2013).

7 Outcomes

This chapter presents a sociocultural theoretical perspective in arts-based self-study research utilizing an integrated learning approach and play-based pedagogies. We found that using these pedagogies was beneficial and allowed the preservice teachers to engage with knowledge through a technique they saw as unconventional for teaching. Students overall enjoyed themselves, were much engaged and chose all the games they wanted to play themselves. This brought comfort and positive energy in the classroom, and students were confident to speak as the indigenous games were knowledge they could share. Using methods that students were familiar with for teaching and integrating them with new knowledge created a balance for the students as they did not become overwhelmed realizing that there was knowledge they were familiar with and could contribute during the lessons. For Makie and Nosipho, this was an act of social justice as students managed to reconcile their indigenous knowledge with academic knowledge.

Engaging in this self-study project, Makie found the value in teaching preservice teachers how to teach early mathematics using cultural artifacts. She observed that the students were growing and developing in their understanding of the integrated learning approach. When they described their artifacts, they were able to connect mathematics with the language and life skills learning areas. This was a lesson for Makie to always strive to get to know her students better. Naudé and Meier (2016) stressed the importance of making students feel genuinely accepted in the teaching and learning process by demonstrating respect for cultural differences and knowledge about their cultural backgrounds.

Nosipho and Makie believe that the vital advantages originate from how the integrated learning approach and play-based pedagogies can promote social justice. Incorporating activities that embrace cultural diversity in our lessons is not a choice but an obligation. We are also mindful that, as much as the artifacts in mathematical teaching and the indigenous games in creative arts teaching are excellent tools, they need to be used correctly to be meaningful to the students. The feedback we received from critical friends engendered different insights on how we could improve our practice. We both want to continue integrating more arts-based teaching methods into our teaching practices as we believe that many preservice teachers may benefit enormously.

8 Conclusion

Arts-based approaches to research expand our knowledge base by including many of the neglected but important ways to construct meaning through artistic expression forms (Weber, 2014). This chapter supports the idea that we can strengthen and reconcile knowledge by employing alternative teaching methods and including cultural artifacts and indigenous games in our lessons. This study makes a particular knowledge contribution so far as it argues that reconciling knowledge by using the integrated learning approach and playful pedagogies can address social justice issues in teacher education. Our collaborative self-study journey suggests that we should advance early mathematics development using artifacts and the indigenous games in creative arts into preservice teacher programmes. From these experiences with our students, we see that teacher education programs need to incorporate activities about sociocultural contexts and create opportunities to link learners' school culture and home culture to enhance learning.

References

Adamu, A. U. (2003, March 14). *The concept of curriculum integration: Its meaning, scope and modalities.* Paper presented at the Workshop on Integrating Qur'anic Education, Arewa House, Nigeria.

Ahmad, N. (2019). Prerequisites and practical implications in Teaching English as a Foreign Language (TEFL) with reference to graduation students in the College of Sciences and Arts, Alnamas, Kingdom of Saudi Arabia. *Journal of English Language and Literature, 6*(1), 1–12.

Ai, B., & Wang, L. (2017). Re-entering my space: A narrative inquiry into teaching English as a foreign language in an imagined third space. *Teachers and Teaching, 23*(2), 227–240.

Alderton, J. (2008). Exploring self-study to improve my practice as a mathematics teacher educator. *Studying Teacher Education, 4*(2), 95–104.

Awopegba, P. O., Oduolowu, E. A., & Nsamenang, A. B. (2013). *Indigenous early childhood care and education curriculum framework for Africa: A focus on context and contents.* UNESCO. Retrieved April 5, 2019, from http://www.iicba.unesco.org/sites/default/files/Fundamentals%20of%20Teacher%20Education%20Development%20No6.pdf

Bailey, A. L. (2007). *The language demands of school: Putting academic English to the test*. Yale University Press.

Bennett, N., Wood, L., & Rogers, S. (1997). *Teaching through play: Teachers' thinking and classroom practice*. Open University Press.

Berry, A. (2009). Exploring vision in self-study. *Studying Teacher Education, 5*(2), 159–162.

Bourdieu, P., & Passeron, J.-C. (1990). *Reproduction in education, society and culture* (Vol. 4). Sage.

Brandt, A., & Chernoff, E. C. (2015). The importance of ethnomathematics in the math class. *Ohio Journal of School Mathematics, 71*, 31–36.

Brüssow, S. M., & Wilkinson, A. C. (2010). Engaged learning: A pathway to better teaching. *South African Journal of Higher Education, 24*(3), 374–391.

Bullock, S. M., & Sator, A. (2018). Developing a pedagogy of "making" through collaborative self-study. *Studying Teacher Education, 14*(1), 56–70.

Butler-Kisber, L., & Poldma, T. (2010). The power of visual approaches in qualitative inquiry: The use of collage making and concept mapping in experiential research. *Journal of Research Practice, 6*(2), 1–16.

Chanock, K. (2007). What academic language and learning advisers bring to the scholarship of teaching and learning: Problems and possibilities for dialogue with the disciplines. *Higher Education Research & Development, 26*(3), 269–280.

Chinn, P. W. (2007). Decolonizing methodologies and indigenous knowledge: The role of culture, place and personal experience in professional development. *Journal of Research in Science Teaching, 44*(9), 1247–1268.

Cook, V. (2006). Basing teaching on L2 user. In E. Llurda (Ed.), *Non-native language teachers: Perceptions, challenges and contributions to the profession* (pp. 47–51). Springer.

Cummins, J., & Yee-Fun, E. M. (2007). Academic language. In J. Cummins & C. Davison (Eds.), *International handbook of English language teaching* (pp. 797–810). Springer US.

Cutter-Mackenzie, A., Moore, D., Edwards, S., & Boyd, W. (2014). *Young children's play and environmental education in early childhood education*. Springer.

Datson, L. (2007). *Things that talk: Object lessons from art and science*. Zone Books.

Department of Higher Education and Training. (2015). *Minimum requirements for teacher education qualifications*. Government Gazette, 38487. Retrieved June 12, 2021, from https://www.dhet.gov.za/Part%20C%20%20Policies/HIGHER%20EDUCATION/14.%20Policy%20on%20minimum%20requirements%20for%20teacher%20education%20qualifications.pdf

Department of Higher Education and Training. (2002). *Language policy for higher education*. Retrieved April 5, 2019, from https://www.dhet.gov.za/Management%20Support/Language%20Policy%20for%20Higher%20Education.pdf

Fielding, L., & Pearson, P. (1994). Synthesis of research/reading comprehension: What works. *Educational Leadership, 5*(51), 62–68.

Garcia, E. E. (1993). Chapter 2: Language, culture, and education. *Review of Research in Education, 19*(1), 51–98.

Garvey, C. (1991). *Play*. Harvard University Press.

Göncü, A., & Gaskins, S. (2007). *Play and development: Evolutionary, sociocultural, and functional perspectives*. Lawrence Erlbaum.

Göncü, A., Jain, J., & Tuermer, U. (2007). Children's play as cultural interpretation. In A. Göncü & S. Gaskins (Eds.), *Play and development: Evolutionary, sociocultural, and functional perspectives* (pp. 155–202). Lawrence Erlbaum.

Hamilton, M. L., Hutchinson, D., & Pinnegar, S. (2020). Quality, trustworthiness, and S-STEP research. In J. Kitchen, A. Berry, S. M. Bullock, A. R. Crowe, M. Taylor, H. Guðjónsdóttir, & L. Thomas (Eds.), *International handbook of self-study of teaching and teacher education practices* (2nd ed.). Springer.

Heinonen, T., Halonen, D., & Krahn, E. (2019). *Expressive arts for social work and social change*. Oxford University Press.

Hlalele, D., & Alexander, G. (2012). University access, inclusion and social justice. *South African Journal of Higher Education, 26*(3), 487–502.

LaBoskey, V. K. (2004). The methodology of self-study and its theoretical underpinnings. In J. J. Loughran, M. L. Hamilton, V. K. LaBoskey, & T. Russell (Eds.), *International handbook of self-study of teaching and teacher education practices* (Vol. 2, pp. 817–869). Springer.

Laridon, P., Mosimege, M., & Mogari, D. (2005). Ethnomathematics research in South Africa. In R. Vithal, J. Adler, & C. Keitel (Eds.), *Researching mathematics education in South Africa: Perspectives, practices and possibilities* (pp. 133–160). Human Sciences Research Council Press.

Lea, M. R. (1999). Academic literacies and learning in higher education: Constructing knowledge through texts and experience. In C. Jones, J. Turner, & B. Street (Eds.), *Students writing in the university: Cultural and epistemological issues* (Vol. 8, pp. 103–124). John Benjamin Publishing.

Letseka, M. (2013). Educating for Ubuntu/Botho: Lessons from Basotho indigenous education. *Open Journal of Philosophy, 3*(2), 8.

Liebowitz, B. (2009). Towards a pedagogy of possibility: Teaching and learning from a social justice perspective. In E. Bitzer (Ed.), *Higher education in South Africa – A scholarly look behind the scenes* (pp. 84–102). SUN Media.

Lindholm-Leary, K. (2012). Success and challenges in dual language education. *Theory Into Practice, 51*(4), 256–262.

Mackey-Smith, K. (2019). Teaching for reconciliation in a multiracial classroom. *The Australian Journal of Language and Literacy, 42*(2), 103–115.

Mardell, B., Wilson, D., Ryan, J., Ertel, K., Krechevsky, M., & Baker, M. (2016). *Towards a pedagogy of play*. Project Zero, Harvard University. Retrieved December 18, 2018, from http://www.pz.harvard.edu/sites/default/files/Towards%20a%20Pedagogy%20of%20Play.pdf

Mazrui, A. M. (2002). The English language in African education: Dependency and decolonisation. In J. W. Tollefson (Ed.), *Language policies in education: Critical issues* (pp. 267–282). Lawrence Erlbaum.

Mbembe, A. J. (2016). Decolonising the university: New directions. *Arts and Humanities in Higher Education, 15*(1), 29–45.

McGlynn-Stewart, M. (2020). Listening to students, listening to myself: Addressing pre-service teachers' fears of mathematics and teaching mathematics. *Studying Teacher Education, 6*(2), 175–186.

McNeil, N., & Jarvin, L. (2007). When theories don't add up: Disentangling he manipulatives debate. *Theory Into Practice, 46*(4), 309–316.

Mitchell, C. (2011). *Doing visual research*. Sage.

Mwakapenda, W. (2008). Understanding connections in the school mathematics. *South African Journal of Education, 28*, 189–202.

Naudé, M., & Meier, C. (2016). *Teaching foundation phase mathematics: A guide for South African students and teachers*. Van Schaik.

Ndlovu-Gatsheni, S. J. (2018). *Epistemic freedom in Africa: Deprovincialization and decolonization*. Routledge.

Nicol, C. (2011). Growing possibilities: Designing mathematical and pedagogical problems using variation. In S. Schuck & P. Pereira (Eds.), *What counts in teaching mathematics: Adding value to self and content* (Vol. 11, pp. 45–60). Springer.

Niranjan, C. (2013). *Using artefacts to support an embodied approach to learn trigonometry: A case study of Grad 10 learners* [Unpublished master's thesis]. University of KwaZulu-Natal, South Africa. Retrieved June 15, 2021, from https://researchspace.ukzn.ac.za/xmlui/handle/10413/11463

Paley, V. G. (1984). *Boys and girls: Superheroes in the doll corner*. University of Chicago Press.

Pillay, D., Pithouse-Morgan, K., & Naicker, I. (2019). "Not just an object": Making meaning of and from everyday objects in educational research for social change. *Educational Research for Social Change, 8*(1), vii–xii.

Pinnegar, S., & Hamilton, M. L. (2009). *Self-study of practice as a genre of qualitative research: Theory, methodology, and practice*. Springer.

Pithouse-Morgan, K., & van Laren, L. (2012). Towards academic generativity: Working collaboratively with visual artefacts for self-study and social change. *South African Journal of Education, 32*(4), 416–427.

Presmeg, N. (2006). Semiotics and the "connections" standard: Significance of semiotics for teachers of mathematics. *Educational Studies in Mathematics, 61*, 163–182.

Riggins, S. (1994). Fieldwork in the living room: An autoethnographic essay. In S. Riggins (Ed.), *The socialness of things: Essays on the socio-semiotics of objects* (pp. 101–147). Moutin de Gruyter.

Samaras, A. P. (2002). *Self-study for teacher educators*. Peter Lang.

Samaras, A. P. (2011). *Self-study teacher research: Improving your practice through collaborative inquiry*. Sage.

Samaras, A. P., & Freese, A. R. (2006). *Self-study of teaching practices primer*. Peter Lang.

Scarcella, R. (2003). Academic English: A conceptual framework. *UC Berkeley: University of California Linguistic Minority Research Institute*. Retrieved April 4, 2019, from https://escholarship.org/uc/item/6pd082d4

Schalkwyk, V. (2010). Collage life story elicitation technique: A representational technique for scaffolding autobiographical memories. *The Qualitative Report, 15*(3), 675–695.

Smit, K. (2015). *Preschool teachers' understanding and implementation of learning through play*. [Unpublished master's thesis]. University of Pretoria. Retrieved June 15, 2021, from https://repository.up.ac.za/handle/2263/50788

StatsSA. (2019). *Mid-year population estimates*. Author.

Stewart, G. (2018). What does 'indigenous' mean, for me? *Educational Philosophy and Theory, 50*(8), 740–743.

Tidwell, D. L., & Jónsdóttir, S. R. (2020). Methods and tools of self-study. In J. Kitchen, A. Berry, S. M. Bullock, A. R. Crowe, M. Taylor, H. Guðjónsdóttir, & L. Thomas (Eds.), *International handbook of self-study of teaching and teacher education practices* (2nd ed.). Springer.

UNESCO. (2003). *Convention for the safeguarding of the intangible cultural heritage*. Retrieved June 14, 2021, from http://www.unesco.org/culture/ich/index.php?pg=00006

University of KwaZulu-Natal. (2008). *Teaching, learning and assessment policy*. Retrieved May 28, 2021, from http://registrar.ukzn.ac.za/Libraries/policies/UTL_Assessment_-_CO03270608.sflb.ashx

University of KwaZulu-Natal. (2014). *Language policy of the University of KwaZulu-Natal*. Retrieved May 28, 2021, from https://ukznextendedlearning.com/wp-content/uploads/2020/02/Language-Policy-of-the-University-of-KwaZulu-Natal.pdf

University of KwaZulu-Natal. (2018). *UKZN annual report*. Retrieved May 28, 2021, from https://z3t9t3v4.stackpathcdn.com/wp-content/uploads/2019/12/Annual-Report-2018.pdf

van Laren, L. (2014). Beyond metaphor drawings to envisage integration of HIV & AIDS education: A self-study in primary mathematics teacher education. *Perspectives in Education, 32*(2), 21–36.

Vygotsky, L. S. (1978). *Mind in society*. Harvard University Press.

Weber, S. (2014). Arts-based self-study: Documenting the ripple effect. *Perspectives in Education, 32*(2), 8–20.

Whitebread, D., & O'Sullivan, L. (2012). Preschool children's social pretend play: Supporting the development of metacommunication, metacognition and self-regulation. *International Journal of Play, 1*(2), 197–213.

Wood, E. (2008). Everyday play activities as therapeutic and pedagogical encounters. *European Journal of Psychotherapy and Counselling, 10*(2), 111–120.

Wood, E. (2013). *Play, learning and the early childhood curriculum* (3rd ed.). Sage.

Wood, E., & Attfield, J. (2005). *Play, learning and the early childhood curriculum*. Sage.

Xulu, M. (2010). Ubuntu and being umuntu: Towards an Ubuntu pedagogy through cultural expressions, symbolism and performance. *Skills at Work: Theory and Practice Journal, 3*(1), 81–87.

Zwiers, J. (2007). Teacher practices and perspectives for developing academic language. *International Journal of Applied Linguistics, 17*(1), 93–116.

CHAPTER 6

Examining the Ethical Implications and Emotional Entailments of Teaching Indigenous Education

An Indigenous Educator's Self-Study

Jennifer Markides

Indigenous education is a space of potential harm for educators who identify as Indigenous. As such, I engage in self-study to interrogate my practices, questions, and insights from teaching Indigenous education courses as Métis and an educator. Through dialogue, I draw out some of the emergent tensions and critically question the ethical implications of my teaching practices, to make meaning from my experiences. I share the discussion as a reflexive and potentially transformative praxis, inviting others to read their own teaching experiences against mine, towards meaning making in new sites.

1   Influences and Potential Impacts

In teacher education, instructors and professors are positioned as experts in the courses they teach. Sometimes, one's identity is taken as concomitant with expertise. Teaching about communities and cultures that are closely linked to one's identity, or to the identities of students, opens educators up to the possibility of experiencing personal harm and/or inflicting harm upon the students (Britzman, 1998; Markides, 2018).

With the rise of xenophobic and right-wing nationalistic leaders who spout racist rhetoric and condone white supremacists as "good people," hatred for *Others* has become more visible in the media and in life; education about difference has never been more important. By taking up the important work of teaching social justice content – in all of its emancipatory forms – and learning from educators' self-study offerings, teacher educators may become better equipped to navigate the treacherous terrain of a socially constructed and highly political landscape (DiAngelo & Sensoy, 2014).

2 Context of the Self-Study

In a time of Truth and Reconciliation in Canada (TRC, 2015a, 2015b), a growing number of educators, both Indigenous and non-Indigenous, are being asked to teach Indigenous education classes in academic institutions. Involvement in teaching these courses is a site of challenging emotional work (Britzman, 1998; Markides, 2018). For this reason, the educators who are taking on these, at times, volatile positions must make time to reflect upon, discuss, and share their personal experiences and reactions to teaching Indigenous education classes, such that we might better understand how the work operates upon the educator. To this end, I look to expand on my previous work (see Markides, 2018) by returning to self-study. Specifically, I dig deeper into the aspects of the teaching that continue to weigh on me, ethically and emotionally, and others that give me immeasurable strength to continue in this work.

3 Researcher's Positioning and Perspective

Situated by my Métis identity, I am part of a distinct cultural group that came into being in Canada during the early days of colonization. Métis settlements emerged as men working in the fur trade married women from First Nations communities and established new cultural practices, created the Michif language, generated commerce that was integral to the fur trade industry, and more (Shore, 2018). Despite having a rich history and strong presence in the Canadian story, Métis were not formally acknowledged as having nationhood and rights as an Indigenous people of Canada. The government's relationship with and responsibility to Métis and non-status First Nations people was only recently recognized by the Supreme Court of Canada in a landmark court case, which began in 1999 and concluded in 2016 (Daniels v. Canada, 2016; Gaudry & Andersen, 2016; Martel, 2018). Being Métis, I am grateful for the tenacious spirit of those who fought to be recognized as an Indigenous group within Canada. Métis have often worked to bridge social, cultural, and political divides, navigating Indigenous and settler relationships for hundreds of years.

While locating myself as a critical, Métis educator in this self-study work, I am cautious of being positioned as an expert in Indigenous education (Markides, 2018). Despite having taught for over fifteen years, none of my experience had prepared me for the assignment of *being* an Indigenous education instructor.

Over the past four years, I have taught four sections of EDUC 530: Indigenous Education in the undergraduate teacher education program through the

Werklund School of Education at the University of Calgary, Canada. In addition to these responsibilities, I have worked as a graduate assistant teacher for two master of education courses in the Indigenous Education graduate program; and I was the instructor for the capstone projects for the same cohort later that year.

It was incredible for me to see where the graduate students started and the growth they demonstrated in the span of the program. I was honored to share their journey and to support them as they completed their final assignments for the course. There is a distinct difference between teaching Indigenous education to a group of students who have chosen an Indigenous Education graduate program, and when the students have to take the course as a mandatory part of their teacher education coursework. When the course is a choice, there is more buy-in from the students right from day one. In the required course, I feel the need to create the sense of urgency and responsibility around the learning. I need it to matter to the students.

My work as an Indigenous educator comprises roughly one quarter of my postsecondary teaching experience to date. The institution that I am affiliated with is situated in a major city, yet serves rural communities through distance courses that utilize the on-line environment. I have taught in both the on-campus and on-line spaces. While my interactions with the students inform my experience of the courses, I am turning inward to interrogate my reactions and responses. The ideas shared in this study are informed by my ongoing reflections, inquiries, and construals of the teaching experiences I have had in my roles as an Indigenous educator.

4   Moving to Self-Study as a Practitioner-Researcher Methodology

The move from being an elementary, Montessori teacher to becoming a teacher educator in the university marked a paradigmatic shift in how I think about my teaching practice – from being a *reflective practitioner* to becoming a *critical and reflexive educator-researcher*, the subtle difference being that "reflection is after and individual whereas reflexivity is ongoing and relational" (Lyle, 2017, p. VII). The shift signals a change from viewing and reviewing my practice for mere personal growth, to considering how critical analysis of my experiences – learning for, from, and through my teaching – connects to the discourse of teacher educators concerned with the professional growth of the field.

As a methodology, "self-study focuses on the development of both the personal and the professional" (Lyle, 2018, p. 2). Significantly over the past 25 years, self-study has been embraced by teachers and teacher educators as a potentially transformative approach to educational research and teaching practice (Samaras, 2011; Tidwell et al., 2009), where the methods used in self-study are flexible, fluid, and ever-adapting. The generation of data and data analysis can occur separately or synergistically at any point (Tidwell et al., 2009), thus illustrating the dynamic potential of self-study – as both generative and in/formative – within education.

The data for this study came from my reflections on the weekly conversations that were held with various members of the Indigenous education teaching team. Additionally, I turned inward to question my responses, reactions, and emotions to the students' comments, questions, and instructor evaluations. This practice mirrors the recommendations put forward by DiAngelo and Sensoy (2014) for students engaging in social justice and inequality courses. Just as I asked of the students, I attempted to follow DiAngelo and Sensoy's guidelines, by: (1) showing intellectual humility; (2) prioritizing informed knowledge over opinion; (3) examining patterns rather than anecdotal evidence; (4) treating my reactions as entry points for gaining greater self-knowledge; and, (5) recognizing that my social position informs my responses to the students and the selection of materials that I put forward in the course. In particular, I interrogated the moments that had me concerned for the students' wellbeing, and my own.

Inseparably, the practice of self-study informs my teaching, just as my teaching practice informs my self-study (Kitchen, 2005). Specific to my work in Indigenous education, self-study allows me to take up the elements of dialogue, navigate the emergent tensions, and make meaning from my experiences (Pinnegar & Hamilton, 2009). For me, this form of study also creates a protective and instructive distance between my vulnerable teaching self and the sense-making process that accompanies my teaching experiences, such that I can make space between my emotions and reactions to form questions, critiques, and assessments of myself in my work.

5   Entering into Dialogue

The act of teaching the course calls on me to bring my identity forward (Palmer, 2017). I am necessarily vulnerable (Wiebe & Snowber, 2012) in this position. I am tasked with justifying the importance of the learning and making the material matter. Put differently, the course requires me to convince the students that Indigenous people, and their experiences, matter. As Métis, I am part of the "Indigenous" that needs to matter.

In all my teaching, I begin with relationship-building. Relationships are the basis of trust and risk-taking in the classroom. Learning something new requires students to take risks in their thinking. To think differently about Indigenous people, many students need to address their existing biases, misconceptions, and often, deeply held and unconscious racist beliefs. I like to believe that the relationship with me is a starting place for some students, especially those who have had little to no contact with an Indigenous person prior to taking the class. They might see me as an exception – or not – to their rules and stereotypes. I see this as the fissure, the weak point in their well-established knowledge structures, that I need in order to break down prior learning, or, at least, a place to build adjacent to their existing convictions.

Being Indigenous, I am looked to as an expert in the class. Early on in the course, I risk my credibility as the instructor as I explain that I actually know very little about only a few Indigenous groups. The term "Indigenous" itself can flatten the complexity and diversity of peoples that the term stands to represent; however, I struggle to find another way to speak to learning in the course that is inclusive of scholarship, stories, and practices of a sampling of many specific First Nations, as well as Métis and Inuit.

Teaching in Treaty 7 territory, there are several groups – including the nations of the Blackfoot Confederacy comprising the Siksika, Piikani, and Kainai; the Stoney Nakoda, including Chiniki, Wesley, and Bearspaw; the Tsuut'ina; and Métis – that the students may recognize from territorial acknowledgements, at very least. These territorial acknowledgements have been offered more frequently, due largely to the TRC's "94 Calls to Action" (2015a, 2015b), where people are formally recognizing that the lands they are on have been inhabited and cared for by Indigenous peoples long before colonization and still to this day. There are over 600 distinct First Nations groups across Canada and numerous others around the world, each with distinct languages, traditions, knowledges, and more. The more I learn about my own community, the more I understand how little I know about the specific communities of Treaty 7.

From my years in school, I learned more about the history and culture of European countries, colonial Canada, and the United States of America, than about any Indigenous group, including my own. The experience of learning about "Indians" from textbooks is not uncommon, even for Indigenous people. And what we were taught about Indians from teachers and through media made it difficult to identify as Indigenous, even within our own family circles (St. Denis, 2007).

I have come to understand that while people's conceptions of Indians and Indigenous people are shifting, my expectation for greater understanding now far exceeds the rate at which most people are changing. In particular, I am very troubled by the notion of "being raised traditionally." Some people hold onto the idea of an "ideal Indian" or that some Indigenous people are more Indigenous than others. The idea that Indigenous people who have grown up on reserves, especially in remote First Nations communities, are somehow an Indigenous ideal is dangerous. This type of thinking creates a false hierarchy of worth or authenticity as Indigenous people. All Indigenous ways of life have been affected by colonial influence. No community has gone untouched.

The Indian Act of 1867, the pass system, reserve systems, community relocations, residential schools, the Sixties Scoop, and more have all had dire consequences for the Indigenous people of Canada. In the span of a few hundred years, many of the traditional ways of living have been banned, oppressed, hidden, lost, or changed forever. While some communities have had greater success holding onto their traditional cultural teachings, none have gone untouched. Therefore, it is erroneous to imagine that there are some "fortunate" Indigenous people who somehow still exist, unscathed by colonization. The notion of a wholly preserved way of life sits in direct opposition with the reality of Indigenous people today. This is not to say that cultural teachings and knowledges are not strong in many places, but instead it is to recognize that the communities whose traditions have survived in spite of colonial rule have undergone significant hardships, pressures, and influences, despite appearances to the contrary. Persons who subscribe to the belief that there are varying degrees of Indigenous further oppress Indigenous people whose realities vary from the imagined ideal or norm. Regardless of when and how any Indigenous person starts their cultural learning journey – from birth, or later in life (Hodson, 2016) – they are continually learning. It is a process with no end.

6   Naming the Emergent Tensions

Regardless of my own journey as Métis, reclaiming and reconnecting to my culture, I have learned a lot about many Indigenous peoples' experiences in Canada, past and present. I have something to offer in Indigenous education. I live in the tension of knowing: I have a responsibility to share what I have learned with others, and the responsibility I have to keep learning, myself. I am an infant in my learning. I will spend a lifetime learning and will not know much – *Can any of us ever know that much about any one complex thing?*

For me, the tension I experience in my teaching manifests in palpable ways. I have great reverence for the subject matter, to the point where I never feel wholly adequate teaching it – *Could I ever do the teaching justice?* I know enough to know that I do not know much, despite the fact that my "not much" is likely much more than many Canadians have been taught in the public education system to this point. My deep respect and unshakeable sense of insufficiency results in varying permutations of nervousness and passion. From my years of teaching, I know that nervousness is not the best place to be teaching from, while teaching from a place of passion is often portrayed as ideal.

I am always excited to teach the course. The learning is meaningful and worthwhile; it has the potential to change the students' lives. I tell them this in the first week, but I don't think that any of them believe me until it happens. In the meantime, I battle my nerves – What if they don't get there? Am I just giving them empty promises that I can't keep? I (over)compensate by providing evidence of a different story. I bring in experts through documentaries, guest speakers, and other media clips. It is like a trial in which I must provide as much evidence as I can to dispel the (mis)truths they have come to know through formal and informal education over the course of their lives.

I work to oust the underlying deficit narrative of Indigenous people (see Fforde et al., 2013) that the students have formed and curated their entire lives. Chimamanda Ngozi Adichie (2009) cautioned against giving power to the single story, specifically the narratives told about a people; instead, she encouraged everyone to look for stories told by the people themselves. In the case of the settler-Canadian narrative told about Indigenous people, the story casts all Indigenous people as failing: failing to take care of themselves, failing to parent in ways the dominant culture sees fit, failing to obey colonial rules and laws, failing to work to better their circumstances. failing to survive the legacies of colonization that are invisible to many settler-Canadians. The story of Indigenous peoples' failure has been created and supported within the oppressive structures of society. Hegemonic systems shaped by the colonizing project have created the conditions that keep the narrative true for those who have no reason to question the status quo. *Systemic racism is difficult to expose, but I try anyway.*

7   Working towards a Big Picture View of Systemic Racism

Billie Allan and Janet Smylie (2015) defined systemic racism as the enactment of oppressive policies and processes within societal systems, structures, and institutions, inclusive of colonization and its legacies. In order to demonstrate this to the students, I present myriad perspectives about the historical wrongs and existing inequalities, as well as providing examples of covert and overt racism, ongoing injustices, and complacent ignorance, in an attempt to create a big picture view of the colonial structures of oppression and racism that have encouraged and allowed people to see Indigenous individuals and groups as less than equal.

As with all instructors teaching the course work, I work from the common syllabus, which includes required readings from critical and community-based research written by primarily Indigenous scholars. The examples I share – in class or as optional, additional sources – feel to me like a bombardment within the span of eight weeks. I hesitate to share them here within the space of a few paragraphs. The stories are often shocking and little known. Together, they can be overwhelming. To give you a sense of the students' experience, I will describe some of the resources I point them towards.

In the subsequent descriptions, I am using emotionally descriptive adjectives as a conscious act of decolonizing my writing towards practices that embrace holistic ways of being in the world (and the academy). I want to capture and include the human experience of the resources, rather than present the stories as a detached list. Importantly, all of the resources involve first-hand accounts of the events and experiences, with the exception of the stories told about people who have passed away (i.e., McCallum & Perry, 2018; Smiley, 2015). An important aspect of the pedagogy engaged when teaching the course is privileging Indigenous voices, while having the students listen with open minds and open hearts.

7.1 *Pointing to Lesser Known Historical Events and Legacies of Colonization*

While many students have learned about the government of Canada's internment of Japanese Canadians during World War II, very few students come into the Indigenous education class having heard of the pass system that saw Indian agents controlling every movement of First Nations living on reserves in the Canadian prairies. Viewing "The Pass System" documentary by Williams (2015), the students witness the troubling testimonials of First Nations people who were illegally forced to live in confinement under Canada's administrative policies. Many of the Indian agents were corrupt with little regard for the sub-standard living conditions the pass system created and imposed on the people. There are many facets of the film that the students find shocking, especially the government's efforts to destroy all evidence of the pass system ever existing once it was finally contested and abolished.

Despite a growing awareness of residential schools in Canada, many students find the first hand-accounts of residential school survivors to be horrific and harrowing. The film "We Were Children" (Wolochatiuk, 2012) is shown in nearly every class in the course at the midpoint in the term. The viewing is, in many ways, traumatic. The students are often visibly shaken. It is a turning point in the course where the weight of the issues associated with the government's racist ideologies of that time are more tangibly felt. Beyond the film, I bring forward stories of other youth who attempted to escape the horrendous mistreatment experienced in residential schools. In a news article, Morin

(2017) recounted the journey of three boys who attempted to travel 130km home through the wilderness in harsh winter conditions. Only one made it home.

The legacies of the residential school era are many and varied. One of the most wide-reaching effects is intergenerational trauma. While "intergenerational trauma" is a commonly used term in discussions around the legacies of residential schools, it is readily apparent that few people understand what experience the concept encapsulates. Again, I turn to the voices of the survivors and their children to provide honest tellings about the legacies of residential school experiences and intergenerational trauma (Calgary United Way, 2019; CBC News, 2018a; Fortier, 2019). The stories reinforce the challenges the survivors have faced when parenting their own children after years of oppression and violence, which include physical, mental, and sexual abuse. Many were taken from their families at very young ages and were not treated with love or care in the residential schools over the vast majority of their childhoods, complicating and/or harming the intergenerational relationships to present day.

Concurrent to the existence of residential schools and the resulting intergenerational trauma, the Sixties Scoop saw many Indigenous children taken from their Indigenous parents to be raised by non-Indigenous families outside of their communities. Some were relocated outside of Canada, in many cases never to see their parents or siblings again. News stories and investigative features (CBC News, 2018b; CBC News: The National, 2018) give insight into the heartbreaking losses of family, culture, identity, and belonging that resulted from the Sixties Scoop. Similar to the previous accounts, students are shocked and in disbelief to learn of the continued mistreatment and governmental over-reach plaguing the lives of Indigenous people across Canada.

7.2 Seeing the Repercussions of Resource Extraction and Encroachment on Indigenous Lands

In addition to the pass system, residential schools, 60s Scoop and resulting intergenerational trauma, many Indigenous communities are still fighting for rights to safe and clean drinking water. Many students question why so many Indigenous communities can be living in areas without access to clean water. The issues in the present can be highlighted by revisiting the past for answers. I share the examples from two communities.

The Sahtu Dene living on Great Bear Lake offer devastating reports of long-term health repercussions from contaminated water supplies, as a result of the radium and uranium mining that took place prior to and during the Second World War (Blow, 1999; Democracy Now, 2014; Henningson, 2013). Men from the community were paid as laborers in connection to the mining. Many of them developed cancer and died as a result of the harmful exposure to the radioactive elements. The government-sanctioned resource extraction supplied the uranium for the Manhattan Project. To this day, Great Bear Lake has dangerously high levels of radioactivity on the land and heavy metals in the water, contaminating the water and food supply, including the fish, caribou, and other vital species within the area.

A second community touched by the pollution produced by industry is in Grassy Narrows, Ontario. The Ojibwe of Grassy Narrows First Nation have been deeply affected by mercury poisoning after Dryden Chemicals Ltd. dumped mercury into the river upstream from the reserve (Orui, 2010; Péloquin, 2016). The contamination has also impacted the residents of Whitedog First Nation. Both the stories of mining at Great Bear Lake and dumping of pollutants into the river upstream of Grassy Narrows and Whitedog First Nations are lesser known stories in Canadian history. These two examples are indicative of the Canadian government's propensity to prioritize industry and economic advancement over the health and safety of Indigenous communities. This can also be seen with hydroelectric damming, resource extraction, and pipeline pathways, to name a few.

In many cases, Indigenous groups have been seen standing against industry and development, speaking for the rights and protection of the land, water, and more-than-human inhabitants (Abram, 1996) of the earth. Indigenous people who stand in opposition to capitalist development on sacred sites and traditional territories, as is seen in "Kanehsatake: 270 Years of Resistance" otherwise known as the Oka Crisis (Obomsawin, 1993) and "Mni Wiconi: The Stand at Standing Rock" in the U.S. (Divided Films, 2016), are demonized and vilified in the media. These Indigenous warriors face violence and racism from both government-run organizations and the public. As seen in these circumstances, the protests are quickly escalated, leading to the use of extreme force – as is more often seen in situations involving people of color. Regardless of the students' political leanings, many of them express anger as they witness the harsh treatment of the Indigenous people who are defending against the disruption of sacred burial sites for the expansion of a golf course and a pipeline.

7.3 Witnessing the Dire Consequences of the Normalization of Systemic Racism

The rights of Indigenous people have been repeatedly violated, historically and at present. Colonization imposed hegemonic and oppressive structures over First Nations, Métis, and Inuit people, leading to the normalization of systemic racism. Seeing Indigenous people as less-than others has led to unethical research testing of skin grafts on Inuit test subjects (CBC News, 2019), and the death of Brian Sinclair, an Anishanaabe man who was left untreated for over thirty hours in the emergency room of a Winnipeg hospital (McCallum & Perry, 2018). Systemic racism has allowed Canadian society to turn a blind eye to the epidemic of Missing and Murdered Indigenous Women and Girls, as well as countless other Indigenous people regardless of their gender identification, where only in recent years has the issue received any real recognition or serious investigative attention (Smiley, 2015). Many factors have contributed to making Indigenous people vulnerable, including the rise of resource-extraction in rural and remote communities. Indigenous women living in close proximity to industry-created man-camps experience greater incidents of rape; however, many of the perpetrators and predators receive no repercussions for their crimes (Haptic Pictures, 2019; O'Feral & Heck, 2020).

The reach of the systemic racism towards Indigenous people extends beyond international borders and has resulted in debilitating global policies around seal hunting that were established on a groundless basis of falsehoods and misinformation, while lining the pockets of profitable animal rights organizations (Arnaquq-Baril, 2016). Additionally, harmful stereotypes and tropes have been treated as acceptable within sports and college cultures, while perpetuating continued racism towards Indigenous people (Little & Little, 2017).

People around the world have romanticized and fetishized the idea of "Indians" to the point of not seeing Indigenous people as equal or having rights. With countless examples to draw from, I attempt to make the systemic racism visible. As the term progresses, I am encouraged by the overwhelming reactions I receive and/or observe from the students; it is apparent that they are moved to advocacy and action. Inevitably, the students begin to see the examples in the media around them and they bring in Indigenous-related news stories along with comments from discussion forums to unpack in class. In these moments, the students are taking up the work of Indigenous education.

8 Reflecting on My Roles and Responsibilities as an Indigenous Educator

While the stories I presented above may seem demoralizing, futile, and hopeless, there are also many examples of community-led resistance, resilience, empowerment, self-determination, advocacy, and action, embedded within them. The strength of Indigenous people is evident despite the unprecedented hardships, inequalities, and injustices that arise from systemic racism.

With few exceptions, I see that the students witness the stories as they are told by residential school survivors, community members, Elders, Knowledge

Keepers, and allies; and they take their words to heart. In both formal and informal conversations, the students demonstrate that the learning has moved them. Some linger after class to share their personal connections. Others send emails that offer candid reflections on the topics and stories. During the follow up discussions and in subsequent assignments, the students speak with conviction about the atrocities experienced in residential schools and other lesser known histories and legacies of colonization. They make claims to their responsibilities within Indigenous education, and share pragmatic examples of how they can carry the work forward in their teaching practices.

Through the uncertainty of the learning and the emotionality of the experiences, the students and I work through distressing curriculum towards "difficult knowledge" (Britzman, 1998, 2013). I realize that this is a challenging pedagogical approach that I am choosing to take on. As a result of my choices, the students may express feelings of shame, guilt, anger, hurt, disgust, sorrow, and more. In turn, I am asking the students to teach from a place of deep emotional work and to share the challenging curriculum with their own students. I am left asking: *Is this ethical?*

9   Meaning Making

While I examine my own experience through self-study, I have become keenly aware that although my learning journey is not identical, it is indeed similar to that of the students. From my learning, I have a responsibility to act and to teach. Through the students' learning, they are developing a sense of responsibility to act and to teach as well, but they may not be as far along in their learning journey as I am. If it is this difficult for me to teach Indigenous education, it might be impossibly difficult for them. Yet, this is the expectation.

How can I, in good conscience, share enough counter examples to move the students, while knowing that there is never enough, or I can never be enough, to prepare them for the work ahead? I try to model the humility and strength that comes from admitting that there is so much more to learn and know in all of our (collective) Indigenous education; and yes, there is a responsibility to teach what we do know along the way. Knowing that we all have a responsibility to teach Indigenous education can be both intimidating and empowering.

For hundreds of years, Indigenous people have been leaders – leading the way in living well with the world, in right relationships with all things (Atleo, 2011; Ermine, 1995; Grande, 2004; Little Bear, 2000; Sheridan & Longboat, 2006; Simpson, 2014; Smith, 1999/2012). Generation after generation have prioritized longstanding community-specific value systems, despite structures that have set out to obliterate Indigenous peoples (King, 2003). We can see this with the Wet'suwet'en in British Columbia. The people are speaking for the land, the water, and the more-than-human inhabitants, also known as sentient beings (Sheridan & Longboat, 2006), who cannot speak for themselves, or at least not in ways that many people will acknowledge or understand. They are also speaking on behalf of their ancestors and the generations to come.

From the settler-colonial narrative, the Wet'suwet'en are a clear example of Indigenous people who are standing in the way of progress – specifically, the building of a pipeline through their traditional, ancestral, and unceded territory. Canadian history is saturated with accounts that illustrate and uphold this ideal. It is only in recent years that more people are beginning to learn differently and to see things from another perspective. Fortunately, many of the resources that new teachers will be using in their classrooms to teach about Indigenous stories, communities, histories, and cultures will be, more likely than not, written by Indigenous people themselves. The information will come from an Indigenous perspective and worldview, as part of an ongoing decolonizing project (Smith, 2012).

I hear the stories of the strong leaders, such as Crow Chief Plenty Coups (Lear, 2006), who have come before us and have made the tough decision in order to give future generations a chance to survive in the face of great hardship and adversity. People who chose to live, when at times other options would have been easier ways out. Leaders who survived massacres, starvation tactics, relocation, isolation, constant policing, residential schools, unjust governance, and oppressive systems. Leaders who have continued to act from places of love, humility, wisdom, strength, and courage. Leaders who educate with stories and patience, providing gentle guidance to those who are open to listening. I am grateful for the leaders in my life – the Elders, community leaders, and Indigenous academics.

Leadership, as seen through an Indigenous lens, is not about being in charge and standing alone; leadership is about standing up and standing together. Indigenous leaders are usually embedded in and supported by rich networks of relationships. They are also often well-grounded in their community's epistemologies, ontologies, connections to place, values, histories, traditions and beliefs. Some leaders are showcased in mainstream media, such as Anishinaabe-kwe water protector Autumn Peltier from the Wiikwemkoong First Nation; and the two-spirit, Amazing Race Canada winners: Anthony Johnson – a Diné artist from the Navajo Nation, and James Makokis – a doctor from the Saddle Lake Cree Nation. These and other leaders may spend their lifetimes learning from and becoming knowledge keepers, spiritual leaders, historians, medicine gathers, ceremonial leaders, grandmothers, fire keepers, and more – all educators. So how is it that for hundreds of years, despite having such strong leaders, that Indigenous people continue to be cast in a negative and disparaging light by so many settler-Canadians?

Now, more than ever, there is a readiness (MacDonald & Markides, 2018, 2019) for people to take up the work of reconciliation. This is being enacted in classrooms, where there is more openness to listen, and more openness to learn. It will take generations of people learning and taking action to see significant societal change, but I believe that it is happening. I have to believe that the world might be a little better for my own children, and their children's children; or I wouldn't have the emotional strength to be able to continue to do this work myself.

While the Indigenous leaders have always been here, advocating and educating from places of wisdom, community knowledge, and values, Settler-Canadians are finally making the courageous move to be "first followers" (Sivers, 2010). As Derek Sivers described, first followers are the people who create momentum for a social movement, having the courage to follow and teaching others how to follow through their actions. As Siksika Elder Clarence Wolfleg noted, this is the first generation of educators who are doing this brave work and beginning to teach differently (McDermott et al., 2021).

In the pre-service teacher education course, I get to work with many of the first followers in the reconciliatory movement. I have the great responsibility and deep honor to support the students' learning as they build up the courage to follow and learn from Indigenous leaders. I am humbled to bear witness to their first steps in this larger social action. While I find the teaching of Indigenous education makes me question my ethical responsibilities to the students, the reflexive process in self-study situates my understanding of the work as part of a larger interconnected picture where we address ethical failings within society. The teaching is simultaneously difficult and rewarding.

10   Concluding Thoughts

In the above discussion, I touch on only a few of the tensions and insights that self-study has helped me to expose from my time in Indigenous teacher education to date. These include: my responsibilities to share what I have been taught while continuing to learn; never feeling fully enough to teach the course despite having knowledge to offer; recognizing that my "having knowledge to offer" heightens my awareness of how much more there is to learn; juggling nervousness and passion; espousing that the course has the potential to be transformative and then having to deliver on that promise; wanting to provide counter-narratives and untold stories in order to dispel myths and raise consciousness while recognizing that the students want and need pragmatic skills and strategies for taking up this work in their classrooms; all, while providing an overview of the oppressive structures and colonial violence that have contributed to systemic racism, within the span of an eight-week course.

I see the dialogue as ongoing, and I invite others into discussions with me and with their own experiences in emancipatory teacher education contexts. From earlier studies with Jennifer MacDonald, we determined that conversations are often what move us forward in reconciliatory work (MacDonald & Markides, 2018, 2019). For me, the dialogue with my experiences, thoughts, ethical questions, grander narratives, and the societal context have moved my learning forward. I have a better understanding of where Indigenous education fits within the larger frame of societal change. My teaching is necessarily dangerous and responsive. It fluctuates between the negotiation of difficult knowledge and the opening of spaces for informed and meaningful action. I am also conscious of the reader's role within the self-study research. Writing through the learning and learning through the writing is a vital part for my own practice. However, I also hope that it offers others a window into my process for coming to know differently about my roles and responsibilities as an Indigenous educator.

As I prepare for the next academic year, I am more wholly aware of my responsibilities as an Indigenous educator. Yet I wonder, will the students be readier for me? Societal change is slow, but I see with each iteration of the course, in each passing year, there is movement, forward steps. Unlike any other class or subject I have taught, the learning journey in Indigenous education has resulted in some of the greatest shifts in people's perceptions, knowledge, and understanding than ever before. In this way, being an instructor for the course can be life changing – immeasurable work, but immensely fulfilling. Teaching and learning can be an exercise in resiliency and renewed hope.

References

Abram, D. (1996). *The spell of the sensuous: Perception and language in a more-than-human world.* Pantheon Books.

Adichie, C. N. (2009, July). *Chimamanda Ngozi Adichie: The danger of a single story* [Video]. TED Conferences. Retrieved May 22, 2021, from http://www.ted.com/talks/chimamanda_adichie_the_danger_of_a_single_story

Allan, B., & Smylie, J. (2015). *First Peoples, second class treatment: The role of racism in the health and well-being of Indigenous peoples in Canada.* The Wellesley Institute.

Arnaquq-Baril, A. (Director). (2016, May). *Angry Inuk* [Film]. NFB of Canada.

Atleo, Umeek E. R. (2011). *Principles of Tsawalk: An Indigenous approach to global crisis.* UBC Press.

Blow, P. (Director). (1999, May). *Village of widows* [Film]. Lindum Films. Retrieved May 22, 2021, from https://www.youtube.com/watch?v=GSReqj1JX-c

Britzman, D. P. (1998). *Lost subjects, contested objects: Toward a psychoanalytic inquiry of learning.* State University of New York Press.

Britzman, D. P. (2013). Between psychoanalysis and pedagogy: Scenes of rapprochement and alienation. *Curriculum Inquiry, 43*(1), 95–117. https://doi.org/10.1111/curi.12007

Calgary United Way. (2019, June). *The #UNIGNORABLE issue of intergenerational trauma | Truth and reconciliation* [Video]. YouTube. Retrieved May 22, 2021, from https://www.youtube.com/watch?v=-mLe6BQ3pD0

CBC News. (2018a, March). *Residential school survivor explains the impact on her family* [Video]. YouTube. Retrieved May 22, 2021, from https://www.youtube.com/watch?v=nJ64DItsIio

CBC News. (2018b, December). *Sixties Scoop survivor finds sister, only to lose her again* [Video]. YouTube. Retrieved May 22, 2021, from https://www.youtube.com/watch?v=w7s78ishGyQ

CBC News. (2019, May). *Inuit break silence on skin graft experiments* [Video]. YouTube. Retrieved May 22, 2021, from https://www.youtube.com/watch?v=E-vh85X8VSc&list=PLeyJPHbRnGaZFu8_xxuXPlYG-j-9cogsx&index=72

CBC News: The National. (2018, April). *Finding Cleo: How a CBC podcast solved the mystery of a missing Indigenous girl* [Video]. YouTube. Retrieved May 22, 2021, from https://www.youtube.com/watch?v=neprXCgokjg

Daniels v. Canada, 2016 SC 12. (2016). Lexum. Retrieved May 22, 2021, from https://scc-csc.lexum.com/scc-csc/scc-csc/en/item/15858/index.do

Democracy Now. (2014, March). *"A slow genocide of the people": Uranium mining leaves toxic nuclear legacy on Indigenous land* [Video]. Democracy Now: Independent Global News. Retrieved May 22, 2021, from https://www.democracynow.org/2014/3/14/a_slow_genocide_of_the_people

DiAngelo, R., & Sensoy, Ö. (2014). Leaning in: A student's guide to engaging constructively with social justice content. *Radical Pedagogy, 11*(1), Article 2.

Divided Films. (2016, November). *Mni Wiconi: The stand at Standing Rock* [Video]. YouTube. Retrieved May 22, 2021, from https://www.youtube.com/watch?v=4FDuqYld8C8

Ermine, W. (1995). Aboriginal epistemology. In M. Battiste & J. Barman (Eds.), *First Nations education in Canada: The circle unfolds* (pp. 101–112). UBC Press.

Fforde, C., Bamblett, L., Lovett, R., Gorringe, S., & Fogarty, B. (2013). Discourse, deficit and identity: Aboriginality, the race paradigm and the language of representation in contemporary Australia. *Media International Australia, 149*(1), 162–173. https://doi.org/10.1177/1329878X1314900117

Fortier, H. (Director). (2019, September). *A mother's voice* [Video]. Telus Storyhive. Retrieved May 22, 2021, from https://www.youtube.com/watch?v=Ip3yGEKGCX4

Gaudry, A., & Andersen, C. (2016). Daniels v. Canada: Racialized legacies, settler self-Indigenization and the denial of Indigenous peoplehood. *TOPIA: Canadian Journal of Cultural Studies, 36*(Fall 2016), pp. 19–30.

Grande, S. (2004). *Red pedagogy: Native American social and political thought.* Rowman & Littlefield.

Haptic Pictures. (2019, October). *Sisters rising | Official trailer* [Video]. Vimeo. Retrieved May 22, 2021, from https://vimeo.com/367084420

Henningson, D. (Director). (2013, February). *Somba Ke – The money place* [Film; Sundance version]. YouTube. Retrieved May 22, 2021, from https://www.youtube.com/watch?v=hzhQBNmIXzA

Hodson, J. (2016). Learning to dance: Pow Wow, Maori Haka, Indigagogy and being an Indigenous teacher educator. In J. Kitchen, D. Tidwell, & L. Fitzgerald (Eds.), *Self-study and diversity II: Inclusive teacher education for a diverse world* (pp. 27–38). Sense.

King, T. (2003). *The truth about stories: A native narrative.* House of Anansi.

Kitchen, J. (2005). Looking backwards, moving forward: Understanding my narrative as a teacher educator. *Studying Teacher Education, 1*(1), 17–30.

Lear, J. (2006). *Radical hope: Ethics in the face of cultural devastation.* Harvard University Press.

Little Bear, L. (2000). Jagged worldview colliding. In M. Battiste (Ed.), *Reclaiming Indigenous voice and vision* (pp. 77–85). UBC Press.

Little, J., & Little, K. (Directors). (2017, August). *More than a word* [Film]. Media Education Foundation.

Lyle, E. (2017). *Of books, barns, and boardrooms: Exploring praxis through reflexive inquiry.* Sense.

Lyle, E. (2018). Engaging self-study to untangle issues of identity. In E. Lyle (Ed.), *Fostering a relational pedagogy: Self-study as transformative praxis* (pp. 1–9). Brill | Sense.

MacDonald, J., & Markides, J. (2018). Called to action: Dialogue around praxis for reconciliation. In L. Daniels, S. Deer, D. Donald, B. Low & D. Wiseman (Eds.), Taking up the Calls to Action of the TRC in teacher education [Special Issue]. *McGill Journal of Education, 53*(2), 213–232.

MacDonald, J., & Markides, J. (2019). Duoethnography for reconciliation: Learning through conversations. *Alberta Journal of Educational Research, 65*(2), 1–16.

Markides, J. (2018). *Being* Indigenous in the Indigenous education classroom: A critical self-study of teaching in an impossible and imperative assignment. In E. R. Lyle (Ed.), *Fostering a relational pedagogy: Self-study as transformative praxis* (pp. 35–44). Brill | Sense.

Martel, K. (2018). Daniels V. Canada: The Supreme Court's racialized understanding of the Métis and section 91(24). In J. Markides & L. Forsythe (Eds.), *Looking back and living forward: Indigenous research rising up* (pp. 145–154). Brill | Sense.

McCallum, M. J. L., & Perry, A. (2018). *Structures of indifference: An Indigenous life and death in a Canadian city.* University of Manitoba Press.

McDermott, M., MacDonald, J., Markides, J., & Holden, M. (2021). Uncovering the experiences of engaging Indigenous knowledges in colonial structures of schooling and research. In M. Battiste & J. Y. Henderson (Eds.), Indigenous and trans-systemic knowledge systems [Special Issue]. *Engaged Scholar Journal: Community Engaged Research, Teaching, and Learning, 7*(1), 25–44.

Morin, B. (2017, September 21). Residential school runaway remembers harrowing journey that killed his two friends. *CBC News.* Retrieved May 22, 2021, from https://www.cbc.ca/news/indigenous/bernard-andreason-tuktoyaktuk-journey-1.4297798

O'Feral, W., & Heck, B. (Directors). (2020, February). *Sisters rising* [Film]. Haptic Pictures.

Obomsawin, A. (Director). (1993, January). *Kanehsatake: 270 years of resistance* [Film]. NFB of Canada.

Orui, T. (Director). (2010). *The scars of mercury* [Film]. Produced independently. Retrieved May 22, 2021, from https://www.cultureunplugged.com/documentary/watch-online/play/6412/The-Scars-Of-Mercury

Palmer, P. J. (2017). *The courage to teach: Exploring the inner landscape of a teacher's life* (20th anniversary ed.). Jossey-Bass.

Péloquin, F. (Director). (2016, June). *The story of grassy narrows* [Video]. PSAC-AFPC. Retrieved May 22, 2021, from https://www.youtube.com/watch?v=9E06pWtCHIg

Pinnegar, S. E., & Hamilton, M. L. (2009). *Self-study of practice as a genre of qualitative research: Theory, methodology, and practice.* Springer.

Samaras, A. P. (2011). *Self-study teacher research: Improving your practice through collaborative inquiry.* Sage.

Sheridan, J., & Longboat, D. R. "He Clears the Sky." (2006). The Haudenosaunee imagination and the ecology of the sacred. *Space and Culture, 9*(4), 365–381.

Shore, F. J. (2018). *Threads in the sash: The story of Métis people.* Pemmican Publications.

Simpson, L. B. (2014). Land as pedagogy: Nishnaabeg intelligence and rebellious transformation. *Decolonization: Indigeneity, Education & Society, 3*(3), 1–25.

Sivers, D. (2010, February). *Derek Sivers: How to start a movement* [Video]. TED. Retrieved May 22, 2021, from https://www.ted.com/talks/derek_sivers_how_to_start_a_movement?language=en

Smith, L. T. (2012). *Decolonizing methodologies: Research and Indigenous peoples* (2nd ed.). Zed Books. (Original work published 1999)

Smiley, M. (Director). (2015, March). *Highway of tears* [Film]. Finesse Films.

St. Denis, V. (2007). Aboriginal education and anti-racist education: Building alliances across cultural and racial identity. *Canadian Journal of Education, 30*(4), 1068–1092.

Tidwell, D. L., Heston, M. L., & Fitzgerald, L. M. (2009). Introduction. In D. L. Tidwell, M. L. Heston, & L. M. Fitzgerald (Eds.), *Research methods for the self-study of practice* (pp. xiii–xxii). Springer.

Truth and Reconciliation Commission of Canada (TRC). (2015a). *Calls to action*. Retrieved May 22, 2021, from http://trc.ca/assets/pdf/Calls_to_Action_English2.pdf

Truth and Reconciliation Commission of Canada (TRC). (2015b). *Honouring the truth, reconciling for the future: Summary of the final report on the Truth and Reconciliation Commission of Canada*. Retrieved May 22, 2021, from http://www.trc.ca/assets/pdf/Executive_Summary_English_Web.pdf

Wiebe, S., & Snowber, C. (2012). En/lived vulnere: A poetic of im/possible pedagogies. In S. Thomas, A. L. Cole, & S. Stewart (Eds.), *The art of poetic inquiry* (pp. 446–461). Backalong Books.

Williams, A. (Director). (2015). *The pass system* [Film]. Tamarack Productions.

Wolochatiuk, T. (Director). (2012). *We were children* [Film]. NFB of Canada.

CHAPTER 7

The Freedom to Be All at Once

My Journey from Literacy to Hip Hop Literacy

Shuaib J. Meacham

As a Black Literacy Scholar and Educator my professional experience has been shaped by the need to reconcile the competing tensions and hierarchical structures that inform the practice "literacy" and the cultural practices and priorities of Black people, particularly Black youth. This is not to suggest that there is a cultural opposition to literacy on the part of Black people and Black culture. In fact, quite the opposite. As the work of Gates (2016) demonstrated, "[there is] an inextricable link in the African-American tradition between literacy and freedom" (p. 12), which has historically been the highest cultural priority among Black people.

However, as Black culture has evolved, the rather rigid and one-dimensional conceptual structures informing literacy, especially within the context of schools and education, have rendered it increasingly irrelevant in the eyes of Black youth (Mahiri, 1998). As not only a scholar but especially as an educator, I have faced a number of challenges that have forced me to examine more culturally relevant literacy practices for their educational potential. This self-study of my journey from literacy to Hip Hop Literacy will examine not only the changes in literacy practice required by such a journey, but more significantly, the mindset required to carry out literacy practices reflective of and informed by Hip Hop culture.

1 The Hierarchical Dynamics of "Literacy"

Literacy has functioned not only as priority practice in the area of education, but also has served as a central organizing principle around which conceptions of effective society have been defined. As Graff (1991) stated, "Literacy was seen as a central variable among that complex of factors that distinguish modern, developed or developing, and advanced societies and individuals from the lesser developed areas and persons of the world" (p. 2).

In order to promote the conceptual integrity of such a vital liminal term, literacy has traditionally possessed a "strong text" (Royer, 1994) conceptual framework. Strong text literacy sees literacy as a structurally singular, exclusively written language practice. This structurally singular and exclusively written conception of literacy was held up, not only as Graff contended, as a "factor that distinguish[ed]" developed from lesser developed societies, but in the case of Black people, the practice of literacy was the factor that distinguished between full and lesser humanity. Therefore, the cultural absence of written literacy was posited as a justification for African enslavement. In other words, slavery was justified, in part, on the premise that "blacks lacked reason, therefore they could not write, and therefore were somehow less human" and were thus suited to be enslaved (Gates, 2016, p. XIV). Since the absence of literacy was seen as the factor that justified Black enslavement, Black people turned the acquisition of literacy into a heroic achievement. As Gates described, Black people produced "the largest body of literature ever created by former slaves and [gave] birth thereby to the African-American literary tradition" (Gates, 2016, p. XIV).

While the Black connection to strong text literacy was pursued for purposes of liberation and social possibility, maintaining a commitment to strong text created inherent tensions for educated Black people, especially for Black Scholars and Educators. Notwithstanding the heroic status accorded to the acquisition and practice of literacy, the oral and rhythmic foundations of Black culture's connections to Africa exerted increasingly stronger levels of influence and prominence. hooks and West (2017) suggested that the foundation of Black intellectual practice resides in part, albeit significantly in what West called the "two organic intellectual traditions in Afro-American life: the Black Christian tradition of preaching and the Black musical tradition of performance. Both traditions, though undoubtedly linked to the life of the mind, are oral, improvisational, and histrionic" (p. 136). To the point, not only do the performative and oral language practices of Black culture exert influence upon Black Scholars and Educators, they often comprise the intellectual foundations from which Black Scholarship and Educational innovations derive their meaning and purposes. This means that Black Scholars and Educators, whose professions require adherence to the practice of strong text literacy, possess an inherent tension with the "organic intellectual traditions" that have historically informed and conveyed Black lived experiences. The question becomes, how does a Black Scholar and Educator, particularly in the academic field of Literacy Education, navigate the professional necessity of emphasizing and propagating strong text literacy, while connecting to the multifaceted, oral and performative literacy conceptions of Black Culture? More specifically, how does a Black Scholar and Educator navigate the technology-mediated and musical literacy contingencies of Hip Hop Culture? I will first examine the self-study research method, with attention to the manner in which self-study is a method particularly suited for the systematic examination of this question. I will then examine the Black cultural contingencies underlying Hip Hop Culture and Hip Hop Literacy, with a focus on the multiple learning and expressive modalities required to be a functional participant in the Hip Hop Literacy experience.

2 Self-Study as a Methodological Vehicle for Documenting the Journey

Self-study is a uniquely appropriate research vehicle for this project because of its three-fold emphasis upon identity, language, and reflection. Coia and Taylor (2009) emphasized the fact that teachers' pedagogical practices are informed by "complex and culturally informed" identities (p. 3), arguing that "Identity is a central concern in self-study of teaching practices" (p. 4). As suggested above, for a Black Scholar and Educator in the field of literacy, identity is central to the Black literacy narrative. Therefore, the journey from Literacy to Hip Hop Literacy is also one of identity. The above-described tensions between the professional necessity of the adherence to strong text conceptions of literacy and the cultural imperative of the two organic intellectual traditions means that a functional professional identity cannot be taken as a given, but must be performed and improvised. Therefore, self-study allows for a vital documentation of this performative practice.

At recent meetings of the Castle Conference and meetings of the American Educational Research Association, scholars whose first language was not English issued challenges to the field, stating that self-study needed to "stretch the boundaries of theories and methods to encompass alternative versions of 'self-study'" (Kitchen et al., 2016, p. 8). While examining the journey from Literacy to Hip Hop Literacy is not one informed by a language outside of English, it is a journey that explores conceptual and intellectual languages that are informed by experiences and perspectives that exist beyond the traditional cultural norms of the Academy. In this study I deeply examine conceptual and intellectual languages that are informed by Bebop Jazz musicians, the music and performances of James Brown and his bands, and the insights of legendary Hip Hop figures Jay-Z, musical executive Steve Stoute, and the multifaceted Hip Hop-informed impacts of designer Virgil Abloh (Zinga, 2017). Dyson (2006) described Hip Hop as a kind of collective reflection on the part of those in the Hip Hop community who deploy the culture as a means of examining vital issues of relevance and impact. The data for this study are taken from a practice of ongoing written reflections about my Hip Hop Literacy experience, which moved from a deep skepticism of and alienation from Hip Hop music and culture, especially with respect to its impact on education, to a radical integration of the music and culture into my professional literacy education experience. It has been my habit, long before I ever learned about the field of Self-Study, to keep an ongoing journal about personal and professional issues and challenges. As Hip Hop culture emerged as a more prominent part of my life, I began to document my learning and work related to Hip Hop in addition to reflections that documented my initial aversion to it. For this study, I reviewed these journals, spanning many years and physical logbooks, and culled the entries that dealt with Hip and its role in my life and work.

3 Constructing a Black Conceptual Language for This Self-Study

As stated above, self-study has been selected as a uniquely appropriate method for this work because of its openness to alternative languages, both languages beyond English and English-based conceptual languages informed by cultural priorities that exist beyond the Western European and American mainstream norms. Gates (1988) posited "signifying" as a foundational African-informed Black cultural practice, which he described as, in part, "repetition … with a difference" (p. 17). Whether it be Black visual art, music, or language use, repetition with often strategically implemented differences is a seminal Black cultural practice. Nealon (1998), while building on the concept of repetition with a difference, attempted to further decolonize Black culture from its Western mooring by taking up Baraka's (1974) contention that Black music and culture be perceived as a verb. Nealon connected Baraka's contention to the conceptual language of Deleuze (2014) to suggest that Black culture as verb "deterritorializes" Black culture by preventing the simplistic duality of the comparison to White culture. Black culture as verb suggests a constant action of becoming and enunciating possibilities instead of becoming a calcified noun within Western cultural typologies and hierarchies. Taken from his observation of Bebop jazz musicians, Baraka emphasized that the practice of constant becoming spoke to a Bebop recognition and assertion that there were no acceptable spaces for their art within the White dominated cultural and musical landscape. Nealon (1998) connected this posture to the framework of repetition with a difference when he wrote:

> Unique contribution of the beboppers was the fact that they reinforced alienation but on the Negroes terms such an alien nation or separateness

> is then a repetition of segregation but with an important difference: This is the repetition that reinscribed the forced segregation of blacks to create a deterritorialization, a line of flight for African-American culture. (p. 85)

Based on this framework, Nealon went on to assert the following:

> we need a critical vocabulary to open the movement of becoming – to enact the *specificity* of the *difference* in *repetition with a difference*. To describe this open-ended movement of transformation, then, we need a force that goes not from *either/or* to *both/and*, but, as Deleuze and Guattari put it, from *either/or* to either or or or or or or or or or or …; not from difference to assimilation, but from difference to difference to difference. (p. 88)

One of the musical responses to Nealon's call for a critical vocabulary that flows from the (verb)al quality of Black culture and thus speaks to the primacy of ongoing becoming may be found in the music of James Brown. Much like the manner in which Bebop sax legend Charlie Parker inspired Amiri Baraka to posit the primacy of the verb in Black culture, James Brown shifted the musical emphasis in his music from melody to rhythm, while maintaining the power of sound. For James Brown, his music became less of a melodic entity and more of a rhythmic force in which all of the instruments in the band contributed to this rhythmic priority. James Brown (Thompson, 2001, p. 11) expressed it in the following manner after the release of his song, "Papa's Got a Brand New Bag":

> I had gone off in a different direction. I had discovered that my strength was not in the horns, it was in the rhythm. I was hearing everything, even the guitars, like they were drums. Later on, they said it was the beginning of funk. I just thought of it as where my music was going. (Marre, 2003)

As Brown described, "everything, even the guitars … were like drums," thus establishing the priority of rhythm within the "process of the verb-like becoming of his music. Perhaps the most singularly identified detail in his shift to the rhythmic emphasis was what Brown famously described as 'The One'" (Marre, 2003).

Technically, "The One" was simply placing the rhythmic emphasis upon the first beat of the measure instead of the second beat, better known as the "downbeat." This signature adjustment opened up a torrent of musical expressions that enhanced the power of that One. The collective effect was a magnetic propulsive dance music that took over Black popular music, called "Funk." While this innovation was relevant in purely musical terms, there are two additional areas of relevance that ultimately contributed deeply to Hip Hop culture and thus my personal journey. First, James Brown's rhythm-first music took on social and cultural significance. James Brown's funk was the soundtrack of Black Power, "Black is Beautiful," and Black Pride.

This surge of Black Pride was revolutionary because "Black" had historically connoted negative phenomena. The "Black" in "Black magic," "Black list," "Black mail," all connote something that was dangerous, evil and ominous. The great Malcolm X (1965/1999), following the teachings of the Honorable Elijah Muhammad, famously took on this pattern to demonstrate the manner in which White society had systemically taught Black people to hate themselves by having Black so singularly associated with the Bad. Just as Black language turned the meaning of "Bad" and made it become something good, "Black" was also transformed into something powerful, desirable, and revolutionary. In his book, *Black Studies, Rap and the Academy*, Baker (1995) discussed the manner in which the Black Power movement, from a cultural perspective, turned the tables on the integrationist intentions of major colleges and universities. According to Baker, these higher education institutions began to admit Black students into their graduate programs under the assumptions that those students would emulate the traditions of the predominantly White-male forebearers who had shaped the culture of the Academy. However, due in part to the cultural influences of Black Pride and Black Power, many of those students had no interest in emulating those traditions, but began to aggressively map out new traditions and practices that would redefine at least a portion of the Academy into their cultural image.

This meant that by the time I arrived in the Academy, there were already strong Black cultural currents that had established the need for ongoing redefinition of academic terms and assumptions that created space for Black lives. Thus in my field of Literacy and in Education generally, there were Black scholars like Violet Harris, Arnetha Ball, Vivian Gadsden, James Anderson, William Trent, Gloria Ladson-Billings, Joyce King and a host of others who made it clear to me that I possessed everything that I needed to pursue scholarship and teaching practices that foregrounded Black experiences and perspectives. Therefore, while I valued the literacy research and pedagogies that promoted the strong text conceptions of literacy, it was my destiny to engage in systematic inquiry that examined literacy from the perspective of the rhythmic and performance priorities of Black Culture. The second important implication of James Brown's shift to an emphasis on the Rhythm was that it played a foundational role in what became Hip Hop music. James Brown is arguably the most sampled artist in the entire Black music canon shaping the norms that informed the sound of Hip Hop. Vincent (1996) argued that the primary innovators of Hip Hop music feverishly sought out the lineage of Black music informed by the rhythmic priorities of James Brown when shaping the sonic Hip Hop landscape.

Notwithstanding the indispensable role of Hip Hop music in the shaping of the impact of Hip Hop on the US and global society (Greenburg, 2018), the music represents but a small part of that influence. To truly understand the influence requires a shift in how Hip Hop culture is regarded. Regardless of the imagery associated with Hip Hop culture promoted by the mainstream media and the controversies that have brought attention to the lyrical content of many of its artists, Hip Hop is at bottom a productive culture of which learning is an essential element. In order to understand and perceive Hip Hop as a productive learning culture, one has to recognize that Hip Hop changed the terms of Black artists' engagement in the music industry. The older, White executives and decision-makers in the industry did not understand the music or the culture and thus depended upon Hip Hop cultural curators such as Russell Simmons to translate the culture for them and demonstrate the business opportunities that were available (Charnas, 2011; Simmons, 2001). What Simmons and others like him knew, that the executives in the industry did not, was that Hip Hop was not a one-dimensional music model. The music was an extension of a multidimensional, multi-modal culture. Hip Hop culture necessarily integrates the creation of sonic landscapes from DJs/Producers, visual art and graphics in the form of graffiti, dance and choreography in the form of break-dancing, and of course the words of the eponymous "rapper" with which the entire music and culture has been identified. This knowledge gap between those leading the entertainment industry institutions and the artists and advocates who knew the culture created heretofore unprecedented professional opportunities for the largely Black and Brown artists to exert unprecedented influence. Artists such as Jay-Z (Sean Carter), Dr. Dre (Andre Young), and P-Diddy aka "Puff Daddy" (Sean Combs) not only became legends in the world of Hip Hop music, but exercised tremendous influence over global popular culture. As Greenburg (2018) stated, "These three kings have built their culture by creating a 24/7 head to toe lifestyle" (p. 4). It is that cultural element of Hip Hop that enabled these visionaries to exert a vast impact with Hip Hop related products and branding.

While the "Three Kings" mentioned above are the most well-known figures associated with the broad impact of Hip Hop upon global popular culture and much has been published about their creative output, comparatively little has been published about the processes that inform their productivity, especially as it relates to their larger public impact. The designer Virgil Abloh, however, not only has been extremely influential in popular culture with his "Off White" clothing company and his prominent role in the career of Hip Hop icon, Kanye West, he has been effusive in his public presentations regarding his productive processes and the manner in which those processes reflect Hip Hop cultural contingencies. Very similar to the Black cultural priorities discussed above, the productive process of Virgil Abloh emphasizes the factor of identity, or as he puts it, one's "design DNA" (Zinga, 2017). Clarity of identity is an imperative for two critical reasons. First, with an established design DNA, one can begin to produce work that comprises an extension of that DNA. This pattern of identity-driven production leads to the second critical factor regarding the primacy of identity – it constitutes the basis for future collaborations. Within this framework, establishing identity is itself a productive act, because the subsequent productivity is driven by that primary factor, creating a critical momentum. As Abloh has stated, "Do the one project that you really believe in and make it exist and have things take off from there … influence emerges from simply doing and making vision public. By making it seen, others will do it, too" (Zinga, 2017).

As the statement implies by using the word, "influence," a synergy begins once one has produced extensions of one's design DNA, others can see it and, in turn, participate, which speaks to the collaborative ethos that reflects this priority. An additional factor in this identity-driven-collaborative practice is the admonition, "Don't be a perfectionist." Because the priority is production and collaborative engagement, the impact emerges from the process and not the perfection of the individual work; there is no need for that more ego-driven outcome. The identity-driven-collaborative process also enables the work to go in multiple directions simultaneously. While Abloh has become most known for his "Off White" clothing line, he has been hired by Nike to connect his design DNA to vintage Air Jordan basketball shoes; IKEA has hired him to design furniture and interior decorations; and Louis Vuitton appointed him as their creative director, while being a Hip Hop DJ. As he concluded, "When perfection stops being a priority, then it is ok to do many things at once."

As I transition to the data of the self-study, it is important to reiterate the points from this section on conceptual language. First, it is vitally important to assert that the "self" under study not be perceived as a cultural noun or object to be classified within the traditional academic typologies, but instead be perceived as a verb, an ongoing performative process that is improvisationally navigating the priorities of the Academy, while creating space for the Black cultural, "organic intellectual" imperatives that have shaped Black life. Those imperatives foreground Black experiences and perspectives that aim to identify and enact an identity that informs all manner of personal and professional work. That identity, like the culture of Hip Hop, is not a one-dimensional expression, but through norms of collaboration addresses multiple needs and contingencies simultaneously.

4   From Alienation to Integration

I initially hated Hip Hop music. I will never forget my first instance of hearing Hip Hop music. It was a shock to my sensibilities and I could not stand it. I was attending a family reunion outside of Washington, DC. in 1978 and I was sixteen years old. At sixteen, my musical tastes were already deeply formed, which set the stage for my initial reaction. That first Hip Hop song was "Rapper's Delight" which begins with a sample of a song that was a hit record earlier that year called "Good Times" by Chic. Therefore, I was initially excited by the song because it began with a very familiar and beloved musical introduction, but instead of the familiar hook proclaiming, "Good Times!" I heard, "I said a hip-hop the hippie the hippie" and I was outraged. What had happened to my song!

However, in spite of my initial aversion to Hip Hop music and culture, there were important personal connections that I was able to make over time that established an openness to the music and the culture that would later inform my cultural practice. In the mid- to late-1980s, I had joined the US Navy, where I had been stationed aboard the Carrier USS Carl Vinson. An aircraft carrier is an enormous vessel that holds upwards of 6,000 crew members. Since I joined the Navy, in part, because I did not yet know what I wanted to do for a career, I spent considerable time in the ship's library, which actually exceeded my expectations with respect to the diversity of the collection and the fact that it contained several books by my favorite author, James Baldwin. When not reading the books in the library, I read the books I checked out during work breaks and it became a norm to have a book with me at all times. Several Black shipmates noticed this practice and asked me why I had books with me all the time. I responded by sharing with them my purpose for reading the books, which, in addition to figuring out what I wanted to do with my future, involved attempting to make sense of the experience of being a Black man in the USA. My shipmates resonated with my purpose for reading and began asking me to share what I was learning from the books. Without any urging or suggestion on my part, they began to go to the library, check out books and share what they were learning from their books with me. This led to nearly all meals becoming focused on discussions of books and literally a movable feast of intellectual discussion from one "mess deck" to the other, depending on which friend was on a dinner break. However, the focus of the discussion was not always on books. Being considerably younger than me, many of my friends were ardent fans of Hip Hop music and culture and when I shared my general dislike for the music, many of them responded that I needed to listen to "Public Enemy." They said that they knew that I would like Public Enemy.

I never listened to Public Enemy while I was in the Navy, but shortly after getting out of the Navy, I recalled the words of my Black shipmates and made a point of purchasing a Public Enemy album. I purchased, "It Takes a Nation of Millions to Hold us Back," and if I had any idea of the impact of the experience of hearing that album, I would have purchased it years sooner. The sonic collage of the walls of samples put together by the producers, known as "The Bomb Squad," combined with the verbal collage of lyrics, by lead MC Chuck D, and the pro-Black samples from the Nation of Islam, Malcolm X and the broad array of speaking truth to power figures was truly intoxicating. I couldn't get enough of it. The sound, the rhythms, the words of power became a soundtrack of the months that immediately followed my discharge from the Navy. I tried to find as much of this type of Hip Hop as I could find, but sadly, this represented an exception and not the norm, from my point of view at the time, so while I truly loved the music of Public Enemy, I did not significantly alter my view of Hip Hop music as a whole. I found a couple of groups that possessed comparable Black culture-focused content that reflected the reading I had engaged in, such as the X-Clan and Poor Righteous Teachers. However, the music and the culture as a whole remained marginal.

It was around that time that my Aunt Jean's best friend, Betty Morrison, a full Professor and one of the first Black female tenured professors in the history of the University of Michigan, began to harass me into going to graduate school. She claimed during my undergraduate years that I would do well in Academia and enjoy the work, but as I did not enjoy my undergraduate experience, the last thing I wanted to do was to return to school. However, my experience in the Navy with my Black shipmates and their sudden embrace of reading created an openness to the idea of going to graduate school. When I entered graduate school, I discovered a field called "Literacy Education" and thought that it might be a path that would lead me to better understand my Naval experience. So I took an introductory class with a Professor named William McGinley. I don't recall the topic of the first paper, but I remember focusing my observations on my reading of Richard Wright's (1977/1988) *American Hunger*, which was the sequel to his better-known work, *Black Boy* (1945/2020). Wright talked about the manner in which literacy had created a bridge between himself and the outside world. Professor McGinley commented extensively on that observation and said that it helped him to make sense of the experience that he was having on his research in Detroit. Soon after that first paper, he began to ask me about my literacy interests, so I told him my story about the Navy and wanting to know how to better promote literacy in school so that students can appreciate the importance of literacy in school and not have to wait to leave school in order to discover its power and importance. He responded by telling me more about his research project in Detroit and invited me to go to Detroit with him. His project involved examining the functions of literacy in a 3rd grade classroom in which the students had published a book. In the research he examined how, once the book was published, the students shared the book with their families and the kinds of discourses that took place around the publication of the book. What was also very interesting was that unlike most of the White teachers in Detroit, who lived outside of the city at the time, this teacher lived in the city and was aware of the many Black literary organizations and other community-based supports for literacy in the city. Professor McGinley, knowing that the field of literacy education had little scholarship that documented Black cultural practices that promoted literacy, encouraged me to undertake my own study to address this absence in the research literature. This research project culminated in a symposium presentation at the National Reading Conference wherein the discussant, Dr. Violet Harris, became my dissertation advisor at the University of Illinois at Urbana-Champaign.

Hip Hop did not enter my life again significantly until I had assumed a faculty position at the University of Colorado at Boulder. Although I worked in Boulder, I lived in Denver where my literacy interests took me to a Black cultural center called "Brother Jeff's Cultural Center and Cafe." Brother Jeff's was extraordinary in that it featured a Saturday evening "Open Mic" in which "the only rule is that there are no rules." People from the predominantly Black community, called "Five Points," would come into the club and often remove paper from their pockets and share whatever they desired to share. But what stood out to me was the impressive number of Black and Latinx youth who shared their work, much of which was obviously influenced by Hip Hop music given the cadence, rhythm and other distinctive features of their writing. Therefore, while prominent research in the field of literacy education emphasized the manner in which literacy was marginal to Black culture, I was able to spend Saturday nights in a club in which late teens and early 20s Black and Latinx women and men shared their writing and the reading and the life experiences that inspired it. That juxtaposition of divergent perspectives and experiences led to an urgency to bring these young people into contact with my University students who had been socialized, not only by the research in their literacy education and teacher education experiences, but by the prevailing media discourse in education that emphasized the literacy achievement gap and the concomitant assumption that the Black and Brown students don't care about literacy. I arranged for several of the young poets to share their work in one of my classes and it was during the ride to the University that led to the next meaningful breakthrough in my journey. While on the way to campus I invited the poets to play their music, which, of course, was the Hip Hop music that had inspired the writing that they shared at the Open Mic. Not too long before that trip to campus, I had been reading Toni Morrison's (1970/2020) *The Bluest Eye* and as I listened to the music, I heard,

> Not strong (Only aggressive)
> Not free (We only licensed)
> Not compassionate, only polite (Now who the nicest?)
> Not good but well behaved
> Chasing after death, so we can call ourselves brave? (p. 202)

When I heard the lyrics, I had them stop the music and go back to make sure that I heard correctly. When they played it again, it confirmed that this Hip Hop music had indeed quoted a Nobel Laureate in Literature. This experience confirmed for me that Hip Hop music possessed considerable educational potential, especially as it related to literacy. I continued to connect the poets at Brother Jeff's to my courses at the University and with the assistance of a local teacher, we established "Young Poet's Night" that brought middle school students in the Denver area to Brother Jeff's where they shared their writing as well as the poetry of Black and Latinx poets who inspired them. It was during one of these events that a cook at Brother Jeff's known to everyone as "Apostle" came to me and asked, "Have you ever considered using Hip Hop in your educational work?" It turned out that "Apostle" was the young man's Hip Hop artist name and he was a prominent local MC (e.g., Hip Hop term for what other people call "rapper"). He was not only an active artist with several album projects, but he was the President of the Colorado Hip Hop Coalition.

One of the primary objectives was to make an impact on education using Hip Hop. We had several insightful meetings during which he shared his vision of Hip Hop becoming a prominent after-school program in schools that connects with the students who don't participate in sports, school government and other more traditional arts practices. We eventually wrote a grant for such a program, which was funded just as I was leaving the area. But the collaboration meant that I went to my next position at the University of Delaware committed to deeply examining the literacy educational potential of Hip Hop.

During my first year at the University of Delaware, I decided to use the transition time to lay the foundation for a serious examination of Hip Hop and literacy. This meant that I had to address my considerable knowledge deficit with respect to Hip Hop music and culture. My plan was to teach a doctoral seminar that would provide me with the opportunity to read extensively about the culture and to listen closely to the music. I was able to read about and listen to the music extensively in that course; however, it was a doctoral writing education seminar that provided a fundamental breakthrough. During the writing seminar, I emphasized non-school-based literacy practices and the manner in which connecting to those practices might provide Students of Color with important literacy support as they learn more traditional literacy practices. One of the students, a middle school reading teacher named Jennifer Bishop, was particularly confused by this aspect of the course because in her extensive training as a literacy educator, she had never encountered the "non-school" literacy practices among "Students of Color" that I had talked about. She felt at a total loss as to how to complete assignments related to these concepts. Then during one school day as she served lunchroom duty, she noticed a large group of Black students gathered around a lunch table freestyling. Freestyling, also known as holding a "Cypher," is an improvisational rhyming competition in which a person bangs out or beat-boxes a beat and the competitors see who can not only rhyme, but use word-play and other forms of creative language use to outperform the other competitor. To her great and enduring credit, Jennifer Bishop ignored the noise, the insults, and even the profanity and observed impressive language skills that she recognized that she could never replicate, particularly within the context of a room of cheering and booing peers. She realized that she might have found her non-school literacy skill that she ironically encountered during school lunch.

She was so excited to have discovered her non-school literacy practice that she didn't wait for the next class session. She called me to explain what she observed and to see whether it indeed qualified as the non-school literacy practice that I had requested. She not only told me about the lunch period cypher, but she invited me to meet with the students who had the strongest reputations as freestylers. They demonstrated their rhyming skills and even embarrassed me when they challenged me to rhyme improvisationally. During our session, Ms. Bishop asked me if there were any ways that their language talent could be used productively in school? Since my primary experience remained my experience at Brother Jeff's, I came up with the idea of creating a poetry writing class, where they could take their composition skills and apply them to writing more formal pieces instead of only rhyming during a freestyle competition. This poetry class led to the students composing pieces that were so impressive that I set up a poetry performance at the University of Delaware attended by my students and several members of the faculty, who provided a powerful experience of validation for the students. Perhaps most importantly, their teacher, Jennifer Bishop, was so impressed that she wrote a grant to purchase recording equipment and software for her classroom, because she knew that the students' ultimate objective was to record Hip Hop music.

During this time, I attended an Academic event called, "Brothers of the Academy," which is an organization started by the late Dr. Lee Jones, who at the time was an Associate Dean at Florida State University College of Education. "Brothers of the Academy" was a research and Academic collaboration network among African American males with PhDs from various fields. When I arrived in Tallahassee, I realized that I had forgotten to bring a toothbrush. Dr. Jones offered to have one of his graduate students drive me to the drug store. This graduate student, Tony Anderson, was a certified teacher as well as a professional music producer. He had participated in a Hip Hop and Education program as a teenager and his goal was to earn a PhD in what he called at the time, "Critical Hip Hop Pedagogy." Mr. Anderson brought a depth of knowledge about both Hip Hop culture and education that would prove critical to my journey into Hip Hop Literacy. Therefore, I invited him to pursue his doctoral studies at the University of Delaware. Mr. Anderson accepted that invitation and began working with the young men whom I had met earlier in the freestyling session. It was the collaboration with Mr. Anderson that helped me to see that the literacy in Hip Hop was inherently multidimensional in contrast to the strong text literacy discussed above. Ms. Bishop received the grant and when the students learned that they would be recorded with professional equipment, it was a game-changer for them. It was a game-changer for me as well because it became readily apparent that technology, or as the students referred to it, "the equipment," was a vital part of their Hip Hop conception of literacy. Every session with the students was preceded with the question, "When will the equipment arrive?" This reflects the fact that, as one of the students told me, the composition is not truly finished until it is recorded. Early research on Hip Hop and literacy emphasized lyrical analysis, equating lyrics with Hip Hop literacy, much in the same way that someone would analyze a poem (Morrell, 2004). But to bring the students' conceptions of their Hip Hop Literacy to completion required that Mr. Anderson attend to the recording equipment, software, CD duplication, and event planning and promotion as a Hip Hop recording could not meaningfully be said to be completed unless it is shared and performed. I was able to observe him work with all of these various elements of the Hip Hop Literacy process wherein students recorded CDs, traveled throughout the United States and even England to perform, built websites, and even held "Stop the Violence" events for their peers featuring their music and performances. Some of them had even used the skills developed from Hip Hop culture to start their own related businesses in the areas of party promotion and DJ services. By the time the students graduated from high school, they had accumulated such an impressive record of leadership and media production that they all applied to and were accepted into four-year colleges and universities.

5 Iowa Hip Hop and the Learning Possibilities of the Recording Studio

As one might expect, Hip Hop and Education in Iowa has been a very different experience from Hip Hop on the East Coast in Delaware. Even though Delaware is no hotbed of Hip Hop culture and music, it is very close to places that are. Downtown Philadelphia is a 45-minute drive away. New York City is two hours, and DC is 90 minutes, so students in Delaware are literally surrounded by urban arts in general and Hip Hop in particular. They can readily see young artists with whom they identify, living out exciting artistic careers. There is no such proximity to urban artistic success in Waterloo, Iowa.

Waterloo has the largest density of Black residents in the state of Iowa and is therefore, in a state that is 91% White, negatively associated with poverty, crime, and educational failure. Most of the city's Black residents migrated from Mississippi and brought with them dispositions toward education and success similar to those described by Richard Wright (1945/2020) in his autobiography, *Black Boy*. Therefore, while Hip Hop music and culture is something that young Black students listen to and enjoy in Iowa, just like youth around the world, it was not something that young Black Northeast Iowans saw themselves doing. In contrast to Delaware where an invitation to record at the school led to a line of students spanning one end of the school to the other in an attempt to get behind the mic, invitations to record in Iowa resulted in confused, questioning facial expressions as if wondering why would I ever invite them to do such a thing. However, in spite of this general disinclination to actually produce Hip Hop music, as in almost any case, there are exceptions. A colleague at the University of Northern Iowa who happened to be a local high school basketball coach, when hearing about my interest in connecting Hip Hop to literacy and education, told me about his freshman point guard who recorded Hip Hop music and thought that a connection to me would be a positive and safe outlet for his player's interests. I met the young man, who expressed interest in working with me on my educational application of Hip Hop. A local community service provider and a retired professor from the University of Northern Iowa approached the Literacy Education faculty about working with them on a literacy program that focused on Black culture. I was the only member of the faculty to respond and when I met with them, I told them about the Hip Hop program that I had been a part of previously and the results we achieved and they said that they would be thrilled if I would implement the program there.

Once the program got started, we didn't have access to professional studio equipment, so we used a mic and speaker that belonged to the point guard. However, I knew that the Hip Hop Literacy process could not be complete until we had access to recording equipment. Because Tony Anderson actually presided over the program in Delaware, I did not have a first-hand perspective regarding how to put together a full Hip Hop Literacy experience. However, the access to the recording equipment came about through what I would learn is a critical aspect of the Hip Hop Literacy experience, the culture. As stated above, the early research on Hip Hop and Literacy focused almost exclusively on the written lyrics. This focus on the lyrics as a way of documenting the literacy of Hip Hop roughly equates to the way that those outside of the culture frequently reduced Hip Hop music to the one quality of "rap." Hip Hop lyrics and rapping is simply one aspect of a multidimensional multimedia culture that collectively produces the music and other media associated with the culture. Hip Hop culture consists of rapping, known within the culture as MCing, which incorporates lyrical composition and dynamic performance that literally "Moves the Crowd," hence, MC; the soundtrack provided by the DJ; dance in the form of the breakers; and visual arts in the form of graffiti artists.

Each of these art forms has evolved significantly over the course of Hip Hop history to the point where MCs/lyricists and the face of the music have often taken the performance skills into the field of acting, including television and movies, film making, and commercials and corporate representation. Filmmaker John Singleton famously told lead MC of the group NWA, Ice Cube, when he starred in the film *Boyz in the Hood*, that if he can write lyrics in the way that he did, then he could write a film. Thirty years later, Ice Cube is known more for making film franchises such as *Barber Shop* and *Are We There Yet?* than anything related to music. Snoop Dogg, in addition to making music and film, has been a corporate pitchman for Chrysler, among a broad range of products. The DJ has evolved into music production as well as film scoring as exemplified by Rza of the legendary Wu Tang Clan, who scored the film, *Ghost Dog*, and even wrote, scored and acted in his own films, *Iron Fist* and *Iron Fist 2*. Graffiti Artists have evolved into graphic designers, who design the covers and logos for many Hip Hop artists. Break dancers have evolved into choreographers who have worked in film, television, and a broad range of other artistic productions. Collier (2003) in his film *Paper Chasers* demonstrated that this culture is so economically viable, that it has been a primary source of employment for many Black college graduates in the South, particularly those with business-related degrees. As the local artists in the Hip Hop community found out about our program, they made sure that we were aware of the various skills and services that they had to offer our program. One of those artists @LyrikalTMG owned a recording studio[1] and invited the artists in our program to record in his studio. This was a game-changer for the program as that meant that we would be able to provide students with the full measure of the Hip Hop Literacy experience.

Once the recording studio became a destination for the students' literacy work, a number of unexpected and unaccounted for learning experiences took place. Again, as I had discovered working with youth in the state of Delaware, a written composition was not considered complete until it had culminated in a musical recording. This meant that the recording studio was a primary motivating factor underlying the students' writing. But the fact that the students were motivated to go to the recording studio did not mean that the studio was not a source of fear and intimidation. While not necessarily a requirement to provide students with the Hip Hop Literacy experience, the professional recording studio is a professional environment that looks much like the recording environments that the students are able to see in the music videos they watch. To suddenly find themselves in the same type of environment can become overwhelming to some of the students. Their initial excitement and motivation to record frequently turned to feelings of inadequacy and fear that they were not good enough. It was at that point that a pedagogy of radical encouragement took place, reminding the students that their verses or "bars," as they called them, were strong and that all that they needed to do was to repeat what they had practiced many times successfully in the classroom. Once the students were talked down from the ledge of not recording their verses, two of the most impactful learning experiences took place. They would successfully record their tracks leading to the relief and satisfaction of successfully overcoming paralyzing fear. Then the look on the students' faces after they were able to hear themselves within the sonic framework of a professional recording was truly inspiring. Even more significant following that initial experience of overcoming the fear, then experiencing the product of their work, was the enthusiasm with which they transferred to the next song.

Another learning advantage of the professional studio environment over the traditional classroom environment was the fact that the people working with the students to record their verses are not educators. They are professionals who expected that the students would conduct themselves in a professional manner. What this meant was that behavior that would be tolerated within a school was not tolerated in the studio, so the students soon learned that if they expected to record their verses, they had to also respect their peers and the other professionals in the studio. On a particularly memorable occasion, one student well known in the program for having difficulty controlling himself was told by the producer to leave and that he wouldn't be able to record that day. Rather than the experience being a source of discouragement to him, he got himself together and returned to the studio on the next occasion ready to do what was necessary to successfully record his contribution to the song. The studio provided all of the students with a tangible example of the fact that there are places in the world that they will want to be a part of that will require them to practice what they are taught in school and that they will have to carry out those practices, not simply because it is required in school, but the places that they desire require it.

The fact that the students had produced professionally recorded music meant that their music was able to join the global media and music distribution network of outlets such as YouTube, Soundcloud, Spotify, Apple Music, iTunes and many others. The program subscribed to a service on Soundcloud that not only shared the students' music but included a data package that documented who listened to the music and where they were from. This led to another area of learning for the students that could now be incorporated into the broad portfolio of Hip Hop Literacy: data awareness and data informed decision-making. According to the data package and for reasons that we never uncovered, Soundcloud data indicated that most of their listens had taken place in Omaha, Nebraska. So we asked the students where they thought most of the listens to their music had taken place? They logically responded, "Waterloo." In response, we were able to show them that according to the data, most of the listens had taken place in Omaha. Then we asked them, if they were looking for people to purchase their music, where would they make sure to advertise? In the process, we were able to demonstrate that any action that takes place online generates data and that to make effective decisions, they need to be aware of and analyze data. This was not a lesson that we anticipated teaching in the program, but the process of producing and then publishing media integrated the students into a global network of media production and distribution that made these areas of learning relevant to them.

As part of this integration into the network of global media, I had asked my Facebook friends to share a link with the students' music and encourage their Facebook friends to listen to the music. Since I have Facebook friends from all over the world, we were able to demonstrate to these young predominantly Black artists from small-town Iowa that people, literally from all over the world, were listening to their music. A graduate student of mine had shared the students' music to his network of Facebook friends, which included scholars and educators from the World Leisure Organization. One of those scholars happened to be the curator of performance talent for their annual Leisure Festival in Hangzhou,

China. He had long wanted U.S. Hip Hop artists to perform at the Festival and after hearing the students' music, he wondered whether we would be able to travel to China to perform at the Festival. This global media connection culminated in a small group of the students accompanied by their producer, @LyrikalTMG, leaders of the Hip Hop Literacy program and other media people from the local Hip Hop culture to support the students traveling to China for a period of ten days to perform at the Hangzhou Citizens Leisure Festival.

The production and distribution of music had changed considerably over the years facilitating the global experiences and the national and international presence of the students' music. However, the most dramatic impact on the program took place this past year during the COVID-19 pandemic. Because of the pandemic, the regular structure of the program of meeting in person and working with the students in groups had to be abandoned. Instruction had to take place via Zoom and the students had to transition from being part of a group and contributing verses to a song, to individual artists who functioned far more independently, coming up with their own topics, finding background tracks and either writing all of the lyrics themselves or collaborating with another artist, which they were able to do via the" breakout room" feature of Zoom. We didn't anticipate how readily the students would take to this independent status and after a couple of weeks to adjust to this different way of operating, they began to come up with a variety of songs on their own which they practiced during the daily sessions and fine-tuned in preparation for the recording session. In a normal summer program session with about 40 students we would record approximately four songs per week and approximately 20 songs over the course of the summer. However, when we had our first recording session with the students, after working exclusively online, the students had a three-hour recording session in which they recorded nine songs. This session was near the end of the 6-week program at which time we had planned a final online performance, so we expected the students to transition toward preparing for the final performance. However, the Monday following their nine-song recording session, they came to the session with four more songs to record. Therefore, we squeezed another session into the schedule before their final performance. This was an exciting development because it accelerated their artistic development substantially. At the end of the summer, instead of four groups producing music on a consistent basis, we had nearly ten individual artists with various combinations and collaborations.

This breakthrough that culminated in a cadre of independent productive artists excited to go into the studio and produce more work has led to the abundance of learning possibilities demanded of Hip Hop's productive culture. The production of the music is step one. Independent artists within the culture require several other media connections. Artists need music videos as a part of the marketing process of their music. They need a web presence featuring branding, logo design and online marketing. They require strategic marketing plans to coordinate this diverse multitude of artistic productivity. The artists can endeavor to learn many of these various skills and competencies themselves or more likely, they can cultivate an ecosystem among other artists that serve to provide each other with productive work that meets the needs of all of the artists, designers, entrepreneurs and technicians working in this productive Hip Hop ethos.

6 Summary Conclusion

As discussed above, the history of Black literacy has been shaped by the cultural imperative to break through restrictive, even enslaving structures. Black writers such as Baraka (1974) have extrapolated that imperative to a broad range of cultural texts, suggesting that Black music and other forms of Black art inhere the same imperatives. My journey from Literacy to Hip Hop Literacy reflects these broader cultural dynamics as the Naval shipmates I worked with embraced literacy because they saw it as a vehicle for fulfilling their personal need to make sense of their experiences as Black men in the context of US society. As I began to work with youth more directly, they too were searching for meaning and identity. They found the possibilities embodied in Hip Hop artistic identities compelling so they sought out not only Hip Hop literacy composition practices, but the technologies that completed those compositions in the form of digital recordings of their work. To help them fulfill their literacy goals and objectives, I needed to connect my work to "the culture," the multidisciplinary community of artists who represent a multimodal range of literacies that collectively produce Hip Hop media. This requires that my conception of literacy become fluid and adaptive, moving from strong-text literacy embraced by formal education contexts to multimedia literacies that represent the norm in the world of Hip Hop.

7 Implications

Toward the outset of this chapter, I identified that one of the tasks of this self-study was to expand the conceptual language that informed the practice of self-study. One of the most salient features of my transition from literacy to Hip Hop Literacy has been an embrace of the collective, collaborative ethos of the Hip Hop cultural ecosystem. In the productive ecosystem of Hip Hop, the writer is not an isolated individual entity who produces from a singular vision. In Hip Hop culture, the writer necessarily collaborates with the producer, who shares and revises the sonic landscapes that accompany the lyrical compositions. In Hip Hop, even the most singular, legendary figures in the art form, such as The Notorious B.I.G. and Tupac Shakur, are also significantly associated with their sonic collaborators, Diddy and Dr. Dre. Although it may be argued that Hip Hop legend Kanye West is known for both his sonic and lyrical creations, he collaborates extensively and derives creative insight from the aforementioned Virgil Abloh, who has declared collaboration to be his primary productive impulse.

This primacy of collaboration and collectivity holds important implications for the practice of self-study from an African American cultural framework. As Gates (2016) captured in his delineation of the Black Slave narrative tradition, the slave narratives were "a communal utterance, and a collective tale rather than an individual's autobiography" (p. XIII). This suggests that the "self" in African American self-study needs to be open to this collective framework, thus expanding the language of the self-study field. Just as the slave narrative and even the Black spirituals, while using the pronoun, "I," were communicating a collective experience that spoke simultaneously in a "double voiced" manner (Gates, 1988, p. 20) to the Black communal audience and to the individual reader, the self in this study, by situating this journey through the work of cultural icons such as James Brown and Amiri Baraka, aims to speak collectively and individually through the term "self." This type of self-representation intends to not only capture my individual experience, but as was argued by Nealon above, my representation of self is not only articulating my portion of the collective navigation of Black scholars, but the collective use of literacy in the effort for Black personal integrity and survival in a landscape shaped by White Supremacy.

The second implication for this self-study can be found in what this exploration of "literacy" means for teaching and teacher education. As stated above, the term "literacy" has been deployed as a mean of denying Black humanity, through narrow exclusionary definitions and understandings of the term. While this same practice is no longer aimed at Black humanity at large, it does exist in schools and in the preparation of teachers in a manner that excludes the educational legitimacy of Black cultural literacy practices. Approaching the year 2021 with Hip Hop being the world's most listened to and purchased musical genre and even the students in the Hip Hop Literacy 319 program in small town Iowa are celebrated by their peers from around the world in China, it is unconscionable that schools are not embracing this art form for its educational potential and possibilities and teachers are not trained to identify the instructional advantages of using strategies that draw from these benefits.

I have found in my work in Hip Hop and education that young students and their families are deeply familiar with these Hip Hop compositional practices such that they may be potential literacy resources for classrooms that seek to take advantage of these broader literacy possibilities. In this way, teachers can engage in the work of Moll (1990) who integrated the educational knowledge of Latinx families into the classroom when that knowledge connected to learning objectives covered in the curriculum. Moll found that such approaches not only enhanced the learning of all students in the classroom, but provided the Latinx students an important experience of cultural belonging in school as they saw the knowledge of members of their community being utilized as instructional resources.

Note

1   https://www.facebook.com/THESTUDIOWATERLOO/

References

Baker, H. A. (1995). *Black studies, rap, and the academy*. University of Chicago Press.
Baraka, A. (1974). *Blues people*. Rabén & Sjögren.
Charnas, D. (2011). *The big payback: The history of the business of hip-hop*. New American Library.
Coia, L., & Taylor, M. (2009). Co/autoethnography: Exploring our teaching selves collaboratively. In D. L. Tidwell, M. L. Heston, & L. M. Fitzgerald (Eds.), *Research methods for the self-study of practice* (pp. 3–16). Springer.
Collier, M. (Director). (2003). *Paper chasers* [Film]. IFC Productions.
Deleuze, G. (2014). *Difference and repetition*. Bloomsbury.
Dyson, M. E. (2006). *Holler if you hear me: Searching for Tupac Shakur*. Basic Civitas Books.
Gates, H. L. (1988). *The signifying monkey: A theory of Afro-American literary criticism*. Oxford University Press.
Gates, H. L. (2016). *The classic slave narratives*. Signet Classics.
Graff, H. J. (1991). *The legacies of literacy continuities and contradictions in western culture and society*. Indiana University Press.
Greenburg, Z. O. M. (2018). *Three kings: Diddy, Dr. Dre, Jay Z, and hip-hop's multibillion-dollar rise*. Little, Brown & Company.
hooks, b., & West, C. (2017). *Breaking bread: Insurgent Black intellectual life*. Routledge.

Kitchen, J., Fitzgerald, L., & Tidwell, D. (2016). Self-study and diversity: Looking back, looking forward. In J. Kitchen, D. Tidwell & L. Fitzgerald (Eds.), *Self-study and diversity II: Inclusive teacher education for a diverse world* (pp. 1–10). Sense.

Mahiri, J. (1998). *Shooting for excellence: African American and youth culture in new century schools*. National Council of Teachers of English.

Marre, J. (Director). (2003). *James Brown soul survivor* [Film]. Eagle Rock Entertainment.

Moll, L. C. (1990). *Community knowledge and classroom practice combining resources for literacy instruction* (ED 341968). ERIC. Retrieved May 24, 2021, from https://files.eric.ed.gov/fulltext/ED341968.pdf

Morrell, E. (2004). *Linking literacy and popular culture: Finding connections for lifelong learning*. Christopher-Gordon Publishers.

Morrison, T. (2020). *The bluest eye*. Vintage Classics. (Original work published 1970)

Nealon, J. T. (1998). Refraining, becoming Black: Repetition with a difference in Amiri Baraka's Blues People. *Symploke*, 6(1/2), 83–95.

Royer, D. (1994). The process of literacy as communal involvement in the narratives of Frederick Douglass. *African American Review*, 28(3), 363–374.

Simmons, R. (2001). *Life and def*. Crown Publishers.

Thompson, D. (2001). *Funk*. Backbeat Books.

Vincent, R. (1996). *Funk: The music, the people, and the rhythm of the one*. St. Martin's Griffin.

Wright, R. (1988). *American hunger*. Harper & Row. (Original work published 1977)

Wright, R. (2020). *Black boy*. Vintage Classics. (Original work published 1945)

X, M. (1999). *The autobiography of Malcolm X: As told to Alex Haley*. Ballantine. (Original work published 1965).

Zinga, A. (2017, October 28). *Virgil Abloh lecture at the Harvard Graduate School of Ddesign*. Retrieved May 24, 2021, from https://www.youtube.com/watch?v=biFlrzTJets

CHAPTER 8

Building the Boat with Funds of Knowledge

Metaphors of a Japanese Immigrant Educator at an Icelandic Preschool

Megumi Nishida

This narrative self-study expresses my transformation as a Japanese immigrant educator at an Icelandic preschool through metaphors. While investigating the concept of funds of knowledge, I recall my interaction with María, a senior preschool educator who called herself "a toy." She taught me the value of using personal resources at work. Data sources are my teaching journal, reflective short stories that I edited based on my journal, mindful walk transcript and my master's dissertation. Reflecting on my teaching journal and short stories, I explore my professional identity transformation by using metaphor of a boat and I am the sailor. At first, my experience as a preschool educator was as fancy but fragile as an origami-made boat. I looked well educated and well prepared, but did not have any flexibility to change my professional attitude from being Japanese. After my origami-made boat was sunk by great Icelandic children, I began to explore how I could reinforce my boat stronger with my resources. María inspired me to look into my Japanese resources and I rebuilt my boat by using my Japanese language and skills I gained in my past. After the boat was built stronger, I became aware of three important resources to support my sailing: theoretical, cultural, and human resources. I continue my sailing and I have tools to build the boat into whatever I desire with funds of knowledge.

1   Prologue to My Voyage

> It's fun to use the body. I am the toy … We have to give something from us … Use the idea you have. Because you are the toy. (María's comment, Nishida, 2013, p. 75)

Calling herself a toy, preschool educator María told me how it would be like to work with children when I was studying about Icelandic preschool educators' professionalism for my master's project (Nishida, 2013). María is an educator at Rocky Preschool with more than 30 years of experience. While I was observing her interaction with children, I witnessed that she would be acting like "the toy." What she meant by her metaphor of toy was that she would use her body and resources to work with children instead of depending on man-made toys and traditional teaching materials. She could tell a story, draw a picture, and dance with children. In her teaching, she was always singing. Therefore, she reminded me of Maria from the movie *The Sound of Music* (Wise, 1965). Each Maria had short blond hair, too. Preschool educator María's message was delivered through lyrics in her singing and that is why I gave her this pseudonym. If educators represent the toy, they need to be flexible enough to meet children's respective needs and ever-changing interests. For me as a former Japanese educator, who could not fit in the Japanese teacher-centered culture (Nishida, 2019), María's attitude of being the toy had a great impact and gave me courage to challenge myself to work as an educator in the Icelandic education system.

This is the saga of me, a Japanese immigrant educator in the Icelandic preschool context, as I seek strategies to gain confidence to develop my professional identity. Metaphors around the sea and building the boat are explored through narrative self-study (Clandinin & Connelly, 2004; Craig, 2018; Kitchen, 2009, 2016). I am the sailor of the boat that represents my experience. I sail on the sea of the Icelandic early childhood education. During my voyage, I keep asking myself the following question to better understand what I am going through: How do I recognize and utilize my resources to enhance my teaching experience, and transform my professional identity through the metaphor of building a boat? There is no set destination for my voyage, but I hope that my saga becomes like a beacon for other educators who may be struggling during their voyage of teaching in the global context.

2   Theoretical Background for Sailing: Icelandic Early Childhood Education and Hjallastefnan

The Icelandic preschool education system has been built upon the history of daycare centers for working women in 1920s (Einarsdóttir, 2006). Since 1994, Icelandic preschool education has been legalized as the first level of education in the Icelandic school system for children under six years old (Preschool Act no. 90/2008) but it was neither compulsory nor free of charge (Einarsdóttir, 2006).

Since Icelandic preschool is called *leikskóli*, meaning playschool in Icelandic, preschool educators seem to perceive their image of preschool work as caregiving and freedom from adults' supervision, which do not put much emphasis on academic aspects (Einarsdóttir, 2006). Although transition from preschool to compulsory school level is challenging, Icelandic parents still expect that children gain social skills rather than academic skills (Einarsdóttir, 2010).

Shortage of qualified preschool educators is becoming a social issue in Iceland (Iceland Review, 2016). Since 2011, the preschool teacher education requires five years with master's degree (Einarsdóttir, 2011). Although Preschool Act states that at least 2/3 of full-time preschool staff should obtain teaching credential (Preschool Act no. 87/2008), in reality, only 40% of all preschool staff in Iceland hold education-related university degree and only 28% of all preschool staff had a teaching license to be legally called preschool teacher in 2018 (Hagstofa Íslands, 2019). To fill the vacancy of a position, preschools are allowed to recruit unqualified staff only if there is no other qualified candidate applying (Preschool Act no. 90/2008).

Hjallastefnan, so-called The Hjalli model in English, is the Icelandic early childhood pedagogical method developed by Margrét Pála Ólafsdóttir since 1989 (Ólafsdóttir, 1996). Hjallastefnan also refers to a semi-private educational enterprise and there are 14 preschools and three elementary schools operated with the same method around Iceland (The Hjalli model, 2018). Because each child is different and their diverse characteristic should be valued (UNESCO, 1994), educators at Hjallastefnan preschool respect children's interests and enhance children's free play regardless of their gender and diverse background (Nishida, 2013).

3 Methods of Sailing: Narrative Inquiry, Mindful Walk and Metaphors

Narrative self-study brings subtleness of knowledge to light through metaphors (Craig, 2018; Kitchen, 2009). While there are different ways of defining narrative, the definition by Clandinin and Connelly (2004) is widely used by self-study practitioners. They explained that narrative inquiry is "a multi-dimensional exploration of experience involving temporality (past, present and future), interaction (personal and social), and location (place)" (p. 576). Kitchen (2009) described narrative inquiry as "a methodology for understanding the personal dimension of teaching" (p. 36). Teaching is a complex business, but narrative inquiry lets me investigate my experience from multiple perspectives with different pieces of stories. Teachers gain and develop teacher knowledge throughout their lives, which is evident when they tell their professional experiences, construct a meaning of a story over time through inquiry process, retell the story, and then continue to live in the story (Clandinin, 2013; Clandinin & Connelly, 2000; Craig, 2011). Therefore we can develop a deeper understanding of our practical knowledge and make our teaching effective (Connelly & Clandinin, 1988). Thus using narrative inquiry in self-study helps me understand how I make meaning from my teaching experience and the context that influences my experience and reflection through stories (Kitchen, 2009). Clandinin and Connelly (2004) emphasized that exploring teacher knowledge gained and developed through narrative "must somehow lie closer to practice, to be studies of practice, studies of what we call personal practical knowledge" (p. 582). I coded my teaching journal and discussed my experiences and thoughts with my critical friend Hafdís. Upon my reflection, I selected relevant moments from my teaching journal that reveal multiple dimensions of my experiences to make a meaning of my metaphors (Bullough, 1994; Connelly & Clandinin, 2004; Kitchen, 2009).

Mindful walk, which is what I have called my culturally responsive data collecting method, enables me to gather narrative data. The basic idea of this method is to voice-record a reflective dialogue with someone, or my personal reflection, in a relaxed walk for the purpose of collecting narrative data. Surroundings and scenery work as a memory-prompt for deeper reflection (Mitchell & Weber, 1999). Recorded narrative should be transcribed by following a qualitative method (Lichtman, 2010). A reflective note can also be added to the journal after the walk. It is supported by the philosophy of research called mindful inquiry (Bentz & Shapiro, 1998). Bentz and Shapiro explained that mindful inquiry intimately links a person's awareness of themselves and their own world through inquiry. It is "a synthesis of four intellectual traditions: phenomenology, hermeneutics, critical social science, and Buddhism" (p. 6). I am aware of the influence of Zen philosophy in my Japanese upbringing (Nishida, 2019). A spiritual practice of Buddhism liberates people from suffering in their lives (Bentz &Shapiro, 1998). Embracing mindfulness in my inquiry process enhances my self-knowledge and wisdom (Karunamuni & Weerasekera, 2019).

Metaphors are used by quite a few self-study researchers to understand their context, practice, experiences and professional identities (Bullough, 1994; Craig, 2018; East et al., 2009; Kitchen, 2009; MacKinnon & Bullock, 2016). Pithouse-Morgan, Pillay and Mitchell (2019) recognized that metaphor is part of artful memory-work. Teacher researchers can express their experiences and understand their education related memories visually for the purpose of teacher professional development. Kitchen (2009) counted metaphor as one of the personal experience methods along with storytelling and autobiography. Because every experience is unique yet genuine, metaphors help us interpret subtleness and complexities of each story. Without having any specific intention, we may use metaphors on a daily basis. In their book *Metaphors We Live By*, Lakoff and Johnson (1980/2003) explained that metaphors are always around us to express our thoughts and action; it is not only a matter of words. When I think about the way I talk, I often use metaphors to Icelandic children to explain something, such as "we walk quietly like a mouse." For young children, I experienced that metaphors work like a scaffolding to support their understanding of a concept as well as enhancing their cognitive development (Berk & Winsler, 1995/2002). Looking at metaphors from a cognitive perspective, Lakoff and Johnson (1980/2003) described that "metaphors we use determine a great deal about how we live our lives" (p. 244). Metaphor "plays a role in human thought, understanding, and reasoning and, beyond that, in the creation of our social, cultural and psychological reality" (Kövecses, 2010, p. XII–XIII). My self-study metaphor of building the boat is effective to explore my professional identity. Bullough (1994) explained that metaphors that arise from his education related life story capture essences of teaching and it is his "on going quest for authenticity in teaching" that integrates his "personal and social identities" (p. 110). MacKinnon and Bullock's (2016) music metaphor expressed their engagement to self-study, providing an example of how self-study researchers effectively use metaphors to articulate their teaching to better understand their experiences positively. Metaphors help me correlate my experiences to understand and reason about my transformation (Lakoff & Johnson, 1980/2003) and know deeply, not just with my head but also with my heart (East et al., 2009).

Without knowing the power of it, I began using metaphor in a rather early stage of my self-study. When I began writing the proposal for my doctoral studies, I first simply used a metaphor of sailing to reflect on my past and express my present and potential future through my narrative (Clandinin & Connelly, 2004). At that point, my intention of using metaphors was rather spontaneous as my analysis of my data was still superficial. However, the more complex my experience became to express, the better served my metaphor of building the boat to express my transformation. Austrian-born philosopher Otto Neurath used metaphors of boats and sailing to explore person's knowledge transformation. His metaphors expressed a core issue between theory and practice (Okruhlik, 1998). I wondered why I envisage a metaphor of sailing and building the boat. My reflection of teaching journal, which I should call my deck logbook, revealed the reason that was hidden in my teaching context.

4 The Context: Sailing on the Sea of the Icelandic Early Childhood

Icelanders may have mixed feelings about being called Vikings after the economic crisis in 2008 (Loftsdóttir, 2010). However, people outside of Iceland still believe that Icelanders are descendants of Vikings who sailed by Viking boats through the rough water to discover a new land. Icelandic descendants outside of Iceland are still proud of their heritage, calling themselves Vikings who are courageous and strong (Eyþórsdóttir & Loftsdóttir, 2015). The first group of settlers came from the Norse in late 9th century, and their language has been protected until today. It means that Icelanders in 21st century speak almost the same language from the time of the settlement (Lacy, 1998). Although the names that appear in my story are pseudonyms except for my critical friend and university colleagues, each Icelandic name has its own heritage, possibly from the Viking age (Lacy, 1998). *Sagas* are the literature from the Middle Ages, known to the world, and they tell stories about the medieval wars, cultures, and people's lives in Iceland (Lacy, 1998). Icelandic people are proud of their culture and supportive to each other in order to survive in a harsh climate. Once I was talking to Hafdís, I realized that Icelanders today still love to tell stories, create poems and use metaphors to express their experiences and thoughts. Vikings are not only courageous, but also creative and respectful to people's sagas and experiences.

I am a Japanese immigrant educator in Iceland. Until my migration to Iceland in 2008, I spent most of my life around Osaka, which is one of the largest cities in Japan. In my undergraduate studies in Japan, I was educated to become a social studies teacher for junior high school level. I never imagined working closely with young children because I did not know enough about their life and perspective. There was no young child around in my life and I was full of bias about children's world. When I became a school manager for children's English conversation school in mid-2000s Japan, there were some preschool-age children whom I met once a week. It was probably my first encounter with young children's world as an educator. Native-English-speaking teachers taught children English and my role was supporting their learning and encouraging parents to support children's homework at home. After the lesson, children often came to tell me what they did in the class. They loved playing board games by using English words and phrases. I simply thought that children could absorb any new information like a sponge, but they did not want to do their homework of listening to the CD with English phrases at home. Children just wanted to play and learning a different language was their parents' desire. Children's major interest of coming to the school would be interacting with teachers to play with. I tended to judge the children as selfish because they wanted to play without studying. I never thought of the reason behind children's crying when they did not want to listen to their homework CD. That was my image and attitude towards children.

When I was enrolled in the master's program in education at the University of Iceland, my image of children was turned upside down. Preschool educators can be passionate about childhood education (Nishida, 2013). Every child is a human being who has voice, just like we adults. It might sound simple, but I never knew it in reality until I began my teaching career at a preschool called *Rocky Preschool* located in a fishing town outside of Reykjavík, Iceland in August 2014.

Rocky Preschool is one of Hjallastefnan preschools (Ólafsdóttir, 2012). The school building is located on the hill by a large community park. Currently there are 164 children aged from 18 months up to five years old, with 38 staff members including administrators working to support children's upbringing. Inside of the school, things are all marked to be correctly placed. There is almost no artwork of children on the wall in order to avoid interrupting children's attention because keeping things simple is their strategy to enhance children's creativity. Educators at Rocky Preschool plan their children's activities under six gender-based courses and each course runs four weeks: respect, independence, communication, positivity, friendship and courage. Educators strive for providing an environment for children to experience the essences of these courses.

When I began working there, my position was a substitute educator who covered absence of any staff member. For example, during my seven working hours a day, I had to lead a group of two-year-old girls, then five-year-old boys, then finish my day by doing dishes in the kitchen. My job responsibility was diverse, which meant that my job required a great amount of flexibility to work in different situations.

Children at Rocky Preschool grow up with sounds of whistles from fishing boats and the scent of the sea. Their life is strongly connected to the sea and fishery (Lacy, 1998). There are fishing boats docked at the fjörd harbor and local people can see fishing boats from their house windows. Every first weekend in June, Icelanders celebrate their national holiday called the fishermen's day. Although the original purpose of the fishermen's day began to promote solidarity among fishermen in 1930s, today it invites everyone in the neighborhood, or even outsiders to enjoy sea-related events such as sailing the boat, looking at seacreature display, eating delicacies and swimming in the cold sea water (Hátið hafsins, 2020). One of the fathers of Rocky Preschool children called Gunni is actually a fisherman. He goes off to the sea for a few days or a week, and comes back with fish and something else to let us look at. Once he brought us a big crab and children were excited about touching its thorny legs. Next time, children took their courage to look inside of the baby shark's mouth. Gunni used to go to see his father off the shore on every other Wednesdays. He was so proud of talking about his fisherman father. In our school, fish is served twice a week for lunch. One of children pointed at Gunni and said, "Gunni's father caught fish for us!" With these living experiences, the sense of respect to fishermen and the sea are fostered among children at Rocky Preschool.

My metaphor around the sea was developed during my mindful walk alone, or with my Icelandic-Japanese daughter Særún. When I began working at Rocky Preschool in 2014, I also began my doctoral studies at the University of Iceland to explore my curiosity about education. In 2016 and 2019, Særún and I spent two summers in Kushiro, Japan. Kushiro is located in the northernmost Japanese island Hokkaido. It is almost like a foreign land for a person from Osaka considering its climate and size. Særún went to local elementary school while I was doing my research at a local teachers' training college. Japanese is spoken across the country, but Osaka dialect is known to people with its very unique intonation and certain use of terms. In fact, many comedians on TV are originally from Osaka. Some Kushiro people thought my talk fascinating and I was invited to talk about the Icelandic inclusive education system for various occasions. Watching their reaction over listening to my story was fun, but I felt that I was a foreigner not only the way I spoke but also my attitude. I was rather outspoken and never shy about meeting new people. I had lived in Iceland long enough to call it my home now. However, Særún and I found some similarities between Kushiro and Iceland. In front of our apartment in Kushiro, there was a large river flowing into the Pacific Ocean. We often enjoyed our mindful walk by the riverbank towards the sea after school. There we always saw fishermen fixing their fishing nets. Seagulls were flying above us. The scenery was almost like déjà vu. We wondered why we felt so, then came to the answer instantly. Its climate, scent from the sea, fishing boats and the size of the town, people's warmth, everything reminded us of our life in Iceland. When my Icelandic colleague Edda joined us in Kushiro in 2019, she agreed with us. Our feeling of déjà vu connected my image of Kushiro to Iceland and inspired my metaphors.

Considering this context, it was natural for me to reflect on my teaching experience through metaphors around the sea and the boat. Narrative lets me share my experience with others, just like the Viking's sagas do for us. I begin my voyage by sailing on the sea of the Icelandic early childhood. Boats represent my experience or condition. I am the sailor of the boats that keep transforming through the self-study voyage to the new horizon of teaching.

5   Findings: Discovering New Land, New Experience, the Voyage Begins

My professional life had begun in Iceland in August 2014. I almost gave up on my career as an educator once I left Japan, but in the new land, people encouraged me to challenge myself once again. It is the country of Vikings; they are brave and supportive. However, at some point, I was struggling with my condition during my voyage of teaching.

5.1 Fancy Origami Boat, Easily Sunk

When I decided to work at Rocky Preschool, María was so delighted to have me as her colleague. My position was a substitute educator to cover people's absence, so I did not work with her on a daily basis. Yet María cared about me and greeted me with a big hug every morning. My Icelandic was insufficient to communicate with others. I took two semesters of Icelandic courses for foreigners at the university, only I wished they taught me how to communicate with young children instead of how to take a job interview. In the beginning of my days at Rocky Preschool, I did not have enough vocabulary to open a dialogue. Moreover, I was rather afraid of speaking Icelandic because I was raised within a culture of no mistake should be allowed. It was stressful because I should be outspoken in my own language. Since I was the only non-Icelandic speaker at work, my colleagues encouraged me to practice speaking with them. So they said, "við tölum saman á íslensku!" (we speak in Icelandic to each other!). Oh no … It was kind of a lonely sailing to begin with.

My job responsibility as substitute educator was quite complex and challenging. I never knew what to do and whom to work with until I arrived at work in the morning and checked on the placement board in the staff room. That moment made me nervous. I was only working part time for a few days a week in order to continue my doctoral studies, so this substitute position sounded perfect. My curriculum vitae looked rather fancy like an origami boat that was made with beautiful *washi* paper. Furthermore, I studied about Rocky Preschool's unique teaching pedagogy of gender segregation during my master's studies. No one questioned my potential to start working with children without any training. They somehow thought that I would be almighty, like a fully equipped boat with the latest technology. Truth was, my origami boat was vulnerable.

In Iceland, using the title of preschool teacher is legally regulated (Preschool Act no. 87/2008). My teaching license in Iceland was only valid for compulsory school level to upper secondary level (equivalent to 1st grade to 1st year of college in the American school system) in 2014. New law allows me to call myself preschool teacher (Lög um menntun, nr. 95/2019), but I am accustomed to calling myself preschool educator for most of my teaching career in Iceland. That was also a reason why I was struggling with my professional title. Because of my Japanese cultural background, I believed that my sense of professionalism should be quite high, but I was not allowed to call myself teacher. I wanted to perform like a professional but I was not "teacher." It was a dilemma for a long time.

In order to be prepared for working at Rocky Preschool, I reviewed Icelandic early childhood literature and education theories that I learned during my master's study. The key to Icelandic early childhood education is to let children learn through play and Icelandic preschool educators respect children's free play (Einarsdóttir, 2006). I wondered: What does it mean to let them learn through play? I felt I knew it in theory, but I could not imagine well in reality. I spoke with other friends who were working at other Icelandic preschools. They all said, "Let them play, they show you how." I just had to begin my sailing on the sea of the Icelandic early childhood education.

I clearly remember my first day at Rocky Preschool on August 11, 2014. It took me a whole hour to get to school from my home in Reykjavík by local bus and on foot. I was a little anxious, so the bus ride felt so long. Around Rocky Preschool, there is lava field with a view of the sea. Sky was high and clear in the late summer. I sniffed scent of the sea water that made me excited to enter the school door. My first assignment was to assist a four-year-old boys' group. I was told that I would be with them often as their group leader would go to university to complete her teaching degree. After a while, I was left alone to watch over the boys' play. As I learned in literature and from friends, I let them play. Calmness before the storm's arrival. In my first entry of deck logbook, I wrote:

> I did not really understand what is 'let them play' in reality … Boys were running around, building a house or something with big pillows … Ragnar seemed to have a big influence over children's play … Ragnar was playing rough. I thought that he would fall (from the table). Should I stop him? How could I say 'stop' in Icelandic? But I knew from my previous research that Rocky Preschool educators are encouraged not to say 'ekki (no)' to children … should I let him learn from the pain? He fell while I was wondering what to do. Of course there was a scream. Luckily he was not seriously injured … My school principal tried to encourage me that things like that happens sometimes and I should be careful but not feel discouraged. (Logbook, August 11, 2014)

From my day one, my forecast of the sailing would not be as calm as in theories. I did not have a nimbus radar. Gradually I began to feel suspicious that my origami boat was not strong enough to continue my sailing, but I did not have enough motivation to reflect on my voyage until the first snow day on October 21, 2014.

Over night, the falling snow piled up knee high. Walking from the closest bus stop to school was hard as snowplows did not clear the way quick enough. I wondered if it was some sort of omen of the day. When I met children at school, they were all joyous. They kept asking staff to let them go out. Since I am from Osaka, where it seldom snows in winter, I had almost no experience of playing in snow in my childhood memory. I had no idea what would happen if I let those excited three-year-old boys go out and play. There were only three boys in the group on that day and it should have been easy enough to watch over them. No, it was not. Once the door was open, they dashed for the outside of schoolyard. They were over excited to be in the first snow for that winter. They were rolling, jumping off the lava cliff that was covered with snow, and screaming with joy. The time for play was very limited as they had yoga lesson scheduled later. The boys were having a blast while I was suffering from a stomachache. My deck logbook sounded miserable:

> I tried to keep them in the same area since we have yoga lesson from 13:30. I knew their excitement over snow, I should have let them explode their energy in snow instead of keeping them in one small play area. Or I should have made the rule clear before going out if I could … There was my uncertainty again. I was not sure whether I should let them go or stop them. Without my word, they just ran. Time was running out … When we went back inside, there was a chaos and I couldn't think about priority … I was in panic. I felt I had no control over children! (Logbook, October 21, 2014)

I did not know what I was doing. During this time period I was confused and my logbook was full of negative words that would tell how stressed I was. It was obvious that I was in a professional crisis. My origami boat was sinking.

5.2   Building the Boat: How Could I?

On the day after my origami boat sank, I was at university. I was so glad that I had a time off from my work; I needed a day to calm down. When I was making a cup of tea for myself at the lounge, my doctoral supervisor Hafdís and my colleague Edda walked by. They casually asked me how I was doing at my work. They probably did not expect, but I was desperate to speak with them about my experience with children in snow. After listening, Hafdís said, "It's time to begin your self-study." She suggested that I keep notes of children's behavior. Does the time of the day matter, or any special occasion? My Japanese cultural habit of controlling was getting in my way, but Hafdís said that my cultural resource would be necessary at some point. When would that be? I had to explore through my self-study voyage. Edda gave me some copies of self-study literature for me to start reading.

I had to rebuild my boat. My origami boat was made with durable washi paper that should not easily get dissolved in water. I had to pull up my origami boat from the sea and investigate why my origami boat sank so easily. My deck logbook on that day reflects:

I always try to keep in my mind to be 'a toy' as María mentioned in her comment. Am I thinking it too much? ... There is no trust with children built yet, of course it is not easy. What do I have? What can I do? I am overwhelmed with my anxiety, I got lost. (Logbook, October 22, 2014)

I began looking for other people's experiences in literature. At the same time, I began paying more attention to surroundings as Hafdís suggested. Otherwise I was overwhelmed by anxiety at my work. I was desperate to find a way to rebuild my boat stronger.

One day I spoke with another university colleague, Karen, who is also a self-study practitioner. I read her doctoral dissertation (Gísladóttir, 2011) and found that she had a similar experience to me. When she came to the class of deaf students, she realized that she did not know the culture of deaf students because she is a hearing person. She could communicate with students by signing, but struggled with her teaching as a hearing literacy teacher. She tried to respect students' resources they brought into classroom and utilized them for her teaching. What did she mean by resources of students? Karen let me borrow the book called *Funds of Knowledge* by Norma González, Luis C. Moll and Cathy Amanti (2005). I did not know that this encounter would become a breakthrough of my professional crisis.

Funds of knowledge is often discussed in a context of immigrants in the educational settings (González et al., 2005; Lefever et al., 2014; Mazurett-Boyle, 2016). The original idea of funds of knowledge has been developed in the U.S.-Mexico context, in which Mexican people had been struggling with historical, cultural, economic and political oppression (Vélez-Ibánez & Greenberg, 2005). Cultural values are developed upon family history and environment that become resources for learners (González et al., 2005). Their resources strongly influence how the learner acts in given society. Learners' diverse resources could be their funds of knowledge. Considering my case, my funds of knowledge as Japanese might contribute to scaffold Icelandic children's learning experience (Berk & Winsler, 1995/2002). As Hafdís said, my Japanese resource could be as an asset and I could take advantage of using it in my teaching. In addition, if I would become aware of children's unique resources, my teaching would be respectful to children's interests. When children's play would be developed based on their funds of knowledge, it could empower them to generate new knowledge.

While thinking of my new learning about funds of knowledge, I realized that the idea of resources sounded somehow familiar to me. Of course, the idea of using one's own resource is exactly what María means when she calls herself being a toy. María says that she uses her whole body in her teaching.

Her way of using resources is efficient to children's learning and discipline. This finding encouraged me to explore my resources to continue my sailing with a stronger boat.

5.3   Row, Row, Row My Boat

After I became more aware of how María's metaphor of being a toy would affect my teaching, I began to observe children closely to find their individual interests. Before knowing about the concept of funds of knowledge, I had been looking at the children as a whole group to control and never paid enough attention to individual needs. In my past teaching experience in Japan, I was always controlling the children to fit them into my schedule. In Iceland, children are to learn through play. Why shouldn't I take advantage of it?

In early November, I was with the same group of seven four-year-old boys that I first had to take care of on my day one at Rocky Preschool. Snow was gone, but it was very windy, which would be called the typical Icelandic winter weather. The boys had been kept inside for a couple of hours and I needed to let them release their energy before our *söngfundur* (singing meeting). It was torturing for them to keep sitting quietly for another hour. What could I do within such a limited time? I wondered what María would do if she were in my situation. She would come up with a creative idea. What would they want? What kind of equipments would be available in the storage? I decided to send them outside to run to feel the wind velocity for few minutes. They first complained about the weather, but I put each of them in a cape and encouraged them to be real Vikings who would beat the strong wind. Being excited, they dashed outside, ran around the play ground yelling, and came back with big smiles. María saw it and came outside to take a photo of seven little Vikings with capes running against the wind. In my deck logbook, I expressed my feeling of accomplishment:

> The highlight of this group time was that they could enjoy being outside even though the weather was not good. Later I asked Stefán who complained the most before going outside. He said, it was fun going out … I could admit to myself that it was a success …? (Logbook, November 2, 2014)

The quote was closed with a question mark. I was not confident with what I did with children. Reflecting on that incident later, I should count it as a success. The reason of success was that I could connect children's needs and interests at the right moment. They had so much energy to release, and I had learned through observation that they would often role play some heroes. If it was not that windy, the cape idea wouldn't have been that effective. It was the moment that I felt that theory and practice were intertwined.

Until this incident, I was struggling with how to make my boat stronger. I was rather passive when I was sailing on the origami boat. I was simply drifting on the sea of early childhood, not knowing where I was heading. I was making an excuse of my insufficient Icelandic. I believed that controlling children was necessary but it would not work without knowing children's interests. Each child has different interests and different resources. I had ignored those important factors and almost forced children into my box. I was the one that needed to change, not the children. Seven little Vikings opened my eyes, empowered me to reconstruct my boat and row it with my own will. My attitude began to change as my deck logbook reveals:

> I also decided to change my way of thinking from 'what I can do with them' to 'what they want to do.' In the past, I was always thinking what I can do for this time being. But it is so self-centered and it does not stimulate children's interests … I learned that they can be respectful if I respect their interests. (Logbook, November 19, 2014)

Finding my own agency let me explore the new path of being respectful to children's interests and initiate their play. If I noticed that they began their way, I would step aside unless they would ask for assistance. I could build a rowboat. Row it with my own agency. I am the sailor of the boat.

5.4 *Building My Boat with Funds of Knowledge*

Since I found my agency to row my boat, I began to gain some confidence. When I was assigned to work with María's group of girls, I tried to observe how she would work with them. It had been a while since I observed María's teaching last. She was always María, who was always singing and playing with children. I learned that Icelandic preschool educators let children play by themselves. María was opposite. She always said that it's fun to work with children and she positioned herself as their friend (Nishida, 2013). I simply thought that she liked children then. As an early childhood education practitioner, I wondered if I liked playing with children. I was not sure because I never tried to reflect on my feeling from this perspective.

A month before Christmas, I got a chance to explore my feeling towards children. I was with a group of five three-year-old girls after lunch time. During this time of the year the day light is very short and I wanted to take the group out to the community park by Rocky Preschool while there was still some light.

There was no snow but hailing a little. It was not actually the perfect condition to play outside, but I couldn't miss this day light. I got them dressed well and took them out to the park. My deck logbook, I honestly expressed:

> I was worried that they might complain about the weather ... We ran ... walked funny around the pond and they never complained. We walked close to the church on the hill, rolled down the hill, jumped off the lava cliff, yelled and ran around. It was fun for me. I think that it is important for me to also feel 'fun' for myself to be able to gain confidence. (Logbook, November 25, 2014)

I finally understood why María kept saying that she was a toy. She uses not only her body, but also her soul to enjoy the moments with children. That fostered a sense of respect between her and the children and she became a part of the children's world. For me, I learned that I also need to feel fun to be able to let children enjoy their life at preschool. In my logbook, I was developing this reflection:

> Recently my way of thinking is shifting like this: 'What can I do as an educator?' – 'What do they want to do?' – 'What are they interested in?' – 'How can I provide the learning space for them to have fun?' (Logbook, December 2, 2014)

One of the strategies would be relying on my resources. It took me some time to recall what Hafdís said to me about my Japanese cultural resource when I was in crisis. I was not feeling as stressed as I used to be in the beginning of my teaching career at Rocky Preschool, but I was not carefully looking into my Japanese cultural resource yet and what that could bring to my teaching.

On April 22, exactly half a year after my origami boat sank, I was invited to sit in the circle of 25 girls aged three to five for 15 minutes for the first time. It was not an easy task to keep young girls' attention for such a long time. My boat was still a simple tiny rowing boat, but I knew that I had my own agency to row it. I had to use my resources to transform my boat. When I sat in the circle of girls, I began singing the Japanese children's song 'Ito-maki,' wind the bobbin up in English. Although my intention of singing in Japanese was simply to avoid drowning again, the children's eyes were fixed on me. I kept singing and moving my hands. Soon they were copying my hand movement. Some even began singing along. The music is also known in Icelandic and therefore they were familiar with it. Later that day, I reflected on this incident in my logbook:

When I began singing in Japanese, they were just silent for a moment. But soon began following me and actually singing together! Especially Sif, Þóra and Ebba loved it and they were so good at copying me. I did not think this could be such fun for them … The movement is simple and the music is familiar to them. (Logbook, April 22, 2015)

Until then, I had had some opportunities to fix my boat. I was gradually gaining my confidence in teaching, but singing in Japanese confirmed that my Japanese cultural resource could help me build a stronger boat. My boat was first fragile as origami, then transformed into a rowboat and then it began to develop into something even stronger. I did not know what would be next, but I began to enjoy my transformation.

6   Epilogue: Sailing Continues

During my sailing of the sea of the Icelandic early childhood education, I discovered three essential resources to transform my boats of experiences: These are theoretical, cultural and human resources.

Theoretical resource is essential for every moment in my sailing. Without knowing educational theories, I could not pull my origami boat up from the bottom of the sea. Cognitive metaphors of sailing on the sea and building a boat let me look into my experience through an analytic lens (Kövecses, 2010; Lakoff & Johnson, 1980/2003). Narrative self-study method works as a compass to decide a direction for my voyage (Kitchen, 2009). Sometimes I was overwhelmed with theories as I tried to follow them strictly but self-study helped me realize my agency that is necessary for sailing (Samaras, 2011). The habit of keeping a teaching journal, which I called deck logbook in this saga, enriched the effect of metaphors. Metaphors supported me to visualize my experiences and opened my eye to a new land.

Secondly, my cultural resources were taken for granted in the beginning. Nor did I even utilize them well enough until my encounter with the concept of funds of knowledge (González et al., 2005). With my presence, children at Rocky Preschool are exposed to cultural diversity which is not easy to explain with a word to such young age group. Using my Japanese language is my strategy to reinforce my boat and scaffold children's learning experience (Berk & Winsler, 1995/2002; Vygotsky, 1978). During my self-study voyage, I realized that the Icelandic culture began to influence my teaching and attitude. I thought that my Japanese identity hindered my teaching as though I was controlling children. Once I decided to take advantage of my Japanese cultural resource, it induced some sort of chemistry with the Icelandic teaching culture that I have been studying in Iceland. I found a balance of respecting children's play (Einarsdóttir, 2006) while maintaining my Japanese teaching value for some aspects (Nishida, 2019). Singing in Japanese to Icelandic children may be the most remarkable strategy to support my sailing. This finding generated new knowledge and motivation of my teaching as an immigrant educator (Lefever et al., 2014).

Finally, I should emphasize that people around me should be the most important resource. María inspires me with a great influence on my thinking about using my resources for sailing from the beginning. I always imagined how she would deal with a tough situation that I was facing during my sailing. She would make it into a song to draw children's attention, for example. I did not refer much in my saga but other colleagues at work give their hands when I was losing my confidence for sailing. They always spoke to me in Icelandic but they never criticized my mistakes, neither in my teaching nor in speaking Icelandic. They were respectful to my endeavor. Sense of inclusion made me feel secure that Rocky Preschool would be my homeport. My doctoral supervisor Hafdís, who actually takes a role of my critical friend during my self-study voyage, shows great interest in my experiences and encourages me to keep writing in order to continue my sailing. She is always ready to jump on my boat to support my sailing through the storm with her critical and provocative inquiries (Costa & Kallick, 1993). My university colleagues provide me relevant literature and a cup of tea when I need to get off my boat and take a moment before sailing to a next land. My daughter Særún inspired me to develop my metaphors during our mindful walk in Japan and Iceland. My three essential resources all become great parts to build my boat.

María called herself being a toy. She still says to her junior colleagues that "ég er dótið," which may be literally translated into "I am the tool" in English. For me, I want to have tools instead of being a toy because I need to have tools to build a boat. My tools may also be transformative. Sometimes I need courage to try a new strategy to improve my boat. I want to be creative to use my resources to develop a unique boat. My tools may be something more internal and invisible, but they are imperative for transforming my boat into whatever I desire with funds of knowledge.

Acknowledgement

A part of this study was supported by The Watanabe Trust Fund at the University of Iceland and Scandinavia-Japan Sasakawa Foundation.

References

Bentz, V. M., & Shapiro, J. J. (1998). *Mindful inquiry in social research*. Sage.

Berk, L. E., & Winsler, A. (2002). *Scaffolding children's learning: Vygotsky and early childhood education*. National Association for the Education of Young Children. (Original work published 1995)

Bullough, R. V., Jr. (1994). Personal history and teaching metaphors: A self study of teaching as conversation. *Teacher Education Quartely, 21*(1), 107–120. Retrieved May 15, 2021, from http://www.jstor.org/stable/23475537

Clandinin, D. J. (2013). *Engaging in narrative inquiry*. Left Coast Press.

Clandinin, D. J., & Connelly, M. (2000). *Narrative inquiry: Experience and story in qualitative research*. Jossey-Bass.

Clandinin, D. J., & Connelly, M. (2004). Knowledge, narrative and self-study. In J. J. Loughran, M. L. Hamilton, V. K. LaBoskey, & T. Russell (Eds.), *International handbook of self-study of teaching and teacher education practices* (pp. 575–600). Kluwer.

Connelly, F. M., & Clandinin, D. J. (1988). *Teachers as curriculum planners: Narrative of experience*. Teachers College Press.

Costa, A. L., & Kallick, B. (1993). Through the lens of a critical friend. *Educational Leadership, 51*(2), 49–51.

Craig, C. J. (2011). Narrative inquiry in teaching and teacher education. In J. Kitchen, D. Ciuffetelli Parker, & D. Pushor (Eds.), *Narrative inquiry into curriculum making in teacher education* (pp. 19–42). Emerald.

Craig, C. J. (2018). Metaphors of knowing, doing and being: Capturing experience in teaching and teacher education. *Teaching and Teacher Education, 69*, 300–311.

East, K., Fitzgerald, L., & Heston, M. L. (2009). Talking teaching and learning: Using dialogue in self-study. In D. L. Tidwell, M. L. Heston, & L. M. Fitzgerald (Eds.), *Research methods for the self-study of practice* (p. 55–72). Springer.

Einarsdóttir, J. (2006). Between two continents, between two traditions: Education and care in Icelandic preschools. In J. Einarsdóttir & J. Wagner (Eds.), *Nordic childhood and early education: Philosophy, research, policy, and practice in Denmark, Finland, Iceland, Norway, and Sweden* (pp. 159–182). Information Age.

Einarsdóttir, J. (2010). Icelandic parents' views on the national policy on early childhood education. *Early Years, 30*(3), 229–242.

Einarsdóttir, J. (2011). *Training of preschool teachers in Iceland*. University of Iceland. Retrieved May 15, 2021, from http://vefir.hi.is/kennaramenntun/files/2011/08/Training-of-Preschool-Teachers-in-Icelandjóhanneinarsdóttir.pdf

Eyþórsdóttir, E., & Loftsdóttir, K. (2015). Vikings in Brazil: The Iceland Brazil Association shaping Icelandic heritage. *International Journal of Heritage Studies, 22*(7), 543–553.

Gísladóttir, K. R. (2011). *I am deaf, not illiterate: A hearing teacher's ideological journey into the literacy practices of children who are deaf* [Unpublished doctoral dissertation]. University of Iceland.

González, N., Moll, L. C., & Amanti, C. (2005). *Funds of knowledge: Theorizing practice in households, communities, and classroom*. Lawrence Erlbaum.

Hagstofa Íslands. (2019). *Menntuðum leikskólakennurum fækkar*. Retrieved May 15, 2021, from https://hagstofa.is/utgafur/frettasafn/menntun/born-og-starfsfolk-i-leikskolum-2018/

Hátíð hafsins. (2020). *Hátíð hafsins 2020*. Retrieved May 15, 2021, from https://hatidhafsins.is

Hjalli model. (2018). Introduction. Retrieved May 15, 2021, from https://www.hjallimodel.com/

Iceland Review. (2016, August 19). *Lack of teachers as school year begins*. Retrieved May 15, 2021, from https://www.icelandreview.com/news/lack-of-teachers-as-school-year-begins/

Karunamuni, N., & Weerasekera, R. (2019). Theoretical foundations to guide mindfulness meditation: A path to wisdom. *Current Psychology, 38*, 627–646. https://doi.org/10.1007/s12144-017-9631-7

Kitchen, J. (2009). Passage: Improving teacher education through narrative self-study. In D. L. Tidwell, M. L. Heston, & L. M. Fitzgerald (Eds.), *Research methods for the self-study of practice* (pp. 35–51). Springer.

Kitchen, J. (2016). Inside out: My identity as a queer teacher educator. In J. Kitchen, D. Tidwell, & L. Fitzgerald (Eds.), *Self-study and diverersity II: Inclusive teacher education for a diverse world* (pp. 1–10). Sense.

Kövecses, Z. (2010). *Metaphor: A practical introduction* (2nd ed.). Oxford University Press.

Lacy, T. G. (1998). *Ring of seasons: Iceland – Its culture and history*. University of Iceland Press.

Lakoff, G., & Johnson, M. (2003). *Metaphors we live by*. University of Chicago Press. (Original work published 1980)

Lefever, S., Paavola, H., Berman, R., Guðjónsdóttir, H., Talib, M. T., & Gisladóttir, K. (2014). Immigrant teachers in Iceland and Finland: Successes and contributions. *IJE4D Journal, 3*, 65–85. Retrieved May 16, 2021, from https://blogs.helsinki.fi/ije4d-journal/files/2015/01/IJE4D-vol.-3-article-4.pdf

Lichtman, M. (2010). *Qualitative research in eduation: A user's guide* (2nd ed.). Sage.

Loftsdóttir, K. (2010). The loss of innocence: The Icelandic financial crisis and colonial past. *Anthropology Today, 26*(6), 9–13. Retrieved May 15, 2021, from https://rai.onlinelibrary.wiley.com/doi/pdf/10.1111/j.1467-8322.2010.00769.x

Lög um menntun, hæfni og ráðningu kennara og skólastjórnenda við leikskóla, grunnskóla og framhaldsskóla nr. 95/2019.

MacKinnon, A., & Bullock, S. (2016). Playing in tune: Reflection, resonance, and the dossier. In D. Garbett & A. Ovens (Eds.), *Enacting self-study as methodology for professional inquiry* (pp. 291–296). S-STEP.

Mazurett-Boyle, R. (2016). Researching our way: Latin@ teacher's testimonios of oppression and liberation of funds of knowledge. In J. Kitchen, D. Tidwell, & L. Fitzgerald (Eds.), *Self-study and diversity II: Inclusive teacher education for a diverse world* (pp. 55–77). Sense.

Mitchell, C., & Weber, S. (1999). *Reinventing ourselves as teachers: Beyond nostalgia*. Routledge Falmer.

Nishida, M. (2013). *Hjallastefnan and professionalism: Preschool personnel's sense of security* [Unpublished master's thesis]. University of Iceland.

Nishida, M. (2019). At the dawn of revolution in teaching: A hybrid educator's prospect of self-study in Japan. In J. Kitchen, A. Berry, S. M. Bullock, A. R. Crowe, M. Taylor, H. Guðjónsdóttir, & L. Thomas (Eds.), *2nd International handbook of self-study of teaching and teacher education* (pp. 1521–1534). Springer. https://doi.org/10.1007/978-981-13-1710-1_54-1

Okruhlik, K. (1998). Otto Neurath: Philosophy between science and policies by Nancy Cartwright, Jordi Cat, Lola Fleck and Thomas E. Uebel. *International Studies in the Philosophy of Science, 12*(2), 175–191. https://doi.org/10.1080/02698599808573591

Ólafsdóttir, M. P. (1996). Kids are both girls and boys in Iceland. *Women's Studies International Forum, 19*(4), 357–369. Retrieved May 15, 2021, from https://www.sciencedirect.com/science/article/pii/0277539596000209

Ólafsdóttir, M. P. (2012). *Æfingin skapar meistarann: Leikskóli fyrir stelpur of stráka*. Almenna bókafélagið.

Pithouse-Morgan, K., Pillay, D., & Mitchell, C. (2019). *Memory-mosaic: Researching teacher professional learning through artful memory-work*. Springer. https://doi.org/10.1007/978-3-319-97106-3

Preschool Act no. 87/2008.

Preschool Act no. 90/2008.

Samaras, A. P. (2011). *Self-study teacher research: Improving your practice through collaborative inquiry*. Sage.

UNESCO. (1994). The Salamanca statement and framework for action. Retrieved May 15, 2021, from https://unesdoc.unesco.org/ark:/48223/pf0000098427

Vélez-Ibánez, C., & Greenberg, J. (2005). Formation and transformation of funds of knowledge. In N. González, L. C. Moll, & C. Amanti (Eds.), *Funds of knowledge: Theorizing practices in households, communities, and classrooms* (pp. 47–70). Lawrence Erlbaum.

Vygotsky, L. (1978). *Mind in society: The development of higher psychological processes*. Harvard University Press.

Wise, R. (Director). (1965). *The sound of music* [Film]. Twentieth Century-Fox Film Corporation.

CHAPTER 9

Developing a Dialogic Space for Moving towards Critical Multicultural Education

A Collective Self-Study

Gunnhildur Óskarsdóttir and Karen Rut Gísladóttir

In this chapter, we engage in an in-depth discussion of a critical multicultural teacher education collective self-study. Because we understand the varied conceptualizations of multicultural education, we define what we mean by critical multicultural education. As detailed by James Banks (1989) in his conceptualization of approaches to multicultural curriculum, we reject a contribution or additive approach, as these tend to reinforce stereotypes and heighten misconceptions. Instead, we define critical multicultural education according to Banks' decision-making and social action approach, which aims to foster transformation via the study of social problems. This meant that we gathered "pertinent data, analyze[d] their values and beliefs, synthesize[d] their knowledge and values" while identifying "alternative courses of action, and finally decide[d] what actions" (p. 18) to undertake to reduce inequities and injustices and foster equity and justice in our School of Education.

Our research study explores a cooperative self-study project that involved 14 university-based teacher educators in the School of Education at the University of Iceland. Over three years, we engaged in self-study to understand how dialogue could aid our understandings of how our cultural backgrounds influence our work as teacher educators. Specifically, we worked to become aware of our identities and educational practices, developing a critical understanding of how we can either resist or reify existing structures of inequity. The purpose of this collective self-study was to document and analyze the process of developing a discursive space that we, 14 university-based teacher educators in Iceland, co-designed and negotiated to mobilize the diverse understandings and experiences of the group to work towards critical multicultural teacher education. The aim was for us to strengthen teacher education through a "diversity-as-asset" lens. Our research question was: What are we, Gunnhildur and Karen (co-authors of this chapter), learning through our negotiation with each other and our colleagues in the process of creating a discursive space for moving towards critical multicultural teacher education? The data collected included focus group interviews, self-interviews, and audio-recordings of meetings. We used art-based analysis methods via the co-construction of sculptures and poems to create a dialogic space (Freire, 1970). Doing so led teacher educators to develop a shared agenda for collective transformation. Ultimately, this inquiry led us to collectively naming and interrogating ideas and approaches to transform our practices as teacher educators, helping us (re)commit to educating teachers in ways that prioritize equity and justice (Kitchen et al., 2016; Zeichner, 2018).

1 Context

Increasing ethnic and cultural diversity of students in the Icelandic school system has produced a need for changes in teachers' and teacher educators' work and classroom practices (Day & Gu, 2010; Guðjónsdóttir et al., 2016). Never before has it been more important than now for teacher education programs to prepare teachers multiculturally, necessitating a collective transformation of the role of teacher educators in Iceland, who predominantly embody dominant Icelandic identities (Sleeter, 2001).

The increasing diversity of students at all school levels also highlights the importance of teacher education programs to develop a multicultural or global vision (Ragnarsdóttir, 2012) to prepare teachers at all school levels for this new reality. According to Souto-Manning (2013), the first step towards developing cultural competence is understanding that everyone is a cultural being. Which is to say, each individual is shaped by their cultural experiences, and those experiences have to be considered and incorporated into pedagogy. In this respect, an essential step for teacher educators is to take the responsibility into their hands. If teacher educators are to work towards increasing student teachers' multicultural awareness and cultivate their courage to put forward their thoughts and understandings in conversations about racial, ethnic, and cultural diversity, they need to engage with these same discursive processes themselves and develop pedagogical ideas, tools and actions that can lead to social change (Kitchen et al., 2016; Mitchell et al., 2009).

We believe that critical multicultural education demands the interrelated transformation of self, teaching, and society (Gorski, 2010; Souto-Manning, 2013). As self-study researchers, we further believe that transforming understanding and educational practices begins with the self and can be further reinforced and developed through interaction with others (LaBoskey, 2004). Working from this perspective, we sought to transform our roles as teacher educators to reconceptualize our practices. Collective self-study was a practical methodology for our transformation. Our inquiry fostered increased meta-awareness of our roles as teacher educators, helping us reconsider the positioning of our diverse backgrounds, practices, and experiences (Kitchen et al., 2016).

2 Aims

The purpose of this collective self-study (Bodone et al., 2004; Samaras et al., 2012) was to document and analyze the process that we, 14 university-based teacher educators in Iceland, co-designed and negotiated a discursive space to bring together the diverse understandings and experiences of the group to work towards critical multicultural teacher education. Through this study, we became aware of our identities and educational practices, developing a critical understanding of either resisting or reifying existing inequity structures. The aim was for us to strengthen teacher education through a "diversity-as-asset" lens. In so doing, we created an opportunity for group members to re-envision their roles and practices as teacher educators (Gísladóttir et al., 2019; Jónsdóttir et al., 2015; Jónsdóttir et al., 2018; Mitchell et al., 2009). Here, we report on our processes of making meaning and making sense of this collective self-study, attending to our positionalities, insights, and experiences in this context. We were guided by the following research question: What are we, Gunnhildur and Karen (co-authors of this chapter), learning through our negotiation with each other and our colleagues in the process of creating a discursive space to develop a shared vision for moving towards critical multicultural teacher education?

This research is defined by a shared commitment to maintaining a dialogical space. In understanding how the dialogical space develops from within, we bring together Freire's (1970) notion of dialogical space and Bakhtin's (1979/1986) notion of interior monologue. We understand dialogical space as an encounter between individuals within a temporalized space. They attempt through shared reflection and action to act upon the world they want to transform. In their attempt to name the world, the world "reappears to the namers as a problem and requires of them a new naming" (Freire, 1970, p. 76). Thus, naming the world becomes a continued "act of creation and re-creation." For dialogical space to thrive, people need to find ways to develop, through dialogue, horizontal relationships built on mutual trust (Souto-Manning & Martell, 2019). For this to happen, Freire asserted, the dialogue must be founded upon love, humility, and faith in humankind; it must be driven forward by hope. Hope, Freire wrote (1970), is "rooted in men's incompletion, from which they move out in constant search – a search which can be carried out only in communion with other men" (p. 80). Hopelessness, to the contrary, is a "form of silence, of denying the world and fleeing from it" (Freire, 1970, p. 80). It is important not to let feelings of dehumanization resulting from unjust order lead to despair but to hope, which is a driving force for continuous "pursuit of the humanity denied by injustice" (Freire, 1970, p. 80). Hope, Freire asserted, "does not consist in crossing one's arms and waiting" (p. 80). As long as we fight, he emphasized, we are moved by hope; and if we are moved by hope, then we can wait. In working towards justice or humanization, dialogue cannot be carried on in a climate of hopelessness. If dialoguers hope for something to come of their effort, they need to engage in critical thinking, which according to Freire (1970) is "thinking which perceives reality as process, as transformation, rather than as a static entity – thinking which does not separate itself from action, but constantly immerses itself in temporality without fear of the risk involved" (p. 80). The undertaking of the humanists is not "that of pitting their slogans against the slogans of the oppressors, with the oppressed as the testing ground, housing "the slogans of first one group and then the other" (Freire, 1970, p. 84). Rather, "the task of the humanists is to see that the oppressed become aware of the fact that as dual beings, 'housing' the oppressors within themselves, they cannot be truly human" (Freire, 1970, p. 84).

Bakhtin's (1979/1986) notion of interior monologue is essential for identifying and interrogating the very foundation of dialogical space. The notion of interior monologue calls attention to how individual monologues are never just monologues. Rather, from a Bakhtinian perspective, dialogue infiltrates every word and has roots stretching into the past, as well as the potential to progress forward into a limitless world. For Bakhtin, "dialogue" describes how the word itself is a battleground in which different voices collide and interrupt each other. This is especially true in the creation of new knowledge or a shared vision. In attempting to understand the complexity of developing a dialogical space for moving toward multicultural teacher education, the concept of interior monologue allows us to interrogate and explore what happens underneath the surface, as ideas are brought into being through lived events or dialogical encounters between individuals and the world.

A shared commitment to creating and maintaining a dialogic space defines this research. Such a commitment allowed us as teacher educators to engage in the critical cycle to name and interrogate practices and identities (Souto-Manning, 2010). The critical cycle offered a framework to investigate experiences thematically, lived realities, and identities as teacher educators. The cycle also allowed teacher educators to critically problematize teaching and work toward practical transformation dialogically (Souto-Manning, 2019).

3 Methods

This research traces how we created a dialogic space across fields of professional expertise and disciplinary backgrounds (Harrison et al., 2012; Pithouse-Morgan et al., 2016; Pithouse-Morgan & Samaras, 2014, 2015, 2019). Methods included rhetorically mapping our existing understandings of multicultural education, dialogically problematizing paradigms to frame differences historically (Goodwin et al., 2008), and developing a shared understanding of multicultural education (Banks, 2013; Kitchen, et al., 2016; Souto-Manning, 2013). In discussing multicultural education, teacher educators troubled how cultural inferiority and deficit paradigms permeated beliefs, identities, and practices. Teacher educators identified and problematized the existing structures of the programs that they work within.

3.1 Data Generation and Data Analysis

Data, collected from August 2017 to June 2020, included self-interviews and focus group interviews, audio-recordings, transcripts of meetings, and group-generated artifacts. First, we engaged in documenting our understandings and experiences of multicultural education via collective self-interviews guided by questions formulated by the group (Meskin et al., 2014). In groups of two or three, we took turns interviewing or being interviewed by each other. These were the questions. (1) What is your understanding of multicultural education? (2) Where does your interest in multicultural education come from, or why have you become involved in multicultural education? (3) Can you name examples of your educational practices reflecting these theoretical underpinnings? (4) Can you identify how you develop an environment, learning spaces, and/or participation in the spirit of multicultural education? Each interview lasted about 30 minutes. Interviews were recorded and transcribed.

Data analysis was iterative and used to build further work. We engaged in art-based methods. We created sculptures that represented specific emphases or combined perspectives from the interviews. The art-based work began by giving participants time to engage with their own interview, identify "emotional hot points" (Cahnmann-Taylor et al., 2009) to share within the whole group. Then, we formed smaller groups and invited participants to negotiate a collective message from their interviews into a visible form, a sculpture that represented a specific emphasis or overall message derived from the interviews. Sculptures allowed us to communicate our insights and understandings to engage dialogically. The purpose of creating the sculptures was twofold. First, to externalize or take something internal and abstract and make it manifest and concrete in the physical world. Second, to use the externalized manifestation to defamiliarize taken-for-granted ideas and assumptions, which are then observable by others. Through the act of seeing it through others' eyes, the research members were enabled to see their thoughts and ideas differently (Lawrence-Lightfoot & Davis, 1997). Explanations of the sculptures were video recorded and transcribed.

Poetic inquiry can be described as "a form of qualitative research in the social sciences that incorporates poetry in some way as a component of investigation" (Prendergast, 2009, p. 560). In our study, it was a way to surprise ourselves and envision new possibilities, affording "the potential to make our thinking clearer, fresher, and more accessible and to render the richness and complexity of the observed world" (Cahnmann, 2003, p. 34). We used poetic inquiry to distill complicated clouds of ideas from the presentations of the sculptures into essential concepts, highlighting the importance of multicultural education on the group. Inspired by "erase poetry" (Faulkner, 2012; Pithouse-Morgan et al., 2014), we read the transcripts from the explanations of the sculptures and erased words that did not hold vital meaning to us in terms of multicultural education, leaving only the words that were important for their collective work. Then, each group rearranged words into poems. Based on these, we extracted the theoretical underpinnings from the poems for our research group. The main theoretical concepts regarding multicultural education developed in the group were 1) belonging, 2) critical dialogue and multiple perspectives, 3) transformation of self, classroom, and society.

3.2   *Participants and the Nature of Our Work*

During the academic year of 2017 to 2018, we had a Fulbright specialist, Mariana Souto-Manning, working with the school of education at the University of Iceland. Her visit aimed to lead specialized academic meetings and workshops with our faculty to focus on critical multicultural matters within the teacher education program and schools. After this year, the School of Education extended her position for three years. During her first year, Mariana held an open lecture for the School of Education about the importance of working with the cultural and linguistic diversity found within schools. Afterward, the faculty members discussed the importance of focusing on how we, in our courses, were preparing student teachers to utilize multicultural approaches in their fieldwork and work with students. Following the lecture, everybody received an open invitation for a research collaboration.

A shared commitment to multicultural teacher education brought together 14 educators with different backgrounds and experiences from diverse, interdisciplinary fields. Nine had Icelandic heritage and spoke Icelandic. Five spoke other mother tongues and were brought up in different countries. Each member had different academic experiences and held different positions within the School of Education, ranging from Ph.D. students and adjuncts to assistant professors, associate professors, and full professors. Some were new and others experienced. Each brought a different theoretical and methodological orientation to the group. Some were familiar with action research and self-study methods, while for others, these forms were new.

Mariana's position included two visits per year. Mariana facilitated the groups' discussion during those visits, pointing out our connection and helping us name and interrogate our practices and identities. In between meetings, we, Gunnhildur and Karen, developed a structure for this collaboration.

4 Findings

The affordances of using self-study to frame our collective work in developing a shared vision and identifying foundational pillars to build our future work upon were twofold. First, it allowed us to identify and analyze how we needed to work with and negotiate across the various experiences, theoretical foundations, and methodological orientations unveiled in our group. By making our processes, highlights, struggles, and negotiations, explicit we became more aware of the nuances embedded in aligning ourselves in a way we could draw on each other's experiences and knowledge. Second, highlighting the process of aligning ourselves revealed practices and approaches important for supporting the development of a discursive space for student teachers as they prepare to become teachers of students of diverse backgrounds. The process we went through involved negotiating a starting point, drawing the map, naming our understandings for developing a shared vision and beginning to name and problematize our identities.

4.1   *Setting Forth*

The process of creating a shared vision for the group did not happen without an effort. Our journey began in April 2015, when Gunnhildur was visiting Teachers College at Columbia University. Gunnhildur was then the head of the faculty of teacher education at the University of Iceland, where she wondered how to strengthen the multicultural aims in the program. While attending a lecture at Columbia, Gunnhildur noticed a woman in the audience who was actively participating in the discussion, asking provocative questions. This woman was talking about multicultural education in much broader sense than Gunnhildur had conceptualized it. She emphasized multicultural education as a good education for everyone, it did include inclusion, it did include race, equity, justice, the education of immigrant children but also the education of dominant populations. Afterward, Gunnhildur approached this woman and got to know her name, Mariana Souto-Manning. They met at Mariana's office a few days later to discuss educational interests, and Mariana gave Gunnhildur her book, *Multicultural Teaching in the Early Childhood Classroom: Approaches, Strategies, and Tools, Preschool – 2nd Grade*, in which she wrote the inscription "with hopes for establishing a partnership."

The book was really an eye-opener for Gunnhildur, who had thought about multicultural issues and their lack in the teacher education program. After this encounter in New York, Gunnhildur knew that Mariana was the one she wanted to work with the faculty at the School of Education. It was something about her critical and warm presence that Gunnhildur believed could lead a diverse group of people together. A year later, Gunnhildur wrote a Fulbright application for Mariana to visit the School of Education two times over a one-year period. During her visits, she wanted her to lead specialized academic meetings and workshops with our faculty to focus on multicultural issues in schools. Gunnhildur also wanted to take this opportunity to develop further links between the University of Iceland and Columbia University, which might lead to research collaboration and further cooperation between scholars and students.

Karen Rut was an associate professor within the faculty of teacher education. As she read about Mariana, she noticed her expertise in sociocultural perspectives on language and literacy and multicultural education, as well as her experience working as a teacher-researcher. These were all components related to Karen's work, and she saw this as an opportunity to engage in deep discussion about those matters. She volunteered to work with Gunnhildur and Arna (another faculty member) on developing a schedule for Mariana's visit. During Mariana's first visit Karen took her on some adventures around Icelandic nature and learned more about her scholarship in the field of multicultural and literacy education and respect for teachers' work. She further learned about how Mariana used innovative ways of collaborating with teachers in schools. Towards the end of Mariana's first visit, she held an open lecture for the School of Education about the importance of working with the cultural and linguistic diversity found within schools. Gunnhildur followed this lecture with an open invitation to participate in further collaboration that focused on these topics. This meeting attracted 12 participants (2 arrived later). Reflecting on the open nature of this invitation process it was very important for Karen, but Gunnhildur was a little disappointed that more people would not show up:

> Karen: This open invitation was important – that those who are willing to commit themselves to this work participate instead of deciding

beforehand who is participating. Then, people might not have the time or be ready to commit themselves wholeheartedly. And the message being communicated around this work, that there were no hurt feelings whether people were going to be involved or not, just this freedom to decide for ourselves if we are ready for this work and what we would like to contribute to it. (Focus group interview, October 2019)

Gunnhildur: We invited people to participate in continuous work and asked to think about if they were ready to commit themselves to the work ahead. I thought more people would show up, but I knew they were committed in various ways and had many things to attend. I did not have much experience in this field, but I knew this was something that our teacher education program needed to address. (Focus group interview, October 2019)

4.2 Drawing the Map

The first meeting of teacher educators was centered on ways we prepare our students for multicultural education practices in schools. We discussed the need to map out current work and understanding about multicultural education within the School of Education. We began to discuss our different experiences and expectations for the work ahead. The conversation traversed several topics: how multicultural education emerged in our educational practices, areas we could do better, and how multicultural perspectives were present in course syllabi. As teacher educators discussed the steps for working towards this direction, they discussed how they could distribute articles on the topic, mobilize beneficiaries, and empower teachers. The discussion then turned toward the critical importance of design-based research. The conversation was rich with different theoretical and methodological orientations. Karen experienced tension when the conversation came to a turning point and began to center on a discussion of the design of a questionnaire to send to colleagues within the School of Education. As soon as the idea of the questionnaire emerged, the focus began to overshadow other ways of approaching the task.

Gunnhildur thought that sending out the questionnaire was an essential way to ascertain how our colleagues approached multicultural education. Karen, however, disagreed. As a self-study researcher, she did not prioritize gathering this information over the first-hand practical transformation the group wanted within their programs. She believed that in sending out a questionnaire, the group uncritically took an authoritative stance, sending out the message that we somehow embody that knowledge. Our task was to make sure that everyone else was including this emphasis in the courses.

Gunnhildur: I myself was focused on sending a questionnaire to all teachers at the School of Education to map out if and how teachers were preparing student teachers for teaching multicultural student groups. I thought it was the fastest way and hopefully would give a good picture of the situation. (Focus group interview, October 2019)

Karen: In this first phase of our work, the big tension arose around the methodological discussion. As a teacher-researcher, I had repeatedly entered research projects assuming we start exploring our own assumptions and understandings about the phenomenon under exploration and expand from there to find out that it was not even on the agenda. The shared commitment to improve teacher education in terms of multicultural education brought this group together. But there are so many ways to do that. I felt confused when, in the midst of honing our work's focus, the idea of sending out a questionnaire became prominent. In my mind, we had not started to map out the various experiences, understandings, and methodological orientations within the group to utilize these resources to their fullest. To bring this all together, I wanted for us to create a space for ourselves. If we would not manage to include the angle of exploring our ideas and assumptions, I saw us risking suffocating some unknown potentials for moving forward. I was ready to push boundaries, frame this first phase of our work as a self-study to examine the group's capacity, and develop different pathways based on what we brought to the group. If it would not work out, I was ready to stand by my methodological orientation and leave the group. (Focus group interview, October 2019)

Gunnhildur left the meeting feeling as though the group was one step closer to understanding how to map out the work happening at their institution. She was aware that not everyone agreed on the questionnaire as the essential step for this work. Karen left the session feeling frustrated with the discussion of the questionnaire. She had collided with some of her colleagues in this discussion. She was concerned that the intensity of her reaction might have done some damage to their new relationships. At the same time, she felt passionate about her point of view. Gunnhildur had never considered doing self-study and found this methodological angle interesting. She agreed that we needed to look at ourselves and our ideas before going any further.

4.3 *Naming Our Understanding*

In the second meeting, the discussion continued where it had left off. Teacher educators exchanged ideas, ranging from sharing publications with other teacher educators on how teachers should think about multiculturalism using existing research in our courses. Karen was discouraged as she did not feel as the discussion provided a space for teacher educators to transform their thinking. In her mind, the group's focus was undergirded by a dominant conception of research, that you read something, interview someone else, and not necessarily the researcher. As Karen struggled to articulate her concern, another self-study researcher within the group stepped in, wondering about our research's purpose and what we wanted to see happen within the School of Education. She proposed we create the questions we would like to send out in the form of a questionnaire and try them out by using them to interview each other in small groups. The group approved the idea of interviewing each other.

Everybody agreed these interviews were essential for the further development of the group's work. Group members talked about how the interviews had allowed them "to put down and reflect upon different views, methods, and experiences," "raise important questions," and "recognize the threads that combine us" (focus group interviews, 2019). Gunnhildur felt that this change in focus had released teacher educators from disagreeing over the questionnaire (Focus group interviews, 2019). Karen felt content and concerned about this decision. She really wanted the group to develop a space where we could listen to each other and take into account our different voices, but having to fight for the direction made her wonder if she was going against her intention and her colleagues were experiencing her as focusing them on doing things her way (Focus group interviews, 2019). Now she found herself suddenly in the position having to convince people that this had been a right decision, knowing that this kind of exploration requires time and is characterized by uncertainty, unfolding by each step in the process, and could take a long time before leading to any "tangible result" (Focus group interview, 2019). In moving ahead, Karen suggested constructing an arts-based framework in which teacher educators would individually begin identifying essential points in their interviews, focusing on what multicultural education was for them. Then they would bring these into small groups to create a collective sculpture. While Gunnhildur found this idea to be exciting, she worried the process would be too time-intensive. Gunnhildur was hesitant because she felt the sculpture idea might detract from the focus of the work (Focus group interview, 2019).

At the beginning of the session, we displayed the materials provided for the art-based analytical work. The session commenced with individual time to engage with each person's interview, identifying points teacher educators wanted to address further in small group discussions. The following points emerged: reflecting on individuals' home culture, assisting immigrant and refugee children who speak languages other than Icelandic, removing hindrances, making the unconscious conscious, identifying students' strengths and language and cultural resources, having courage, addressing prejudices and privileges, securing the participation of people of foreign background, reflecting on one's disposition, and finding pathways to collaboration. Other topics also emerged: bilingual children, poverty, gender equity, equal opportunities, participation, social position, positive attitudes towards others, and the school should reflect society. In small groups, teacher educators listened to each other's points and then moved forward to creating the sculptures to distill a shared understanding of multicultural education. When the sculptures were ready, each group explained how their work represented their understanding of multicultural education.

The final step in developing a shared vision for our group was to use transcripts from each group's explanation to craft poems. We read through the transcripts and erased words that did not hold vital meaning in multicultural education, leaving only the words we thought were necessary for our collective work. Then we rearranged the words into the following poems.

personal journey
institutional journey
societal journey

speaking from experience
without shame
about poverty
social position

dialogue
listening
the courage to say
I want this included

starting with ourselves
do I have prejudices?
how can I overcome that?

Children
as creators
of opportunities

the classroom
reflection of society
equity and respect

> the teacher
> learning and growing
> creating opportunties
> supporting students
>
> students
> participating
> their voices heard
> requires structure
> support

The artistic process described here provided us with a pathway for capturing and representing the multiple experiences found in our group, which comprised the theoretical foundation from which the group would grow. Finally, we began to identify foundational pillars to build our future work through a dialogic engagement with the poems. These were
- Belonging (Who gets to belong? What are the terms of belonging? Who gets othered?)
- Critical dialogue, encompassing the consideration of multiple perspectives (What do we know? How's what we know informed by dominant perspectives and values in Icelandic society? How can we recognize the problematics of not naming power in/and identity?)
- Transformation of self, classroom, and society (How can we start acknowledging the categories and spaces of privilege and disprivilege we occupy? How can we abandon notions of normalcy and notions of who and what is and isn't Icelandic? How can we learn from our own cultural locations and positionings in society? How can these learnings inform our classroom practices? What do we need to teach in order to cultivate a more inclusive, equitable, and just society?).

4.4 *Naming Our Identities*

Working on the foundational pillars, "making sense of each different groups' emphasis and trying to combine them, was a hard mental work" (Focus group interview, 2019). It took the group up to nine months to name them. Many group members felt we had finally "accomplished something" when they emerged (Focus group interviews, 2019). Our learning journey continued. In May 2019, Mariana came for a week visit. She shared that "there was already a lot of knowledge and experience in place in terms of multicultural education" and that "part of what the commitment of the group was, was to think about multicultural education as really being part of teacher education, as a matter of equity, as a matter of justice and injustice" (interview with Mariana, 2019). While she was facilitating the process, her work was "to recognize what was already in place and mapping the strengths of every single member." To enrich the group discussions this week, she had selected some articles that had recently been published related to the landscape of teacher education. We started this week's discussion with a little activity, which entailed Mariana reading aloud the picture book *Looking Like Me* by Walter Dean Myers, illustrated by Christopher Myers and inviting us to think about the multiple ways we can be described and how these affect our positionalities and inform our sense of belonging. Then, reflecting on the book and on the ways we are described across contexts, we spoke in pairs about our positionalities and what positions we brought to our research, eventually attending to how these showed up in our theoretical and methodological understandings. Then we were tasked with introducing our partner to the whole group. Through this introduction, we began to name different aspects of our identities and recognized how power and privileged were inscribed and reinscribed in our positionalities.

In introducing each other, we began to name how our colleagues had traveled around the world, lived in different places, were good listeners and observers, liked to collect people's experiences, were critical and reflective, were interested in children's perspectives and children's agency, different cultural identities, how they used qualitative or blended methods in their research, and how the idea of self-study and teacher research was important to them (transcripts of meetings, May 6th, 2019). In this discussion, one pair shared how after they had stopped talking together, sharing professional and personal information, they wondered why they had emphasized who they were in the ways they did and how some aspects of their identities had been left behind a little bit. Mariana thanked them for bringing that up, explaining how in becoming a community, there were parts of ourselves that we would have waited to share and other parts that we assumed to be welcomed (transcripts of meetings, May 6th, 2019).

The group discussion evolved. We further shared how we aligned with the idea of social justice, multicultural education, inclusive education, and critical thinking, reflection, and problem-solving. Several group members highlighted how they were always striving to improve, always wanting to develop, aware that they would never get where they wanted to be. Mariana highlighted how what we were talking about was so important, to embody the process and understand the process's importance, instead of thinking that there is always a solution. She further explained how often we have a problem and want the solution. Still, it was so important to work through a process towards a possible solution in confronting a problem, and we might never get *there* because the *there* keeps moving.

Through this discussion, Mariana kept underscoring how the members of the group had complementary experiences in terms of collecting different perspectives on phenomenon under study and accenting the self in experiences in terms of thinking about more sociocultural approach trying to understand how people experience through questioning, to question, to move towards problem-solving and implicating the role of self. She drew our attention to that even if we were drawn to different methodological approaches, they complement each other well, and it did not mean that one was better than the other.

As we shared each other's cultural backgrounds, it was interesting to note that none of us mentioned their cultural background. Karen's partner shared with the whole group how Karen said she was a teacher-researcher, literacy person, an Icelandic teacher. These were all aspects Karen had just shared with her. Then she added that Karen had said she was a hearing person, which she thought was remarkable because she would never say that about herself despite the fact she was also a hearing person. Mariana thanked them for bringing up the hearing person, reminding them that we need to be aware that "just because we don't feel the need to say something it does not mean it is not there" (transcripts of meetings, May 6th, 2019). Then she encouraged us to really think about how it is that "we don't mention, and by not mentioning we invisiblize and marginalize, and that we cannot change something until it is named." In that way, a critical multicultural perspective has to attend to power, and we all have power. We all hold power over somebody, and somebody always holds power over us, so it is a complicated perspective.

Within the group were five group members that were immigrants to Iceland. In the introduction of the two of them, their identity as immigrants was foregrounded. For one, her partner introduced her saying that her "immigrant identity was at the core." Her partner also highlighted her knowledge of languages. In the beginning, she had said she spoke four languages, but as they spoke further, she realized the languages she knew were six. At the end of the partner's introduction, she herself stepped in, explaining how it had just been at the end of the discussion that she had mentioned how she was a Muslim, not finding out her partner's religion in return because the time for the pair discussion ran out. For the other group member named an immigrant, the additional explanation followed that "she did not really want to be labeled like that."

In responding to these introductions, Mariana pointed out a couple of things. First, it was thinking about "who gets labeled and who doesn't" (transcripts of meetings, May 6th, 2019). She pointed out how two of the group members had "identified themselves as immigrants," others had identified themselves as "having lived in different places but not necessarily identify with those places." She posed the questions of "how do people get labeled, and what does that mean?" She wondered if they had to identify as an immigrant. The first person she heard identifying herself as an Icelandic teacher or a teacher of Icelandic, not even Icelandic, was Karen Rut. No one said, "I am Icelandic," because that is just the dominant identity. She emphasized how "we need to think of what is rendered visible and invisible or what is visible and rendered visible like 'but this language is not counting. I haven't used it'" (transcripts of meetings, May 6th, 2019). And we need to think of what that does mean for our work in terms of mapping the assets of the community, even though these assets may not fit in the community because it is not rendered needed or necessarily desirable within the context of Iceland. It is important to acknowledge that we are having difficulties doing identifying, it is a hard work. One of the greatest challenges is that the assets may not just be on the surface … so the question is "how do we get to the knowledge that may be further hidden like, at the last minute you were exposing you were Muslim. That is a big part of your identity, but maybe because it does not line with the dominant Icelandic expectations of the norm it gets hidden. We need to become aware of and name the privileges that we hold because we are all privileged in some ways and disprivileged in other ways. Just think about the invisible categories in our statements because we don't feel like we need to say them. Like none of us said, college-educated (everyone laughs). We are all privileged because we are all college-educated. What are some of the other things that we are privileged in, and which are some of the ways we are disprivileged?" (transcripts of meetings, May 6th, 2019).

5 Discussion and Implications

In "Teachers Learning about Themselves through Learning about 'Others,'" teacher educators Mary Louise Gomez and Amy Johnson Lachuk (2017), used Holland et al.'s (1998) argument that the "self" always is "embedded in social practice, and as itself, a kind of social practice" (p. 28) to explore how student teachers can become better teachers of children from whom they are culturally different. Gomez and Lachuk argued that Holland et al.'s work helped them better understand how a self acts in "socially and culturally constructed realm[s] of interpretation in which particular characters and actors are recognized, significance is assigned to certain acts, and particular outcomes are valued over others" (Holland et al., 1998, p. 54). Such figured worlds mediate a persons' behavior and inform how people see the contexts in which they are located, and view ourselves and others' behaviors (Gomez & Lachuk, 2017).

As we discussed our positions and privileges we saw evidence, just as Gomez and Lachuk did in their exploration of one student teacher's identities and positionalities, of how "the dialect we speak, the degree of formality we adopt in our speech, the places we go, the emotions we express, and the clothes we wear are treated as claims to and identification with social categories and positions of privilege relative to those with whom we are interacting" (1998, p. 127). In our discussions of our privileges, we positioned ourselves relationally, bringing forth evidence of how we are viewed within established social hierarchies. That no one thought of naming our shared and taken-for-granted privileges is just one examples. But also, how persons who were not born in Iceland automatically identified themselves as "outsiders" is another.

Gomez and Lachuk (2017) explained how Holland et al.'s work engaged with Bakthinian dialogism:

> Bakhtin explained that the spatial and temporal contexts in which persons are situated are key to what persons know, do, and understand. Because persons are in continual dialogic relations with themselves and others, persons need to examine their identities in relation to how they imagine who they are and why they behave in ways they do. (p. 459)

Using Bakthin's concept of dialogism to understand how teachers can better teach students from diverse backgrounds is useful, Gomez & Lachuk (2018) argued, because it is through "dialogue with one another, we come to know who we are – what we believe and how it may be possible to act in particular places and spaces" (p. 100). In our discussions with each other, we witnessed firsthand how we "get ourselves from the other" (Holquist, 1990, p. 22 as cited in Gomez & Lachuk, 2017, p. 459). Our discussion of our privilege illuminated how we, as teachers and persons, inhabited two concurrent yet separate spaces – that of "I" and that of "those who are different from me" (Holquist, 1982, as sited in Gomez & Lachuk, 2017). We saw how in discussing who we were, what identities we brought to our teaching and our relationships, how we literally envisioned ourselves against what Gomez and Lachuk referred to "a milieu of the Other" (2017, p. 459).

Through this process we are learning that although it may be a hard "mental work" to negotiate a shared understanding of critical multicultural education, it may even be more intense to engage in the identity work involved in transforming teacher education towards that understanding. We are learning how in working with diverse persons with diverse commitments and viewpoints, including those whose identities reflect dominant categories in Icelandic society, certain features must be present to create a shared vision. We need to create spaces where individuals can bring in knowledge, experiences, and understandings. Such a space cannot be judgmental or evaluative but must be open-minded and inclusive of diverse vantage points.

If we are to be true to developing these spaces, we need to approach it with curiosity and humility, searching for ways to develop horizontal relationships built on mutual trust (Freire, 1970; Souto-Manning, 2019) with both colleagues and students. Building these relations does not happen without critical self-reflection. We are learning that if we are not to risk pitting our slogans against "the slogans of the oppressors, with the oppressed as the testing ground housing the slogans of first one group and then the other" (Freire, 1970, p. 84), we must find ways to slow down to attend better and listen to one another and what is emerging in between us. In short, we need to be present and mindful of each other.

Finally, our dialogic encounter and how the discussions facilitator, Mariana, helped us name and lay meaning to our utterances by naming privileges and inequities and posing critical questions to the group illuminates how every utterance is just the tip of the iceberg on the surface, with a whole slew of feelings and experiences down in the depths that needs to be named and worked with. Through our ongoing personal and professional dialogue in relation to critical multicultural education we are revealing hidden assumptions and power hierarchy affecting how different group members are impacted to perceive themselves. As power hierarchy exists in all groups, we are learning how important it may be for us to capture our own dialogue to explore how we are (or are not) listening and being responsive to each other. We need to be accountable to each other, but most importantly to ourselves, ensuring that we honor and respect each person.

Ultimately, collective self-study puts us on a challenging, albeit productive, pathway towards furthering our personal and professional development in multicultural teacher education. Self-study provided us with the space to develop individually and collectively, serving as a site for strengthening our relationships, aligning our practices, affirming our commitments and problematizing our identities. Self-study research served as a powerful avenue for identifying, problematizing, and transforming our individual and collective understandings of our roles and practices as teacher educators (LaBoskey, 2004).

References

Bakhtin, M. M. (1986). *Speech genres and other late essays* (V. V. McGee, Trans.). University of Texas Press. (Original work published 1979)

Banks, J. A. (1989). Approaches to multicultural curriculum reform. *Trotter Review, 3*(3), 17–19.

Banks, J. A. (2013). Multicultural education: Characteristics and goals. In J. A. Banks & C. A. M. Banks (Eds.), *Multicultural education: Issues and perspectives* (8th ed., pp. 3–23). John Wiley.

Bodone, F., Guðjónsdóttir, H., & Dalmau, M. (2004). Revisioning and recreating practice: Collaboration in self-study. In J. J. Loughran, M. L. Hamilton, V. K. LaBoskey, & T. L. Russell (Eds.), *International handbook of self-study of teaching and teacher education practices* (pp. 743–784). Springer.

Cahnmann, M. (2003). The craft, practice, and possibility of poetry in educational research. *Educational Researcher, 32*(3), 29–36. https://doi.org/10.3102/0013189X032003029

Cahnmann-Taylor, M., Souto-Manning, M., Wooten, J., & Dice, J. (2009). The art and science of educational inquiry: Analysis of performance-based focus groups with novice bilingual teachers. *Teachers College Record, 111*(11), 2535–2559.

Day, C., & Gu, Q. (2010). *The new lives of teachers.* Routledge.

Faulkner, S. L. (2012). Frogging it: A poetic analysis of relationship dissolution. *Qualitative Research in Education, 1*(2), 202–227. https://doi.org/10.4471/qre.2012.10

Freire, P. (1970). *Pedagogy of the oppressed.* Continuum.

Gísladóttir, K. R., Guðjónsdóttir, H., & Jónsdóttir, S. R. (2019). *Self-study as a pathway to integrate research ethics and ethics in practice.* Springer.

Gomez, M. L., & Lachuk, A. J. (2017). Teachers learning about themselves through learning about "Others." In D. J. Clandinin & J. Husu (Eds.), *The Sage handbook of research in teacher education* (pp. 457–472). Sage.

Gomez, M. L., & Lachuk, A. J. (2018). Cultivating an informed empathy: An aspiring teacher examines his talk and actions. *The European Educational Researcher, 1*(2), 23–39. https://doi.org/10.31757/euer.122

Goodwin, A. L., Cheruvu, R., & Genishi, C. (2008). Responding to multiple diversities in early childhood education. In C. Genishi & A. L. Goodwin (Eds.), *Diversities in early childhood education: Rethinking and doing* (pp. 3–10). Routledge.

Gorski, P. C. (2010). *The challenge of defining multicultural education.* https://www.edchange.org/multicultural/initial.html

Guðjónsdóttir, H., Óskarsdóttir, E., Wozniczka, A. K., & Gísladóttir, K. R. (2016). Námsrými byggð á auðlindum nemenda. *Netla – Veftímarit um uppeldi og menntun.*

Harrison, L., Pithouse-Morgan, K., Connolly, J., & Meyiwa, T. (2012). Learning from the first year of the Transformative Education/al Studies (TES) project. *Alternation, 19*(2), 12–37.

Holland, D., Lachicotte, W., Jr., Skinner, D., & Cain, C. (1998). *Identity and agency in cultural worlds.* Harvard University Press.

Jónsdóttir, S. R., Gísladóttir, K. R., & Guðjónsdóttir, H. (2015). Using self-study to develop a third space for collaborative supervision of master's projects in teacher education. *Studying Teacher Education, 11*(1), 32–48. https://doi.org/10.1080/17425964.2015.1013026

Jónsdóttir, S. J., Guðjónsdóttir, H., & Gísladóttir, K. R. (2018). Að vinna meistaraprófsverkefni í námssamfélagi nemenda og leiðbeinenda. *Tímarit um uppeldi og menntun/Icelandic Journal of Education, 27*(2), 201–223. https://doi.org/10.24270/tuuom.2018.27.10

Kitchen, J., Fitzgerald, L., & Tidwell, D. (2016). Self-study and diversity. In J. Kitchen, D. Tidwell, & L. Fitzgerald (Eds.), *Self-study and diversity II: Inclusive teacher education for a diverse world* (pp. 1–10). Sense.

LaBoskey, V. K. (2004). The methodology of self-study and its theoretical underpinnings. In J. J. Loughran, M. L. Hamilton, V. K. LaBoskey, & T. Russell (Eds.), *International handbook of self-study of teaching and teacher education practices* (Vol. 2, pp. 817–869). Springer.

Lawrence-Lightfoot, S., & Davis, J. H. (1997). *The art and science of portraiture*. Jossey-Bass.

Meskin, T., Singh, L., & Van der Walt, T. (2014). Putting the self in the hot seat: Enacting reflexivity through dramatic strategies. *Educational Research for Social Change, 3*(2), 5–20.

Mitchell, C., Pithouse, K., & Moletsane, R. (2009). The social self in self-study: Author conversations. In K. Pithouse, C. Mitchell, & R. Moletsane (Eds.), *Making connections: Self-study & social action* (pp. 11–23). Peter Lang.

Pithouse-Morgan, K., Coia, L., Taylor, M., & Samaras, A. P. (2016). Exploring methodological inventiveness through collective artful self-study research. *LEARNing Landscapes, 9*(2), 443–460. https://doi.org/10.36510/learnland.v9i2.786

Pithouse-Morgan, K., Pillay, D., Naicker, I., Morojele, P., Chikoko, V., & Hlao, T. (2014). Entering an ambiguous space: Evoking polyvocality in educational research through collective poetic inquiry. *Perspective in Education, 32*(4), 149–170.

Pithouse-Morgan, K., & Samaras, A. P. (2014). Thinking in space: Learning about dialogue as a method from a trans-continental conversation about trans-disciplinary self-study. In D. Garbett & A. Ovens (Eds.), *Changing practices for changing times: Past, present and future possibilities for self-study research.* Proceedings of the tenth international conference on Self-study of teacher education practices, Herstmonceux Castle, East Sussex, England (pp. 167–170). University of Auckland.

Pithouse-Morgan, K., & Samaras, A. P. (2015). The power of "We" for personal and professional learning. In K. Pithouse-Morgan & A. P. Samaras (Eds.), *Polyvocal professional learning through self-study research* (pp. 1–20). Sense.

Pithouse-Morgan, K., & Samaras, A. P. (2019). Polyvocal play: A poetic bricolage of the why of our transdisciplinary self-study research. *Studying Teacher Education, 15*(1), 1–15. https://doi.org/10.1080/17425964.2018.1541285

Prendergast, M. (2009). "Poem is what?" Poetic inquiry in qualitative social science research. *International Review of Qualitative Research, 1*(4), 541–568. https://doi.org/10.1525/irqr.2009.1.4.541

Ragnarsdóttir, H. (2012). Empowering diverse teachers for diverse learners: A program in International Studies in Education and its implications for diverse school settings. In A. Honigsfeld & A. Cohan (Eds.), *Breaking the mold of education for culturally and linguistically diverse students: Innovative and successful practices for the 21st century* (pp. 229–236). Rowman & Littlefield.

Samaras, A. P., Guðjónsdóttir, H., McMurrer, J. R., & Dalmau, M. C. (2012). Self-study is a professional organization in pursuit of a shared enterprise. *Studying Teacher Education, 8*(3), 303–320. https://doi.org/10.1080/17425964.2012.719127

Sleeter, C. (2001). Preparing teachers for culturally diverse schools: Research and the overwhelming presence of whiteness. *Journal of Teacher Education, 52*(2), 94–106. https://doi.org/10.1177/0022487101052002002

Souto-Manning, M. (2010). *Freire, teaching, and learning: Culture circles across contexts.* Peter Lang.

Souto-Manning, M. (2013). *Multicultural teaching in the early childhood classroom: Strategies, tools, and approaches, Preschool-2nd grade.* Teachers College Press.

Souto-Manning, M. (2019). Toward practically-just transformations: Interrupting racism in teacher education. *Journal of Education for Teaching, 45*(1), 97–113. https://doi.org/10.1080/02607476.2019.1550608

Souto-Manning, M., & Martell, J. (2019). Toward critically transformative possibilities: Considering tensions and undoing inequities in the spatialization of teacher education. *Teachers College Record, 121*(6), 1–42.

Zeichner, K. (2018). *The struggle for the soul of teacher education.* Routledge.

CHAPTER 10

A Racialized Canadian Professor's Self Study

Teaching about Multiculturalism during the Trump Era

Manu Sharma

1   Introduction

In this self-study chapter I examine my professional journey and positionality while teaching in mid-west Wisconsin, under President Trump's political influence. I had the honor and the important opportunity to teach a Foundations of Multicultural Education course to undergraduate students from across various disciplines. This course was a required course that fulfilled the university's American diversity requirement (3 credits) for graduation. The students in my classes were mostly from rural backgrounds, lower-middle class, and white females. As a passionate advocate for social justice-based teaching and research, a Canadian citizen, and a racialized woman, I faced many conflicting experiences within myself about teaching. In particular, I studied how my positionality was responded to, how my choice of curriculum for my course was received (the curriculum development), my beliefs around social justice and communal responsibility towards my students (my ethics and sense of responsibility). I use a self-study methodology to engage with reflections I kept on my daily teaching, syllabus changes, as well as correspondence with my critical friend, Dr. Julian Kitchen. With the use of these personal and professional sources I provide insight on some of the challenges, opportunities and possibilities I encountered while teaching in Wisconsin.

2   Positionality and Background Context

I grew up in Toronto as a first generation Canadian-Indian. My public schooling experiences bring back memories of exclusion, racism, and unkindness. I recall feeling that my elementary school teachers did not want to help me do well academically and did not care for me as they felt I was a lost cause. It was tough going to a school in which all of my teachers and most of my classmates were white and unkind. With this elementary public school experience in the back of my mind, I had many similar experiences in middle school and high school. It was not until post-secondary schooling that I was able to develop my skills to critically think, question, analyze and develop a deeper understanding of myself. In particular, my graduate studies helped me realize that what I was most passionate about was making public education equitable for all marginalized students and teachers. I had worked as a part-time public school teacher for a number of years while completing my post-secondary graduate studies and learned how being a teacher still left a gap in being able to assist the vulnerable marginalized students. As a teacher I did not have the autonomy to always teach as I wanted to, nor was I able to critically challenge initiatives that were pushed onto teachers by principals and school districts. Thus, as life went on, I became a racialized Canadian woman in her thirties who decided to change her career from being a classroom teacher to being a professor, working a number of years as a sessional instructor and ancillary academic faculty in three Canadian universities.

As a scholar who had previously taught at three Ontario based universities and was dedicated to the cause of making education equitable and trying to reach as many future professionals as possible who would interact with children, I was delighted to continue my work in a new context. Thus, I accepted the tenure-track position as an Assistant Professor in the mid-west of the United States. Elated at the opportunity to teach in a tenure-track position at a mid-sized university in Wisconsin, located in a quaint town in a rural setting, my family and I decided in August 2017 to make the move south across the Canadian border. At the time, President Donald Trump began his second year of his presidency and I heard rumors that the motto "Buy American and hire America ... make America great again" had seeped deeply into most rural parts of America. In my eyes, I was hired to teach about social justice issues and concerns in America in a political time of uncertainty, which permitted an opportunity to make a real difference by educating the future teachers of America and other professionals who would work with children in some capacity; and this was invigorating.

2.1   *Location and Duration*
I flew in mid-August to get settled into my home environment, to which I was lovingly received by a colleague and his wife from the University. This particular couple became sincere friends of mine and their generosity and kindness will never be forgotten. After having three weeks to settle in, the first class of the required American diversity course, *Foundations of Multicultural Education*, began.

The university I taught at for two years (2017–2019) was an American mid-sized university situated in a mid-western college town. The campus was a serene and beautiful campus that offered students a home away from home. Most students lived in residences on the campus.

2.2 *My Courses*

As I learned more about my position, I realized I was the sole person teaching about multiculturalism or social justice directly and thus my assigned course was the main source for students to learn about social justice. I felt the importance, value and ethical responsibility that I had to teach about multiculturalism. Thus, I was excited to teach the three sections of Foundations of Multiculturalism (FoM) in the Fall of 2017. Each section had on average 28–30 students. Each class met 3 times a week for 50 minutes, thus 450 minutes of instruction every week for 16 weeks. I taught each section back-to-back with a ten-minute break between. In addition, I taught the School and Society course in the Fall of 2017, the capstone course for most students in the Bachelor of Education program. In the 2018 winter semester, I taught the FoM course to another 3 sections, again back-to-back, with one additional section in the evenings, three times a week. I was awarded a course release for working on a research project. In the Fall of 2018 I taught the FoM course to 3 sections, again back-to-back along with teaching School and Society course. In the Winter of 2019 I taught FoM course to 4 classes, three of them were back-to-back and one in the evening. In total, I interacted with approximately 390 students in the 13 FoM sections and with 60 students in my School and Society classes. It is important to note that FoM was the only social-justice-based course being offered to fulfill the American diversity credit that was required by all undergraduate students, and I was the only instructor who taught this on campus. Thus, my analytical reflection is informed by my theoretical orientation and the two years of teaching experiences in the mid-west.

2.3 *Context of Trump Era*

Trump was inaugurated into the White House on January 20, 2017. I began teaching in the mid-west of the United States in September that year; thus President Trump had been in office and making political changes for seven months by the time I arrived. To give some political context to this self-study it is important to identify some plans and actions that President Trump enacted on the topic of immigration. With alignment to his campaign slogans President Trump created four pillars for immigration reform. In his first State of the Union address on January 30, 2018, Trump outlined his administration's four pillars for immigration reform: (1) a path to citizenship for DREAMers;

(2) increased border security funding; (3) ending the diversity visa lottery; and (4) restrictions on family-based immigration (Pew Research Center, 2019).

Each of these pillars had a series of events that were carried out under the orders of President Trump. For example, in September 2017 President Trump ordered an end to the Deferred Action for Childhood Arrivals (DACA) ("Immigration policy of Donald Trump," 2020). In February 2018 an active separation between family members entering the USA was executed, following a zero-tolerance policy of family separation that took place on the Mexican border, which did not allow parents or relatives to bring in children with them into the States ("Immigration policy of Donald Trump," 2020). Moreover, in 2019 there were several unannounced immigration and customs enforcement (ICE) raids, and ICE have arrested, fined and/or deported hundreds of undocumented immigrants. Such examples demonstrate the political anti-immigration atmosphere to which my students and I were regularly exposed on the news during my teaching in the mid-west between 2017–2019.

3   Theoretical Framework

Drawing on neo-Marxist framework, this chapter takes a critical approach in looking at my teaching experience at a mid-western university. In particular, I follow work in critical pedagogy in order to analyze my teaching and my relationships with my students through critical-political lens, that is, by being aware of political conditions and circumstances that influenced my work in Wisconsin during 2017–2019. In this regard, the work of Freire is especially relevant and helpful in understanding my experience about teaching about multiculturalism to mostly White rural American students. Freire (1970) believed that education could not be separated from politics; as such, the acts of teaching and learning are considered political acts in and of themselves. Therefore, in education that is aimed at liberation (which in the Freirean anti-colonialist context that means education in general), teachers and students must be aware – or be made aware – of the politics that surround education, including political circumstances, tensions, and events. A result of this position is that what teachers teach as well as the way they teach serves a political agenda; there is no way around it. And since teaching is done through communication, teachers use and bring with them political notions into the classroom (see also Kincheloe, 2008).

Furthermore, Freire's work is especially helpful for my analysis since in his critical pedagogy he stressed oppressors–oppressed relationships. Founded on German idealism (and particularly Hegel's philosophy), Freire (1970) described the complexities articulated in the educational context of the relationships between those in power who govern education and those to be educated. For Freire, education must entail uncovering oppression circumstances. But this should not be done in a top-down manner when the educator tells the oppressed about their situation; the oppressed individuals must play a role in their liberation. In the same vein, oppressors must be willing to rethink their way of life and to examine their own role in oppression if true liberation is to occur. This pedagogy suggests the rejection of the "banking model" of education and adopts a dialogic education where the teacher and the students examine together their positionality and beliefs (Freire, 1970, p. 58).

On this theoretical backdrop, teaching a course about multiculturalism in education to rural middle-class White students at a mid-west university during Trump's presidency – and by a racialized female immigrant – just augments the political anchors Freire talked about. I faced an educational challenge that requires careful attention, as my students can be regarded as members of both sides of the oppressors–oppressed distinction. A dialogic education with them, aiming at encouraging them for self-reflection and hopefully for the possibility of transformation with regard to contemporary political issues, was not easy. In the following section, I will describe why I used self-study methodology for this chapter and what data sources were used in this research.

4 Methodology

I used a self-study methodology because I wished to reflect, analyze and understand what my teaching meant to me in the space and positionality continuum I found myself in. I wanted to decipher why there was so much anxiety around teaching practices and delivering this course for me and thus I chose to do a self-study on this matter (Loughran, 2002). As Kitchen (in press) claimed, self-study

> researchers go beyond reflecting in and on action by also considering their personal and professional identities. They recognize, as Connelly and Clandinin (1988) articulated, that "'personal knowledge' … determines all matters of significance relative to the planned conduct of classrooms." (p. 2)

Thus, the data is derived from my personal course journal on the three sections of Foundations of Multiculturalism class I taught during my first semester at this mid-sized Wisconsin university, course syllabi over the semester, my previous and current teaching experiences, my positionality in the US context, communications with a critical friend, and course evaluations.

4.1 Journal Entries and Course Syllabi

Bullough and Pinnegar (2001) support collecting and reflecting on journal entries as they explain tensions between oneself and their context. I kept my teaching reflections and notes in a journal that I would write in regularly after teaching my three back-to-back sections. It was a good way to process things that I was unsure of in my teaching based on students' participation, and it also was a great way to help improve my course syllabus for the next semester.

4.2 Teaching Experiences and Positionality

My teaching experiences from Canada and my positionality as a first generation Canadian-Indian woman informed how I taught and what I emphasized in my teaching. For example, I heard myself give examples from my elementary school teaching experiences about how Bank's (2010) model of multiculturalism needed to be enacted. Another example is that I would aim for inclusivity and embracing multiculturalism as that would help create better schooling experiences for marginalized students, as I recalled the painful memories of my elementary school experiences. It was evident that my teaching experiences and positionality impacted my teaching in the mid-west.

4.3 Critical Friendship

Loughran (2002) argued that the process of collaboration is essential in self-studies because it allows researchers to check data and interpretations and frame and reframe understandings. Schuck and Russell (2005) contended that critical friendships have often become a way of establishing the trustworthiness in self-study.

In this self-study, the role of a critical friendship was offered by and fulfilled by Dr. Julian Kitchen who contributed to a spirited conversation that was composed from his letters sent via email to me and my correspondence back to them as I reflected on my teaching experiences in the US.

Dr. Kitchen is a Professor at Brock University who has decades of experience teaching teacher education students in the context of social justice-based courses. His positionality contrasted with mine and thus provided perspectives that were informed by his lived experiences. Dr. Kitchen is a White male and I am a racialized female. Furthermore, during my teaching examined here he was living in Canada under a liberal government and I was a Canadian living in the US as an "alien resident" under a conservative US government. Thus, critical friendship was helpful in bringing this chapter together.

4.4 *Course Evaluations*

Lastly, I used official students' course evaluations in order to help me reflect on how students felt about this course and me. I recall examining the data points on the course evaluations and how there were certain patterns that emerged across the course evaluations in each section and over each semester. These patterns helped me analyze and deeply reflect on my teaching experiences in the mid-west and about how my positionality was received by my students.

5 A Thick Description of My First Semester Teaching the Course

As usual, I was very excited to teach and had all my materials prepared and ready to go as the students of the first section walked into the room. I had a table at the front of the room with all my materials for the three sections of this course that were about to commence. My PowerPoint was up, the 24-page syllabus was photocopied on colored paper, sheets of colored paper and markers were available for name cards, an ice breaker activity, an attendance folder, a Get To Know You student questionnaire, and an online website on Desire to Learn (D2L) platform was all set up and ready to go for each of the three classes!

The first class session was about to begin in ten minutes. As the students trickled in one by one or in small groups, they sat at the tables that I had put into a great big horseshoe style to encourage a way of getting to know everyone and see everyone during class discussion. I had some background music playing that students may have recognized from the top 40 hits of the summer to help create a cozy atmosphere.

I asked some students to start making their name cards based on my demo name card located at my seat among the students in the horseshoe. Soon there was a rippling effect and all the name cards were complete. I stopped the music to formally introduce myself to the class and gave them a chance to ask me any questions they had. And then,

> I vividly recall a male student raising his hand and asking where I was from, because clearly, I was not from the USA portrayed by my accent. As I answered that question, by sharing that I was from Canada and just relocated here over the summer, I noticed his hat states "MAKE AMERICA GREAT AGAIN." This made my heart race because it seemed that patriotism was in the class and I was not in support of it. Then this student continued to ask, 'Did Canada not have any jobs anymore?', and I felt

that the undertone was that I was not an invited or welcomed person to this community, at least not in his eyes. So, as my mind calculated what to say in a professional manner and my heart raced, I said, 'I guess the University wanted someone like me to help move conversations around multiculturalism forward during this political time and they could not find anyone internally.' (Multicultural Course Journal, September 6, 2017)

Next, I asked the students to engage in an icebreaker activity. After the completion of the activity, I unpacked the purpose of the icebreaker with the students to ensure that the reasons beyond getting to know one another were understood. Most of the students were surprised to learn that the game was a way to learn about where in the world they had culturally connected with others and what interactions they had with different diverse populations. For me this was the opportunity to learn about what experiences students had with immigrants.

Then, I went on to guide students briefly through the 24-page syllabus which provided a detailed class outline for each of the 45 classes we would have together. I also simultaneously pulled up the online D2L website which showed all the readings picked from a variety of peer reviewed articles and some book chapters, assignments and their rubrics, and any additional resources. To end the class, I handed out their student questionnaire that was a confidential document to complete and hand it back to me the next class.

In the second section, the changes that I made were: I did not ask students if they had questions about me but rather I told them I taught in several universities in Canada and taught in public schools internationally; I reduced the amount of time on taking up the purpose of the ice breaker; and I extended the time of examining the syllabus and the online platform.

> I realized that I pulled back on the class participation and made it more teacher-facilitated as I felt uncomfortable in the first section. I found myself reading the students' clothing and hats, looking for political messages, and low and behold I found them, many proud Americans wearing, American flags, and slogans from the recent elections. (Multicultural Course Journal, September 6, 2017)

By the third section, on this first day of school, I was able to quickly go through the planned lesson and decided to focus on the level of professionalism in students' work ethic, and as a result, the satisfying level of growth and insight they would receive.

> I wanted them to think of this required course as important, relevant and interesting so that it could make an impact on their thinking. I recall saying that this course was a foundations course which is different from a methods course, the distinction was that unlike methods courses that are practical and provide you with templates on what to do when one teaches, this course would make students think critically and deeply about social justice issues that cut across school life experiences, which don't have one universal answer or a fix-it-solution. (Multicultural Course Journal, September 6, 2017)

Knowing that this course did not have one set of answers to the large and complex social justice issues involved in multiculturalism, on the questionnaire I asked students how they felt in situations where there was no one explicit answer and sometimes there may be no answer. With respect to having a lack of closure on social justice issues, many students later revealed on their questionnaire that this made them very uncomfortable. There was a desire to know exactly what was the problem, how to solve it and then be done with it. I shared back with the students in our third class together what the main themes were that emerged out of the student questionnaire and spoke to the concerns around not having closure or an answer on some of our complex discussions that pertain to issues of multiculturalism in the USA.

> Moving forward, in all three sections of this course there was resistance to reading academic articles and doing daily assignments, that was shared with me via emails. I was surprised by the lack of enthusiasm by the majority of students to read and do the class work for this three-credit course. (Multicultural Course Journal, September 25, 2017)

In response, I had to address each section about changes I would make to the readings and workload. I added more book chapters that were easier to read and reduced the number of pages that needed to be read per week from 40 pages to about 30 pages. Many students were pleased with this as they were comfortable with textbook like chapters that laid out information in a direct manner. I was told by more experienced faculty members in the Education Department that previous students who took this course read from a textbook and that was best. I found myself justifying my decision on having a plurality of readings from different authors from different texts to provide multiple perspectives on any given social justice issue.

Next there was an issue with the assignments. I explained to each of my class sections that I had developed a scaffolded approach to their learning every week. I shared that from the theoretical readings on Monday we move to the applied case studies on Wednesday and then we connect what we learned to the lived experiences that students had in the field experience in St. Paul, Minnesota. This field site was about 30 to 40 minutes away from the campus. In other words, the class met three times a week, and I had created a format in which every Monday I would provide an opportunity to facilitate a reading discussion based on the assigned readings for the week, on Wednesdays I would facilitate an analysis on the weekly case study on the same topic and on Fridays I would facilitate a dialogue on the reflection based on the tutoring and class assistance experience they had in St. Paul. Unfortunately, the students brought the dialogue back to the number of assignments they had to do in a week. To this I responded that each of the assignments I had created was to help mobilize their learning in a way that was constructive.

> I felt myself becoming disappointed in their lack of interest to learn more deeply about social justice issues. (Multicultural Course Journal, September 25, 2017)

With a deep breath, I proceeded to think out loud with the students about what assignments could be refined.

Many students said they were not happy with the assignment for Mondays which required them to come up with two critical questions based on the readings to share with their weekly assigned partner. They also suggested that they wanted me to lecture on the topic instead of facilitating a dialogue.

> This made me wonder whether they were uncomfortable with the topic or did not want to do the work to engage with one another on these topics. Perhaps it was a bit of both of these reasons that they wished for the facilitated dialogue to be removed on Monday. (Multicultural Course Journal, September 25, 2017)

Later that week, I offered that I would lecture for 25 minutes and provide the remainder time for doing an exchange of the critical questions and asking me questions to further understand the readings. I also reduced the number of case studies they had to analyze throughout the course and I also minimized the number of reflections they had to complete on their field experience. I was hoping these changes would have created more enthusiasm in the students for completing and engaging in the dialogue about the topics in this course.

As the course progressed and we got to the mid-point of the semester, I found there was a great deal of resistance to conversations around white privilege.

> I had planned this topic, five weeks into the course as I thought it would have been an appropriate time to have gained class trust, vulnerability and willingness to have such a conversation. (Multicultural Course Journal, October 4, 2017)

I had arranged for students privately to do the Harvard implicit bias test (Project Implicit, n.d.) based on race and then write a reflection on it before coming to the class. I reminded them that this was just one insight but not an ultimate universal truth about themselves.

Despite the music played as they walked into the classroom (a regular routine I had to help lighten the mood) and warm welcome I gave them, many were not interested in talking that day. I reiterated that the Harvard implicit bias test was not 100% accurate and that there were spaces in its formatting, questioning, and the process that could be challenged, and I asked them to think of what these challenges were. In each of the three class sections of that day,

> I had only 1–2 students speak up and it was often the ones that did not see themselves as being White or those that identified with being White but with financial instability. The ones who were not White shared that they were adopted into nice Minnesotan and Wisconsinite families so never felt any difference, and the ones with financial hardship experiences spoke of how their families worked hard and made the American dream come true for their generation. (Multicultural Course Journal, October 4, 2017)

In response, I shared that not all people in financial hardship would be able to pull themselves up to get out poverty because their race prevented them. I explained how only White people had an opportunity to own and farm their land up into the 1850s, as I knew the context of most of my students was coming from farm-based rural settings. This was a hard insight for many students to hear – I saw the body language shrink – and then I added that but of course hardship is never easy and it is important to acknowledge how our ancestors helped us get to where we are today. As for the point on adoption, I knew the topic on immigrants would come up later in the course.

> However, in the back of mind I thought, how interesting that these students who were not part of the White race identified with the White culture and privileges and did not seek out to find out their heritages even though in class there was an activity (Flower Power) that asked students to investigate their heritage and other identity factors. Was this a strong

> case for assimilation into the American identity? I wondered if their adoption was acknowledged outside their community, where people did not know them and thus saw them as racialized people who were not American? I wanted to know more but could not go there in this limited and fragile time, so I left it for myself to reflect upon. (Multicultural Course Journal, October 6, 2017)

Nevertheless, there was a sense of anger and resentment that came across heavily towards me. I was uncomfortable with the tension and thus tried to focus the class on content such as what Peggy McIntosh (1990) argued in her article on the invisible knapsack, what was shared in a YouTube video entitled "A million dollar race," and the Harvard test; but for some reason this content was not promoting any discussion. As a result, I decided to allow students to speak in small groups of 4–5 instead, without me facilitating the discussion to ensure an opportunity to debrief. As soon as I did this, there was a great deal of chatter and I stayed a good distance away from each group to stay good on my promise for them to have a personal discussion. Each group was given the opportunity to report back to the class with one or two salient points but this was not compulsory or graded. The hope was the invitation lowered stakes of participation and allowed for a thoughtful close to this discussion. Unfortunately, not many groups wished to engage in this and as a result I thanked them to engage in discussion and hoped that in the near future they would be willing to engage in it again on a larger class scale.

As the semester came to an end, it was almost time for course evaluations to be done. I always felt nervous around this time because learning about controversial topics and looking inward on oneself is challenging and not everyone enjoys this process despite my best intentions to create a safe and trusting environment and meticulous planning.

> Also, as a faculty member that still needed to get tenured and promoted, I knew that course evaluations would impact and influence my career trajectory and this made me anxious. (Multicultural Course Journal, December 6, 2018)

I knew that other faculty members who were not tenured and were hired at the same time as I was did not have to teach controversial material that implicated their personal identity, and I wondered if this would be considered when my file was examined.

It is important to note, that the following three semesters in which I taught the FoM course to ten more sections, I tweaked my syllabus by adding: (1) more current events that were in the news pertaining to our course such as political decisions made on immigration, (2) videos that demonstrated how profiling of suspects who shot open fire in schools were done with a bias when the suspect was racialized in contrast to being White, (3) podcasts as an alternative to readings, and (4) equity based in-class activities. All these content and delivery changes in FoM occurred because I realized students were not desiring to put in the effort to read because discussing these topics was controversial and uncomfortable. Thus I hypothesized that making the learning process more easily accessible and experiential based would bring more dialogue into the class space, and it did. I also changed the assignments to be more scaffolded and reflective than analytic and transformative, as I realized students were at many different entry points on the equity continuum, and my social responsibility was to push them a bit further.

6 Discussion: Drawing out Thematic Findings and Their Complexities

One of the main components of self-study methodology, formerly known as methods of narrative inquiry, is to ensure that the teaching and learning process is improved after the analysis of the teaching has been completed (Mishler, 1990). My aforementioned thick descriptions of teaching experiences have provided me an opportunity to self-reflect by drawing on all of my data sources and my lived and teaching experiences. After examining the data sources carefully, the major themes that arise out of analysis are (1) my positionality as a racialized Canadian woman, (2) the impact of Trump's political messages on my course, (3) the lived experiences of students, and (4) the impact of student evaluations on the tenure review process. Collectively, these findings draw out the complexities that were unexpected. In what follows, I will explain each of these thematic findings.

6.1 My Positionality

Although I am aware "it is crucial that teacher educators engage in rigorous self-study in order to develop self-understanding and an understanding of education for others" (Kitchen, 2005, p. 18), I am not sure that I have developed in either of these ways. I have gained insight on the complexity of my positionality and teaching about multiculturalism under a nationalistic government.

In particular, as I now reflect back on the decision of allowing students to speak in small groups about white privilege and the activities I provided instead of having a large facilitated discussion, I worry that my lack of debriefing the above class may have created solidarity amongst the student voice, which was heavily influenced by students who were very vocal and often held patriotic views and anti-immigrant sentiments. This makes me question the level of safety and trust a teacher educator should provide, as it was unclear when this level of safety can be used to create a stronger divide between teacher and student and also allow for a dominant perspective to take hold of smaller groups. Thus, in retrospect, I think this centralized my worry about being read as a Canadian-Indian young woman with a racialized background and with an agenda that was perceived as transforming students to acknowledge, care and respect marginalized people.

> Once I started to question what impact my positionality had on my teaching and sense of belonging to this community of rural White middle class Westerners, I started to question the interactions and impact I had on my students. I wondered if all the open conversations I had about being honest about my pedagogical choices, content selection for the course, and changing the assignment tasks would have occurred if I was a White male in his mid 40s and was American? Could it be that my positionality had a major impact on how I and the course I was delivering was received? (Multicultural Course Journal, October 6, 2017)

I shared the above sentiments about my positionality with my critical friend, Dr. Kitchen, who responded with insights on his own positionality and insights on the political climate in the US with the following:

> White and male privilege are accorded to me even when they may be uncomfortable with my identity as gay; presenting as a non-threatening and reasonably masculine certainly helps. I choose to be out, unlike some, because it both allows me to use my privilege for others and as a way of choosing to relinquish some privilege. You also note that there was much one way talk, implying that silence does not equal agreement though. (Letter correspondence from Julian Kitchen, November 3, 2018)

After re-reading and thinking about Dr. Kitchen's correspondence, I notice how he made a point of emphasizing that he chooses to bring his positionality into his classroom discourse. This opportunity to choose is not something I had when it came to my positionality, as I was already pinned to be a racialized young woman and my accent made it clear that I was not American. The assumptions and stereotypes attached to my positionality were already obvious and thus, I had to work hard to demonstrate my genuine intentions in teaching in order to get students to think critically for themselves. That is, I had to be explicit in my pedagogy to let students see the transparency in any given lesson. For example, when debriefing the activity of the Harvard Implicit Bias test, I said that we would examine the purposes of the test based on its website and we were going to open it up for a critical discussion, so that the students could challenge and critique what the purpose and process of the test was according to students themselves.

I also believe my lived experiences were not welcomed in the classroom as they were seen as biased and one-sided in the first semester of classes. Therefore, I made sure my direct voice was removed from the classroom space. I remember over the semesters purposefully using authors' names who wrote the chapter to be central in class discussion so that I was not seen as putting forth these social justice arguments but rather it was the author who put them forward. Lastly, I recall using equity issues, based on case studies, as another pedagogical tactic to get students in a position of power to analyze cases with different perspectives in mind such as of a teacher, student, parent, community member and principal, while simultaneously getting them to consider perspectives they may not be familiar with in a non-confrontational manner. In hindsight, I believe this layer of extra caution would not be necessary had my positionality been that of a White male.

6.2 *The Impact of Trump's Political Messages on My Course*

Reflecting back on the "make America great again" comment made in the very first class I taught in the mid-west, I assume I was trying to let the student know that I was not taken aback by his impolite questions and was aware of the political climate, as well as had what it took to teach such courses. I recall that I continued to assert and defend myself by sharing that I had taught about social justice issues directly and indirectly at three previous Canadian institutions and thus had the work experience to help facilitate some conversations in this particular area of work and research. In retrospect, that may have sounded like I was justifying my presence to this student who did not know me for more than 10 minutes at that time. Politics and power dynamics were felt almost immediately in the classroom space.

Another example that impacted students' thinking when we learned about illegal and legal immigrants was President Trump's campaign that argued for building a wall to keep illegal immigrants out. Students would conflate illegal immigrants with immigrants in general (anyone who was not White), and then with a negative connotation. Thus, students in my class often talked about immigrants generally and were not worried by President Trump's decision on sending immigration officers to schools. Such actions, therefore, supported the sentiment that multicultural immigrants were not invited and were not part of America. Trump's tweets were influential to my students who brought them forth as an affirmative perspective of their beliefs to re-own America, especially when we examined the topics of immigrants in one of our classes. I noticed there was a sense of pride and empowerment in many of my students because they were fairly vocal and shared stories of times of financial trouble and unemployment, and stood in solidarity with the political messages and actions being taken to rid the country of illegal immigrants and undocumented immigrants without any hesitation. Knowing this about some of my students' views, I felt an immense sense of moral responsibility to expose all of my students to perspectives of immigrants, what they contribute to the US, and how they too have personal stories. Again, I shared this burning desire to fulfill this moral responsibility through teaching with Dr. Kitchen, my critical friend, and he wrote back the following:

> Teaching about equity, diversity and social justice in the United States right now is incredibly important and challenging work. The President seems scarier than ever and the views he expresses more reified in the populist/Republican movement/structure. The Kavanaugh affair prompted a conservative backlash, immigrants/refugees are again under attack, transgendered people may be written out of definitions of gender according to leaked reports, and the Saudi government's assassination of a journalist in a Consulate is minimized by the president. The white 'tribe' in Middle America seem drawn to these narratives and coalescing as a solid voting block. And you are teaching members of this tribe in the heartland of the rural Midwest. Every day must be intense. You must always be always asking what you can do to make a difference in the thinking and actions of the decent young women and men in your classes so that they resist the pervasiveness of Trumpian thought.
>
> As I have expressed in relation to my own classes, I think we have an ethical obligation to present students with alternative perspectives and invite them to consider the voices of minoritized and marginalized groups. (Letter from Julian Kitchen, October 22, 2018)

Dr. Kitchen's insights had me thinking about the ethical obligations of presenting students with different perspectives on multicultural issues, especially those dealing with immigrants in the US context. Although I agreed with presenting different views as I used a variety of readings, case studies, and in-class activities, I also thought that it was insufficient, for example, with respect to Trump's response and actions taken against illegal and undocumented immigrants that were dehumanizing and unethical. I am not convinced that it is enough to invite young minds to think through different perspectives when they still come to a conclusion that dehumanizing ICE raids and deportations are acceptable. This acceptance of ICE raids and deportations was the conclusion of many of my first semester class students. I find it frightening when educators are put in a position where they are limited in how they can respond to conclusions that students share that demonstrate values of dehumanizing and unethical treatment towards fellow human beings. Thus, while I believe that educators have an ethical responsibility to facilitate learning from different perspectives, I also believe they have to acknowledge that they have limited control of how students draw their conclusions. Nevertheless, I urge educators to promote and uphold the dignity and value of all human beings especially in contentious conversations.

6.3   *The Lived Experiences of Students*

I validated and heard my students but I am not sure they heard or were open to receive the information from other perspectives, despite it coming from academic and non-academic literature, and/or experiences during their field placement. I was careful not to bring my personal life story into this space as they did not ask me for it when I offered everyone an opportunity to share their lived experience; this is despite making suggestions I was working multiple part-time jobs to financially support myself during my postsecondary education. Thus, although I agree with Russell (2002) that "accepting responsibility for, and genuine caring about, the interpersonal relations that are so embedded in teaching really matters" (p. 4), I wonder: is this a two-way commitment? Do students also have to respect and be open to learning from the educator? What happens if the educator feels intimidated, or isolated, or cornered, or unsafe based on class comments? I would contend there needs to be care and safety on both sides of student-teacher relationships.

When a student asked a question that had an unwelcoming undertone on the first day, I felt cornered and unsafe to continue making myself available to them in this manner. I understand it was only one student, but if one student could think such a thing, I wonder how many thought it and just didn't say it. I became even more aware of my positionality and the thoughts students had.

Later in the course when students shared that the course was difficult with respect to readings and assignments, I was disappointed and felt myself alone in the passion to pursue teaching about multiculturalism. I wondered how to get my students to care and feel passion for a course that they were required to take but did not wish to be there. I know students have their own lived experiences and views on life, but there seemed to be a lack of overlap between their lived experiences and my lived experiences, a discrepancy that was brewing my worries.

I can understand the lack of excitement for required courses. But given the current political climate in the US and in Wisconsin in particular, I thought this course was extremely important and could be utilized to open up serious conversations around multiculturalism in a positive way. As the semester went on, I was concerned about the impact I could make, as I knew many of the students in this required course were going to be future teachers, some would be speech pathologists, and others would work with young minds in some other capacity. I reached out to Julian Kitchen and he asked me to reconsider what was possible in the duration of a single course. He wrote the following back to me:

> But how far can we move them in a single course? My line of thinking in our dialogue has been that we begin where they are and move them as far as is reasonable within our limits as instructors of a single course. Just as we accept kindergarten students who cannot read and do our best to adapt the curriculum to their present knowledge/skills, so too we need to begin where they are. My teacher candidates are not as aware of social justice as I would like, and your students are less advanced still. But they are good people with the capacity to grow as people and as professionals. (Letter correspondence from Julian Kitchen, December 27, 2018)

I wished that students would examine their own life experiences and identities (Schön, 1983) and acknowledge the realities of different marginalized groups through this course's content and field placement, with the hope of better understanding themselves and those they work with at the urban schools. Unfortunately, often there was a tension between what I wanted to achieve in terms of exposure to these social justice topics and then acting upon them, on the one hand, and a passive, sometimes disagreeing, desire to just fulfill the American diversity credit by this course, on the other.

I felt external pressure to bend to the demands of my students, due to my tenure evaluation requirements. I remember the level of internal conflict I had when decreasing the readings and moving from peer-reviewed articles to chapters. It was difficult as it meant content on large topics of social justice was limited or omitted.

6.4   *The Impact of Student Evaluations on the Tenure Review Process*

My teaching evaluations would be looked at closely for my promotion and tenure review, which was coming up soon, and I knew these evaluations would count as this was the predominant course that I was responsible for teaching. I was the only instructor in our department teaching three sections of this Multicultural course to approximately 90 students in the first semester, and in the second semester I taught the same Multicultural course to another 120 students.

I agree with Russell (2002) that official course evaluations have an underlying assumption "that all teaching is telling and that each teacher stands alone in the assessment of teaching." In addition, I think standing alone in the assessment is problematic, especially when teaching is seen as a relational event. Fitzgerald et al.'s (2002) articulation of a problem with course evaluations is closer to what I think: "we all are at a disadvantage when students respond to an instrument developed for linear teaching ('teaching as telling') but are participating in classrooms developed for interactive teaching" (p. 208). The interactive teaching in the Multiculturalism course is essential to consider when a lot of course content is relearned through activities done in class such as Four Corners, debates, surveys, and listening to podcasts. Thus, when students do not openly engage in these activities by sharing multiple perspectives, thinking outside of their own perspective, and being ready to reconstruct their views and values on contentious topics, then the teaching becomes one-sided and ineffective.

I agree with Fitzgerald et al. (2002) that

> [m]any of the items [on the course evaluation] are consistent with a teacher-directed pedagogy and linear information processing model of learning … This narrow representation of education limits our vision of what "good" education might be, and privileges a particular mode of learning. (pp. 213–214)

In addition to the limitation on what constitutes good education or good teaching and the responsibility of being the only instructor in the department that taught this course, there is no space on these evaluations to consider the context of the subject matter being taught. I contend that the more contentious and personal the course content is, the more challenging it becomes not only to teach but to evaluate fairly, given that self-growth and learning that is directed to go beyond one's comfort zone is not always a welcomed approach by students. And when it comes to questions about the instructor on the course evaluation, there is no space to share that the positionalities of the instructor and the student are different, which leaves a gap as to why a student feels uncomfortable with the instructor and the content. These particular concerns around the course evaluation are especially pertinent as they impact the career trajectory of racially marginalized faculty members who are put in the position of teaching such challenging course material with very limited support, if any.

When the course ended and the course evaluation summaries became available, I found out, unsurprisingly, that students did not feel very comfortable in my class. There were no reasons provided why they felt uncomfortable as the relevant item was a quantitative scale-based survey question (i.e., "I felt comfortable asking questions and/or expressing opinions"), but the average was 4–4.5 on a scale out of 6. This score was lower than scores I experienced in Canada and was the one result that brought the average of my course evaluations down. As an educator who always strives to do my best, I was unsure how to make sense of this level of "discomfort"; my current reflections lead me to believe it had to do with my positionality and this course content. I also found out that no other current faculty in the department ever asked to teach or ever taught this course, only sessional instructors had taught it, so I found myself alone in this particular situation.

Thus, with reference to my course evaluations, the statement that troubled me the most was "I felt comfortable asking questions and/or expressing opinions" as it did not account for the context of the course, the political intensity, students' lived experiences, and my positionality. And if wanted to understand what this statement meant for my particular course and me, I had no one I could speak to that could relate to how the following pieces created such challenges in my teaching: my positionality, American politics, the difference in lived experiences between my students and myself, the contentious course content, the lack of students' interest in social justice and multiculturalism, and course evaluations. Thus, retrospectively, I do not think teaching evaluations can accurately capture all the work that goes on in teaching such a controversial course nor the complexity of classroom dynamics, especially when the instructor is a racialized person. In other words, as it is quoted in Fitzgerald et al. (2002):

> [t]eachers have every right to be demoralized by such a simplistic approach [in course evaluations] – the nuances of teaching cannot possibly be captured this way. No uniform set of questions will apply with equal force to the many varieties in which good teaching comes … There is only one honest way to evaluate the many varieties of good teaching with the subtlety required: it is called being there. We must observe each other teach, at least occasionally – and we must spend more time talking to each other about teaching. (Palmer, 1998, p. 143 as cited in Fitzgerald et al., 2002, p. 216)

In light of this, I recommend having peer evaluations done by colleagues observing the classroom. Moreover, I recommend that the colleague doing the teaching review would engage in a discussion with the instructor before and after the observed class, and that the instructor will have an opportunity to explain about the particular context of their teaching. Thus, the challenges around positionality, teaching content, student interaction and creating safe spaces to speak can be heard from the instructor's position. In addition, I would recommend that the questions in a course evaluation are revised to offer students an opportunity to self-reflect on their own positionality and how that impacts their evaluation of the course and the instructor in additional to standard course evaluation questions.

By reflecting on my experience teaching in Wisconsin, with a focus on the contents of my course, teaching practice, positionality, experiences with students and faculty, and course evaluations, I conclude that each of these elements is essential to understanding my experiences. In one of my early correspondences with Dr. Kitchen I conveyed this sentiment and contemplated on the responsibilities involved in ensuring that students in the teacher education program leave my class as ethically and equity minded teachers. On this matter, he had a thoughtful and sincere advice:

> My advice is to keep up your efforts and not to be discouraged by minimizing and resistance. But don't force them to reconcile contradictions yet. Let the ideas be the sand in the oyster that may produce the occasional pearl. And be pleased that you are advancing their thinking, even though you will never be satisfied that they have moved far enough forward. I take some solace in the thought that a conservative teacher candidate might as a teacher be more understanding of the challenges faced by minority students and might take steps to make them more welcome, even if they cannot fully embrace diversity. (Letter correspondence from Julian Kitchen, October 8, 2018)

Although I think Dr. Kitchen has a point in acknowledging where individual students may be and how far we as educators can carry them in their equity mindfulness trajectory, I also believe it is important to keep expectations high. By keeping expectations high, I argue that educators need to continue to push students past their spaces of comfort and teach to the notion that in discomfort there lies growth. When class discussion is provocative, challenging and uncomfortable, while ensuring no person is being bullied or shut down, it can have a greater impact that can bring about a greater transformation compared to a situation where comfort is the main priority. I am thankful to have had about twelve students out of the 390 students who wrote me a few lines of sincere gratitude in emails and cards about my classes over the two years teaching in Wisconsin. In their sentiments many of them conveyed that my classes pushed their levels of comfort and thinking to a place that at first they did not like, but in the end were thankful for, as it made them understand issues of equity and the importance of responding to them. Learning about the impact these few students felt makes me proud as I know they have developed the practice and mindset of holding themselves and others accountable to daily inclusive and equitable practices and behaviors, which I hope will have a lasting impact.

7 Conclusion

I share Myers' (2002) view on self-study being a form of self-analysis that leads to improving institutions. This concept of improving institutions links back and supports my four discussion themes.

The fourth theme of the impact of student evaluations is well addressed by Fitzgerald et al. (2002) who stated, "until the institutional structure gets transformed, we are cycling through these tensions for accountability (tenure file, student assessments, grading) as individuals" (p. 219) instead of examining factors such as the positionality of the educator, course content, political environment, power politics, how course evaluations are structured and are used in the tenure process.

The third theme of acknowledging students' lived experiences in classroom spaces requires educators to be reflective and analyze their own teaching and learning process in order to improve students' learning. However, as mentioned previously, if teaching is a relational activity then there needs to be an opportunity to hear and learn the perspective of the educator and the student. This, in turn, improves the quality of education being offered in the institution.

The second theme on the impact of Trump's political messages on my course is essential given that politics are ever present in education. Given the strong and impactful exclusionary messages and actions President Trump has shared with the American people on immigration, it is essential that educational institutions carefully scrutinize these political influences. If educational institutions wish to be inclusive spaces for all and aim for progressive thinking then politics must be examined critically by students.

Lastly, with respect to the first theme of positionality, it is important to note that racialized instructors have a different perspective to offer as their bodies are markers of identification that are often stereotyped and their roles in the academy are seen as an exception and not the norm. In other words, positionality is a central and often highly influential variable for racialized instructors, which impacts their work and the way they reflect on their teaching experiences.

I am now back in Canada since September 2019. I teach classes that are composed of 90% international students and I hear their enthusiasm to learn in Canada while sharing insightful narratives from their respective countries. Having insight on the contributions international students can offer in postsecondary institutions compels me to recommend to institutions around the world that it is important to learn with first-hand knowledge what assets potential immigrants bring and how educators benefit from an inclusive classroom. I am glad and thankful to know that the political climate in Canada is more inviting and accepting of immigrants. As for my positionality and course evaluations, it is yet to be seen how international students evaluate my teaching abilities. Every geographical and political context is important to acknowledge as it impacts both student's and teacher's positionality, especially in an active participation-based class that discusses contentious equity issues. The contextual variables and positionality factors are essential as they heavily influence teaching and learning practice.

Acknowledgements

A special thank you to Dr. Julian Kitchen and Dr. Doron Yosef-Hassidim for closely reviewing earlier drafts of this chapter.

References

Banks, J. A. (2010). Approaches to multicultural curriculum reform. *Multicultural Education: Issues and Perspectives, 7*, 233–256.

Bullough, R. V., Jr., & Pinnegar, S. (2001). Guidelines for quality in autobiographical forms of self-study research. *Educational Researcher, 30*(3), 13–21.

Fitzgerald, L. M., Farstad, J. E., & Deemer, D. (2002). What gets "mythed" in student evaluations of their teacher education professors? In J. Loughran & T. Russell (Eds.), *Improving teacher education practice through self-study* (pp. 208–221). Routledge.

Freire, P. (1970). *Pedagogy of the oppressed*. Continuum.

Immigration policy of Donald Trump. (2021, April 30). In *Wikipedia*. https://en.wikipedia.org/wiki/Immigration_policy_of_Donald_Trump

Kincheloe, J. L. (2008). *Critical pedagogy primer* (2nd ed.). Peter Lang.

Kitchen, J. (2005). Looking backwards, moving forward: Understanding my narrative as a teacher educator. *Studying Teacher Education, 1*(1), 17–30.

Kitchen, J. (in press). Improving teacher education through the self-study of practice. In R. Tierney, F. Rizvi, K. Ercikan, & G. Smith (Eds.), *International encyclopedia of education* (4th ed.). Elsevier.

Loughran, J. (2002). Understanding self-study of teacher education practices. In J. Loughran & T. Russell (Eds.), *Improving teacher education practices through self-study* (pp. 239–248). Routledge Falmer.

McIntosh, P. (1990). Unpacking the knapsack of white privilege. *Independent School, 49*(2), 31–36.

Mishler, E. (1990). Validation in inquiry-guided research: The role of exemplars in narrative studies. *Harvard Education Review, 60,* 415–442.

Myers, C. B. (2002). Can self-study challenge the belief that telling, showing, and guided practice constitute adequate teacher education? In J. Loughran & T. Russell (Eds.), *Improving teacher education practice through self-study* (pp. 130–142). Routledge.

Palmer, P. J. (1998). *The courage to teach: Exploring the inner landscape of a teacher's life.* Jossey-Bass.

Pew Research Center. (2019, May 17). *Key facts about US immigration policies and proposed changes.* Retrieved May 14, 2021, from https://www.pewresearch.org/fact-tank/2019/05/17/key-facts-about-u-s-immigration-policies-and-proposed-changes

Project Implicit. (n.d.). *Implicit association test.* Retrieved May 14, 2021, from https://implicit.harvard.edu/implicit/takeatest.html

Russell, T. (2002). Can self-study improve teacher education? In J. Loughran & T. Russell (Eds.), *Improving teacher education practice through self-study* (pp. 3–9). Routledge.

Schön, D. (1983). *The reflective practitioner: How professionals think in action.* Basic Books.

Schuck, S., & Russell, T. (2005). Self-study, critical friendship, and the complexities of teacher education. *Studying Teacher Education, 1*(2), 107–121. https://doi.org/10.1080/17425960500288291

CHAPTER 11

Navigating Shifting Waters

Reflections from a Critical Anti-Racist Teacher Educator

Leanne Taylor

1   Introduction

Teaching is both a process of learning and unlearning. Teaching for social justice and equity is "socially, culturally, and politically constructed," "complex" and "changing" (Lee, 2011, p. 4). Social justice practice can also be "challenging, emotionally taxing, and at times risky" (Taylor & Diamond, 2020, p. 4). To teach for social justice is to reshape policies and engage pedagogies that will equip students, particularly those underserved, with the knowledge, tools and learning opportunities necessary to transform society (Chubbuck & Zembylas, 2008, p. 274). But effective socially just practice recognizes that teaching is also about storytelling: we are both the tellers of stories and the characters within those stories (Connelly & Clandinin, 1990; Taylor & Diamond, 2020).

As a Black, multiracial teacher educator, associate professor, and mother I have been thinking about and living issues related to equity and social justice education for some time. I am an insider in a teacher education program (Cochran-Smith & Villegas, 2015), and therefore familiar with (and have experienced) many of the challenges, pitfalls and opportunities involved in social justice-focused teacher education. However, as a reflective and responsive practitioner, I am also aware (and take into account) my different identities and note that these positions are neither static nor simplistic. I can speak to my experiences of racism but also to how I have benefited from colorist and social class privilege (Tilley & Taylor, 2013). Bell et al. (2016) reminded us that "our memberships in racial or ethnic groups, class status, gender identity, and categories of age are linked and impact how we show up in the classroom and how students see and interact with us" from the moment we connect (p. 399). As we prepare teachers to engage in social justice practices, we are most effective when we understand that who we are informs our approaches to teaching and shapes our interactions with students (Tilley & Taylor, 2013).

Richard Milner (2007) once asked:

> What was it that I, as an African American male educator, brought into the learning environment of my college classroom that could enable or stifle the students' (preservice teachers) learning about race and racism in education? That is, how did my racialized experiences influence my curriculum development and teaching? (p. 585)

Like Milner and hooks (1989), I consider how teaching strategies get lived out differently depending on a host of factors connected to my gendered and racialized location (Taylor & Diamond, 2020). In this chapter, I share stories of how I navigate the messy and often shifting waters of resistance, emotions, and White dominance in the teacher education classroom. It is my hope that this self-study can help teacher educators reconceptualize their practice and enhance their understanding of possible approaches to address resistance and tensions involved when teaching against race and racism in teacher education contexts.

2 Conceptual and Theoretical Framework: Critical Race Theory, Self-Study and Counterstory

My pedagogy is grounded in critical theoretical perspectives that shed light on how institutional and epistemological racism can affect teacher educators' experiences in the profession. These perspectives start from the position that classrooms are cultural and political sites that often reproduce power hierarchies. Critical theories of race and racism offer guidance on not only how to be a better anti-racist educator, but are, as Milner (2007) and others argued, useful tools to unearth and critique the racism embedded in teacher education policies, practices, and research.

The following five central tenets comprise a critical race theory (CRT) perspective (James, 2021; Milner & Laughter, 2015; Solorzano & Yosso, 2001):

1. Race and racism are central to critical analysis, although understood to intersect with other forms of oppression such as gender and class.
2. Challenging dominant perspectives and ideology, including White privilege, neutrality, meritocracy, colorblindness and equal opportunity is essential, as these perspectives serve to uphold power relations, police boundaries, and position non-White people as other.
3. Educational institutions are contradictory spaces that carry the potential to both oppress and emancipate. A commitment to social justice therefore

must seek to actively eliminate racism, sexism and poverty and also empower subordinated groups.
4. The centering of experiential knowledge recognizes and validates the knowledge of people of color, often through storytelling and other types of narrative. CRT exposes deficit perspectives and builds on the strengths of racialized groups.
5. Its interdisciplinary and transdisciplinary perspective draws connections across fields of study (sociology, history, law, education, etc.) and analyzes race in both historical and contemporary contexts.

I draw on CRT in an effort to reflect on my practice and experiences within teacher education as a racialized teacher educator. This perspective, and those of other racialized faculty, can help shed light on the ongoing and shifting tensions present within the teaching profession. It also recognizes that critical and anti-racist teaching is a "necessary disruption" to the status quo (Ohito, 2019, p. 3). Racialized teacher educators must navigate racism across micro and systemic levels, and in covert and overt forms of exclusion and hostility found in complex expressions of resistance, hate, and violence (Henry & Tator, 2009; Henry et al., 2017; Wing-Sue, 2010). On the other hand, the same racialized faculty are increasingly called upon to share their anti-racist knowledge, expertise, resources, and recommendations. Moreover, CRT keeps central the reality that racism persists systemically and structurally, despite individual intent or action (James, 2021). When we understand critically how antiracist teaching functions (and the context in which we operate), we are better able to understand:

> *how* those of us who identify as antiracist pedagogues teach (i.e., pedagogies, disposition), as well as *what* we teach (e.g., artifacts, texts), *why* we teach (e.g., motivations, ideological commitments), and *who* we teach. (Ohito, 2019, p. 3)

In addition to these four factors, Ohito (2019) highlights that we must also be tuned into how "*who we are*" informs the process of teaching (p. 3). I am interested here in what I bring to the classroom as a Black, multiracial teacher educator and how that informs how I think about and address issues of race and racism in teaching. This perspective highlights how institutional and epistemological racism can affect teacher educators' experiences in the profession.

2.1   *Self-Study as Counter-Story*

To study the self is not an easy challenge. (Milner, 2007, p. 586)

As Dinkelman (2000) explained, self-study is useful for helping teacher educators understand "something important about [their] practice that [they] did not know before, something [they] only came to know about as a result of self-study" (p. 7). In the tradition of critical race theory (Ladson-Billings & Tate, 1995; Yosso, 2005), I engage in self-study as a form of counter-storytelling. Counter-storytelling, as Solorzano and Yosso (2002) wrote, involves "telling the stories of those people whose experiences are not often told" (p. 32). The emphasis on storytelling challenges the storyteller to present an honest depiction of her experience and asks the listener to consider the assumptions and perspectives informing their own understandings (Hannon, 2020). The counter-story is useful for "exposing, analyzing, and challenging the majoritarian stories of racial privilege" and can "shatter complacency, challenge the dominant discourse on race, and further the struggle for racial reform." However, stories are not only responses to dominant narratives; they also help "strengthen traditions of social, political, and cultural survival and resistance" (p. 32). By focusing on my story, I consider my position as both teller and listener and ask: "To what extent is the non-White teacher educator transformed through anti-racism?" (Umangay, 2019, p. 288).

In this self-study, I build on my personal observations, struggles, successes, and emotions as I reflect on my experiences as a Black, multiracial teacher educator seeking to challenge forms of oppression in my teacher education classrooms. The literature on Black teachers and teacher educators draws attention to how teachers' racial and cultural identity and experiences inform their work (Brown, 2004; hooks, 1989; Maloney, 2017). Racialized teachers bring to the classroom pedagogical approaches that may differ from their White colleagues.

> Black teachers, similar to all teachers, are texts themselves – they are a form of the curriculum; however, these teachers' pages are inundated with life experiences and histories of racism, sexism, and oppression, along with those of strength, perseverance, and success. Consequently, these teachers' texts are rich and empowering – they have the potential to help students better understand the world … and some of the complexities of race and racism, for example, in meaningful ways. (Milner, 2007, p. 590)

Although racialized teachers can bring their critique and lens to their teaching, they can also be "ridiculed for being too radical or for not being 'team players'" and can feel "isolated because he or she offered a counterstory or counternarrative … to the pervasive discourses and views of their mostly White colleagues" (Milner, 2007, p. 590). These combined experiences inevitably influence how racialized teachers teach and engage with their students. By considering "whose stories are privileged in educational contexts and whose stories are distorted and silenced" (Solorzano & Yosso, 2002, p. 36), I attempt to add to the conversation about social justice teaching.

To prepare my self-study, I drew primarily from experiences teaching undergraduate, graduate and teacher education courses. I reference personal reflection journals from my teaching over the years and draw on various articles and chapters I have written on the subject (e.g., Kitchen & Taylor, 2020; Taylor, 2000, 2017; Taylor & Tilley, 2013; Tilley & Taylor, 2013). I also consider academic presentations and conversations with racialized students and various colleagues. In what follows, I outline some of the central tensions I have observed in my teaching practice and share my approaches and considerations about teaching to highlight what has worked, which challenges remain, and how I seek to address difficulties.

3   Placing Tensions in Context

The recent rise of the Black Lives Matter movement and other social justice protests has pushed many educators to re-evaluate their pedagogy, curricula, and positionality so that they might better account for the needs of racialized students in their classrooms. The sales spike in critical, anti-racism literature (reported by Forbes as increasing 6,800% in the months following George Floyd's murder) has prompted increased attention to social justice practice (McEvoy, 2020). Despite these shifts, critical scholars understand that "all is [still] not well with teacher education" (Brown, 2013, p. 10). The various challenges and tensions that come with teaching for social justice in particular are well documented (Adams & Bell, 2016; Kitchen & Taylor, 2020). And, as George Lipsitz (2019) pointed out, our anti-racism victories are often not permanent as we face a resurgence of different expressions of racism.

> radical racial justice movements face the enormous challenge of fighting the resurgence of overt forms of racism in the neo-fascist era of Trump, *and* the covert forms embedded in neoliberal institutional policies that endorse sanitized and de-radicalized forms of antiracism, diversity, multiculturalism, and colorblindness. (Blake & Ioanide, 2019, p. 27)

The less visible neoliberal agenda positions students as consumers of higher education and decries pedagogical approaches that can cause discomfort

(Dutta et al., 2016). In the context of teacher education, pre-service teachers, most of whom are White, middle-class, straight women (Sleeter, 2018) "come to their teacher education programs lacking experiential or content knowledge about culture, difference and inequality in both societal and school-based contexts" (Brown, 2013, p. 10). These gaps "reflect the culturally monolithic experiences that characterize the lives of many White students, [and] also illustrate the limited content knowledge that students acquire about sociocultural knowledge in their K-12 schooling" (Brown, 2012, p. 10). Discourses of race and racism are hardly fading, but persist differently. Teachers, administrators, parents, and students all "co-create the worlds of others based on physical appearance" (Taylor, 2017, p. 185). Racial liberalism can assert a "ubiquitous, globalizing, sanitizing narrative about race" (Mahtani, 2014, p. 136).

As I reflect on this contemporary historical moment of anti-racism struggle amidst post-racial discourses, I find myself asking new and renewed questions about my practice. In the following sections, I consider three broad challenges and tensions I face and reflect on how I have adapted my teaching practice and employed strategies to work through this shifting terrain of critical anti-racism education: (a) student resistance and defensiveness; (b) emotional intensity; and (c) meeting racialized students' needs. There are many other challenges teacher educators endure. My goal in this chapter is to explore how I have attempted to re-think my practice, approach, and strategies and see differently what works and what I can be doing better. The self-study has also helped me ground my perspectives, feelings, and challenges that surface when teaching social justice content.

4 Navigating Student Resistance and Defensiveness

One of the guarantees of social justice teaching is that it will, at some point, generate discomfort. In fact, the process of unlearning necessitates some form of conflict and cognitive dissonance as students' previous knowledge and assumptions are challenged (Gorski, 2009). Conflict, of course, is not always negative, nor should it always be avoided – it can also be a sign of growth and the beginning of critical awareness. While our goal should not be to create unnecessary discomfort in the classroom, nor "allow people in privileged positions to hijack a conversation," we must prepare for and be willing to welcome its inevitable arrival and various faces (Gorski, 2009, p. 55). Doing so requires an understanding of how power circulates in the room. As a critical educator, I recognize that there is power in the classroom and that power "is never unidimensional" (Giroux, 1983). On one level, I have power as a professor: I assign grades, set the content, direct discussions, can write recommendations for jobs and/or graduate study, have a stable income, and experience relative job security. On the other hand, my students have some power to challenge my authority: they can file complaints with the department chair or dean, or provide poor course evaluations. But when addressing racism in class, these power relations often take on a different shape. Racialized faculty may face strong resistance from White students who do not accept the existence of systemic racism (Han, 2013). Though troubling, this resistance is not surprising – students' rootedness in liberal discourses of multiculturalism, celebratory understandings of difference, and minimal exposure to social justice related courses contribute to their feelings of discomfort.

My experiences as a critical race educator have led me to reflect on the ways resistance to critical discussions of racism find varied forms of expression in my classroom. In nearly every class I teach, the majority of students begin the course reluctant in some way to name their privileged White locations and identities (even in exercises designed to support them in doing so). Although many are sincere in their desire to learn more, they often claim that they fear sounding or appearing racist and struggle to understand racism as systemic and structural. Most begin with (and some hold on to) neutral, celebratory expressions of diversity, colorblindness and meritocracy and resist "content that challenges [their] understanding of the dominant stories of Canadian history" (Dion, 2007, p. 331). Students tend to cite exceptional achievements of prominent Black and Indigenous figures who have achieved success as evidence of a post-racist society. Some celebrate interracial mixture and the rise of multiracial families and identities. This "seductive nature of 'positive stereotyping' masks the racism and structural inequity that exist in society, and as such, is often quite harmful" (James, 2012, p. 479). Celebratory discourses can also inflict harm on dark-skinned bodies as a focus on multiracial people as symbols of progress "ensures that the specific histories of black bodies are elided and erased" (Mahtani, 2014, p. 44; Taylor, 2017).

At various points in my teaching career, students have expressed their frustrations in person and sometimes on course evaluations, claiming that the content is too difficult or unsettling. Others "willfully ignore" (Sensoy & DiAngelo, 2017) research and course content about racism and have questioned readings and lectures by either criticizing the validity of research or demanding more statistics and further evidence as proof of racism. My focus on critique in my courses, including critical theory, is sometimes (mis)read as permission for students to challenge (or criticize) incidents of racism as inaccurate, exaggerated or outdated. Other forms of resistance present as requests to move past "the 'big questions' toward concrete teaching tools and practical solutions" (Marom, 2017, p. 173).

In most of my courses, students are required to write critical reflective papers on the readings. They are asked to provide brief summaries of the articles and then offer their thoughts on what they are working through, thinking about, or what they feel they still need to learn. These responses give me an opportunity to engage with students and provide one-on-one feedback. I typically enjoy reading these responses and appreciate the effort and time most students put into crafting reflective thoughts grounded in course readings as they work to improve their understanding and self-awareness about oppression and privilege. In most cases, students are quite open in their comments and are trying to learn and do better. However, I at times find myself suspicious about student responses and consider how these spaces of reflection can also be places that reinforce racism. Webb (2001) suggested,

> reflection and reflective teaching are not sufficient methods, by themselves, for teachers to examine their ideas of teaching because reflection privileges the "epistemology of the individual" ... That is, reflection as a process of thinking alone does not account for the beliefs and biases that guide the thinking in the first place ... teachers' "mainstream academic knowledge" and "personal/cultural knowledge," ... can be negatively affected by reflection if the process of reflection does not simultaneously interrogate teachers' beliefs about racial and ethnic minorities. (p. 246)

Written responses can expose the privilege of Whiteness and create the option to disengage from challenging content. In courses that address a broad range of social justice issues, including ableism, classism, and heterosexism, students can sometimes easily opt out of deep discussions of racism. I am also aware that in reflections, students can choose to be silent on certain issues, tell me what they think I want to hear, and go out into the world with power restored (see Milner, 2007, p. 601).

In Taylor and Tilley (2013) I wrote of a White student who, in her reflection, denied claims of racism articulated by a racialized author in a reading and claimed that the real problem was poor communication. "The student's focus on improving communication as the way to address structural racism emphasizes individual acts and reflects liberal support of individualism – it does not address power relations and privilege and how they operate in contexts of difference" (Taylor & Tilley, 2013, p. 76). Although I provide feedback intended to encourage deeper connections, if students do not "engage with controversial topics education is reduced to measurable knowledge in a realm of political correctness" (Marom, 2017, p. 173).

In this contemporary moment of anti-racist and Indigenous activism, including the Black Lives Matter movement, decolonization, and reconciliation the tone of the classroom seems visibly different. This year I witnessed several new responses to difficult material. In class presentations, White students began including trigger warnings (warnings that material may cause distress) in their seminar presentations as well as in their reflection papers when addressing examples of racism, residential schools, and other topics related to oppression (Sanson et al., 2019). The examples and content my students were introducing were no more challenging than material covered in my past courses; in fact, I would argue they were quite general and key content in any social justice course. Nevertheless, students included trigger warnings in an attempt to create what they felt were safe classroom spaces. During a seminar presentation, I jotted the following on a post-it note next to my computer: "*Safety for whom?*" Then, I wrote the following reflection after class:

> Where are these trigger warnings coming from? Is this a new norm? Should I make a comment in class about when it is appropriate to use trigger warnings? How will students respond? How do I suggest that trigger warnings may not always be necessary without dismissing the traumatic responses one might legitimately have? I am concerned that these warnings might shut down some important conversation that can push students' learning in the class. Am I now expected to provide trigger warnings to talk about racism with White students? Will this leave the impression that teacher candidates should send home warning letters to parents in order to cover difficult topics (e.g., residential schools) that are clearly outlined in the curriculum. Do I need to provide "trigger warnings to talk about my experience"? (Reflection, February 11, 2021)

I recognize that trigger warnings have "long served as activist tools for recognizing [marginalized] people's lived experiences in social space" (Reed, 2019, p. 130). They have also been used to provide people with a history of trauma with a warning that material or graphic images may trigger a post-traumatic stress reaction, providing the option to avoid material or regulate emotions (Sanson et al., 2019). My concern is how these warnings have come to be expected, normalized and perhaps co-opted in classroom contexts in ways that hide (and thereby reinforce) relations of power and structural inequities. This to me suggests that expressions of resistance have shifted and are shifting in my practice. The trigger warnings in my class were not framed with the goal to protect the traumatized from further harm, but to protect sensitive students who may be shocked or horrified by powerful examples of racism.

Reed (2019) wrote that "for many students who experience the daily impact of racism, sexism, homophobia, transphobia, and endemic sexual violence on college campuses, the university never was a trauma-free space" (p. 135). However, "The co-opted language of trauma and safety protects the vested interests of white anxiety and their centrality in the universe and university" (p. 136). This tension illuminates how I "must contend with the contradictions of a neoliberal university that at once vilifies radical thought and cashes in on the market value of a sanitized antiracism divorced from praxis – precisely by attempting to replace discussions of institutional racism with respect for so-called 'difference'" (Reed, 2019, p. 136).

I am not suggesting we ignore the very real potential for our actions and content to re-traumatize minoritized students in our class. My question is: how do trigger warnings and other actions grounded in language of safety double as an excuse to disengage, avoid, and resist conversations that are necessary and required in social justice teaching and learning? I am aware of calls to move beyond "the rhetoric of classroom safety typical of liberal individualism" (Dutta et al., 2016, p. 345). As Marom (2017) wrote "an extreme form of PC has become a silencing mechanism and a barrier for critical engagement, as seen in the many current disputes around 'microaggressions,' 'safe spaces,' and 'trigger warnings' in institutions of higher education" (p. 174). While I appreciate many students do not wish to re-marginalize students and I understand most are consciously trying not to offend or be culturally irresponsible, the side effect can be an absence of controversial discussions that would transform and enhance learning.

4.1   My Approach

When faced with any form of resistance, I remind myself in each course that my goal and purpose is to teach for critical consciousness. My social justice teaching involves "challenging pedagogical approaches in classrooms that: support treating all students the same, advocate 'equality over equity,' ignore differences, avoid conflict, and inevitably resist exploring knowledge assumed useful to only a few" (Taylor & Tilley, 2013, p. 81). Liberal and neoliberal approaches to schooling restrict the necessary work involved in productive and transformative education. Ultimately, my goal is to help teacher candidates do more than just feel more comfortable teaching a diverse group of students. I want them to also critique, challenge, and improve the system. As Freire and others contend, being a critically conscious educator requires "profound love, humility, faith, and trust to enter into dialogue *with* their students to disrupt inequity" (Kohli et al., 2019, p. 25). Critical consciousness and equity-focused thinking and engagement does not happen through information-transfer but through an ongoing continual and evolving engagement. So, I have come to play the long game. As Kohli et al. (2019) put it, critical consciousness "must be a fundamental part to their ways of understanding and being in the world" and "must involve cultivating teachers with capacities to recognize, interrogate, and transform injustice" (p. 25). This informs how and what I teach and how I help move students through resistance. The focus then must be on building this recognition of injustice and building capacity to act.

I anticipate resistance and begin each course letting students know that we will be challenging our assumptions and views. I also keep content focused on structural concepts to encourage students to move beyond their deep-rooted opinions, engage in intellectual humility, and think critically through facts (Sensoy & DiAngelo, 2017). When students understand the underlying structures of inequity, they are more easily able to move past their guilt and fear. In my practice, I seek to challenge tendencies to engage in "oppression Olympics" – discussions that focus on hierarchies of oppression or reinforce binaries. I do this by intervening in discussions and in critical reflections and assignments that help students make connections.

For example, when students push back against readings and content and question its relevance to their teaching, I reassure them that we will fill their toolbox with teaching tools in time – but that until we understand clearly what the problem is, we can never know for sure which tools are best suited for the job. Put differently, a surface understanding of the problem will only leave us with surface solutions – some of which can do more damage than good when taken to classroom contexts. As I wrote in Kitchen and Taylor (2020), this approach is grounded in an understanding of the importance of threshold concepts. Threshold concepts are essential if students are to "progress toward bigger learning goals and understandings" and overcome "cognitive bottlenecks" in their learning (Gorski et al., 2013, p. 1). In social justice teacher education, key threshold concepts include, among others, privilege, discrimination, and the main "isms." The most effective educators with social justice goals in mind draw on pedagogies that move students across the threshold. They recognize that "once an individual ... *crosses* a cognitive threshold, the likelihood of reverting to previous ways of knowing is extremely slim" (Gorski et al., 2013, p. 5).

In my teaching, I encourage students to be patient as they build their structural understanding of concepts and issues so that they will be armed with tools that will do the best job. I often ask students to consider theory as a guide to help them decide if they should use a hammer, wrench or a hacksaw to solve a problem. When I frame theory in this way (and the importance of critical theory in particular), students are more open to settling into the process and thinking deeply about the ideas and issues.

How one engages in the teacher education classroom is informed by their positionality (Tilley & Taylor, 2013). I try to call students in through story and experience. I include my personal narratives, observations, challenges and missteps to shed light on the complexities of race and racism as lived. I try to present myself in a way that encourages open dialogue and generates meaningful questions (even when I know those questions might be difficult to process for me). For example, I have shared my published articles detailing some of my multiracial experiences in order to complicate understandings of racial identity and to draw attention to intersectionality (Taylor, 2000). In other cases, I offer examples of racism by referring to my daughter's experiences. I have shared at various times how at age five my daughter told me she wished to change her skin color, hair, and eye color in response to a racist remark from a child at school. I follow up with details on how I responded to her and to her teachers the next day. I ask students how they might approach the situation in their classrooms. These stories not only illustrate where racism exists and how it gets expressed in schools, but open opportunities to reflect on how we might respond when they do. I also share stories to point out my own blind spots. As a multiracial woman whose Blackness can be visible and invisible depending on context (Taylor, 2000; Tilley & Taylor, 2013) I demonstrate the complexities of racism by highlighting the ways bodies can be privileged, celebrated, exoticized and demonized.

I am aware of the risks that come with personal sharing in class. Some students have responded with expressions of pity and concern for my well-being that can be uncomfortable. I tend not to share personal stories until I have built rapport with students. Most generally respond well and thank me for sharing stories that make the course material relatable. My hope is that they will see my willingness to be vulnerable as an invitation to do the same. I also expose parts of my world so that other racialized students do not feel that they must. But I do not overvalue my experience as a sacred text – I stress that racism is not just individual actions. We cannot dismiss these incidents as "one-offs" or from "bad seeds." I use them as opportunities to discuss how they reflect larger processes that are often rendered invisible.

To address my earlier concerns about reflection (Webb, 2001) I use reflective exercises as a "tool for critical inquiry and a way to connect theory and practice" (Marom, 2017, p. 182). In reflection papers, I push students to not merely dump feelings but to ask more meaningful questions that help them consider the relationship between their positionality and their observations. I ask students to refer back to readings and make connections to concepts.

Case studies have also been useful to help students enter into difficult conversations, weigh various perspectives, and move through bottlenecks. Students are brought right into the problem and collectively engage in discussion about the inequity, tensions, barriers, emotional responses, and solutions or strategies (short term and long term). In order to keep the critical edge, I introduce case studies through a critical anti-racist and equity literacy lens (Gorski & Pothini, 2018). Equity literacy is an approach that has been useful to guide me through the difficult conversations. I find this approach, since using it, has helped move students through the bottleneck and come to not only recognize but also discover how they can redress racial (and other) inequities in their practice. When students engage from this perspective, they are better able to zero in on the problem and then consider how they can move toward change. The approach moves students beyond surface understandings of culture by keeping equity and injustice central in the conversation (Gorski & Swalwell, 2015). Students are pushed to interrogate their assumptions and expose blind spots but employing an equity literacy lens and developing their ability to recognize subtle expressions of discrimination, inequity and bias; respond to inequities in thoughtful ways; redress inequities by considering not just interpersonal biases but also structural change; and cultivate and sustain approaches that are free of discrimination even when difficult (Gorski & Swalwell, 2015).

Ultimately, the goal to critical teaching cannot be to create happy environments: "an uncritical focus on achieving happiness and comfort in our classroom has its costs – distracting us from the important work of disrupting our classrooms as we try to move students to new understandings about sensitive issues and 'difficult knowledge'" (Taylor & Tilley, 2013, p. 81). However, I have found it is good practice to consider my tone, timing and choice of words when responding to students. Facilitation techniques should keep students engaged but not condone problematic comments such as "'all lives matter," "I don't see color – I'm color-blind" or "I don't understand why some people don't want us to say Merry Christmas in schools anymore." Tone is useful when providing written feedback as well. I draw guidance from other social justice educators such as Bell et al. (2016) who suggested responding in the following way: "*Thank you for sharing your perspective. That is a sentiment many people have. Throughout the class we'll be discussing why people believe that and the impact that approach may have on creating equity*" (p. 72, original emphasis). In other contexts, I ask students to explain more about why they hold a particular view ("can you tell me more about that?" or "can you explain what you mean?").

Such approaches allow the instructor to seek clarity on students' perspectives before responding. When I engage in discussions in this way, I am better positioned to correct misunderstandings, engage the class in deeper discussion, or decide whether it is appropriate to move on to different content. It also helps protect me from making unhelpful comments that may reflect my personal and emotional responses to racism. However, as I note in the next section, such emotional response is not always avoidable or problematic.

5   Balancing the Emotions of Teaching for Social Justice

"The interplay between justice and emotions is complicated," wrote Chubbuck and Zembylas (2008, p. 275). Social justice teaching is "bound up with the emotional lives of the individuals involved and the social and political circumstances in which those individuals and groups live and express their emotionality" (p. 276). Often the conversation centers on the emotions of novice teachers from dominant groups who wrestle with powerlessness or guilt associated with teaching for social justice (Dlamini, 2002). However, "among teachers of color, other emotions emerge, including anger, frustration, and discouragement over being marginalized and silenced in school discourse about unjust educational practices" (Chubbuck & Zembylas, 2008, p. 286).

The past few years have generated heightened and shifting emotions. Like many others, ongoing events of racist violence, hate speech, and political controversy have shaken, devastated, but also emboldened me. Hallander (2019) wrote, "emotions can contain educational possibilities because emotions, whether we want them or not, can *do* something" (p. 470). This raises two important questions for me as I reflect on my teaching practice: What do I want emotions to do in my classroom and what do I do with my emotions? My degree of comfort with emotions (mine and those of my students) will inform how comfortable I am addressing some concepts and expressing different ideas in class.

> It is much harder for someone who is directly targeted by oppression to have a dispassionate view. Acknowledging one's own feelings of outrage at injustices perpetuated on our group can help an instructor be more empathic and understanding of participants from other groups who react intensely to examples of injustice. (Bell et al., 2016, p. 408)

To move into spaces of discomfort and be vulnerable also requires consideration of the "structural conditions that constitute the pedagogical context"

(Dutta et al., 2016, p. 351). In the neoliberal university, my emotional responses push up against discourses of "effectiveness and efficiency" that depend on "predetermined standards and measurement of outcomes" (p. 351). Dutta et al. pointed out that "These shackles in higher education are neither new nor unique" (p. 351). Moreover, from the first day of class, teacher educators are "'marked' according to the students' constructed understandings of race and difference" (Tilley & Taylor, 2013, p. 415). Sarah Ahmed (2012) reminded us of the contradictions women of color scholars face:

> The woman of color isn't a real scholar; she is motivated by ideology: The woman of color is angry. She occupies the moral high ground. The woman of color declares war by pointing to the complicity of white feminists in imperialism. The woman of color is racist (and we hurt, too). The woman of color should be grateful, as she lives in our democracy. We have given her the right and the freedom to speak. The woman of color is the origin of terror, and she fails to recognize violence other than the violence of white against black. The exercising of this figure does more than make her work: *it is a defense against hearing her work*. (p. 162)

I consider Ahmed's comments in relation to my experiences teaching. I am aware that students may see me – a multiracial woman – and ask: "Does she have authority?", "Does she have experience to back up what she is saying?", "Will she push her agenda on us?" In an article I wrote with my White colleague, Susan Tilley, we noted how students treated us differently despite teaching the same content. Susan was often viewed as "objective," and "scholarly," while I was perceived as "bitter," "radical" and as pushing my political agenda (Tilley & Taylor, 2013, p. 417). I wrote the following reflection about students' responses to my feedback on their assignments that asked them to consider deeper connections to the material:

> When I try to get one student to complicate her social class analysis by also considering how it intersects with race and whiteness, she complains [in class] that I am trying to make her and the students in the class into social justice and anti-racist activists. She says that if that is my goal, then the word race should be in the title of the course. (p. 422)

Racism operates to ensure that when certain people expose problems, they can be constructed as *being* the problem (Ahmed, 2017). Feeling problematic can shift one's posture. Bell et al. (2016) reminded us that "social justice education is not only cognitive but also affective" (p. 407). Our academic and teacher training does not often prepare us to address the complex emotions we might feel when exploring issues of injustice or when interacting with students. I have come to recognize that how I personally deal with "emotional intensity" informs how I am able to manage emotions constructively in class (Bell et al., 2016, p. 408). I am aware of how my emotions can shape and inform my interactions with and responses to students. Several years after the previous experience, I wrote the following after teaching a teacher education class.

Today's class was difficult. I am struggling with an encounter I had after class. Three white male students asked to speak with me after class about a group assignment. I found myself alone in the room looking up at them – all close to a foot taller than me. They asked how they were supposed to create a lesson that addressed concepts of racial inequity when their teaching areas were physics and science. "I don't see how we can do this – it seems more appropriate for an English class." They even added, "I can see how this would be meaningful for you as someone in social justice, but what exactly are you expecting us to do here?" "Can we focus on something else instead that would be more useful for our teaching?" These questions are not new to me – it usually takes time for TCs in STEM to consider how a critical anti-racist and socially just approach can inform their teaching. But they usually come around and find opportunities. But this encounter feels different. *None of them could look me in the eye* – they seemed to look everywhere but "at" me. I felt so uncomfortable – hypervisible – so self-conscious in that moment. Do I feel unsafe? Not entirely – not in a physical sense. But I definitely feel more non-white and non-male than I have felt all term. What about me is so threatening that they won't look at me? Sometimes I wonder if I am imagining this – but I think I know better (Reflection, February 20, 2020).

In that encounter, my posture changed. I abandoned, briefly, the openness and warmth I had tried so hard to bring to the classroom all term. I became Professor Taylor and referred them to several articles and resources – including many we had read already in the course – that provide examples of teaching ideas and strategies they could employ in their subject areas. Then I found myself asking them: "'Why do you think you might be resisting the assignment?" "Are you saying kids in physics and science are protected from experiencing racism in your classroom?" "Are you suggesting that the content you are choosing to teach effectively reflects students' diverse experiences?" "Are you saying that teachers do not bring biases and assumptions about student capabilities to their classroom?"

The exchange felt like a power battle. In that moment, I did not wish to be particularly thoughtful, encouraging, or supportive. It did not help that the content for that class had included discussion and research about institutional racism, educational streaming, and the disproportionate representation of different groups in particular fields of study and in higher education. This was not the first time I was in this position and it will not be the last. But it was a reminder of how racialized teacher educators can sometimes find themselves "stepping lightly across terrain to which [we are] not securely fastened" (Tilley & Taylor, 2013, p. 417). I read their comment, *"this would be meaningful for you as someone in social justice"* as implying this is not relevant for White folks. I am reminded of how, at times, "the work of White professors requires less 'proving' as they are already seen as legitimate in the eyes of individual students and the institution" (p. 417). I wondered how would they approach my colleagues differently? How would my colleagues respond? Emotions "are not peripheral by-products of events, but rather they are constitutive forces for (trans)forming individuals, social interactions, and power relations" (Chubbuck & Zembylas, 2008, p. 280). Emotions in the classroom are politicized and the "allocation of power is manifested in who gets to express and who must repress various emotions" (p. 280).

There are other emotions that surface too. For example, in the wake of George Floyd's murder, I received several emails from current and former White students looking for opportunities to expand their understanding of anti-racism practice. I always oblige but am aware of the toll it takes. I am also aware, however, that my voice as a racialized instructor affords some students permission and guidance on how to act. I have come to recognize that there are different types of emotions involved here – on the one hand there is resistance to my position/body/approach but also added demands and expectations placed there too.

Chubbuck and Zembylas (2008) used the term "critical emotional praxis" to "denote critical praxis informed by emotional resistance to unjust systems and practices in our pedagogies and our everyday lives" (p. 276) and position emotions in socially just teaching as "transformative" (p. 279). "Emotionality is frequently marginal to discussions of socially just teaching or at best is regarded as an effect rather than as a constitutive component in a teacher's actions and the implications of those actions. However, emotions do play, at best, a constitutive role in challenging the prevailing norms" (p. 275). Engaging with emotions in my practice, including being in tune with feelings about different perceptions of inequity, can contribute to rich and transformative educational discussions and practices.

5.1   *My Approach*

We never know who will resist or how students will respond. I begin by including the following "Educational Philosophy" on many of my course outlines:

> It is understood that, as every member of the class brings in different perspectives and experiences, we are all (students and instructor)

co-learners. Students are encouraged to think critically and apply academic knowledge to real-world examples, while reflecting upon their social locations and experiences. Students will be exposed to a range of diverse perspectives and are encouraged to reflect on the ways in which these perspectives compliment or contradict traditional educational perspectives and their own understandings.

One concern I continue to wrestle with is whether my commitment, focus and emotions might inadvertently shut down dialogue across differences. I am generally careful to keep an openness but recognize that at times creating safe space also means interrupting racism in the room. When that racism feels personal, those conversations are more difficult. "Since facilitators are not immune to being triggered, we need to recognize the comments and signals to which we are most susceptible" (Bell et al., 2016, p. 409). Critical social justice educators recommend that instructors, when triggered, can "pause, take a deep breath, and try to refocus our attention to the situation at hand" (p. 409). Other methods include using self-talk to shift our reactions and regain composure, as well as recognizing when we need to pause, take a break, and free-write before rejoining the larger group. Other strategies include using the moment to pose reflective and thoughtful questions to help the class process the situation. I personally find it helps to have a regular journaling process and a good support system among colleagues and critical friends. I am often fueled by my conversations with colleagues and when possible seek out semi-regular debriefing opportunities where we can support each other and gain different perspectives. I also find comfort and gain perspective by researching and writing about my practice. I read voraciously – taking in not only academic or teaching resources, but a range of social justice literature, novels, non-fiction, news, and social media. Knowing when to step back and reflect can also be a key survival strategy in this field.

The more I encourage openness and dialogue, the more I also risk being exposed to microaggressions, racist comments, or assumptions about my experience. I balance this risk by ensuring I always keep a structural focus on oppression and guide students back to the threshold concepts. When the course remains structured around theoretical principles of equity and critique, I am afforded more latitude that does not leave the discussion personal or personalized and thus easily dismissed. This work requires ongoing self-care, recognition, and awareness of how I am responding in the moment. Being overly taxed emotionally ultimately does not serve myself or students. I am in this for the long haul – this means taking note of the emotions and learning when I need to forge ahead and when I need to step back.

6 Supporting Racialized Students

> This teacher education program caters to white people. (Black teacher candidate)

I seek to employ strategies that help students combat hesitancy about addressing racism and other forms of oppression in schools. In the US and Canadian context, the majority of those who enter teacher education programs are White, monolingual, middle-class women (Picower, 2009; Sleeter, 2018). Given these demographics, teacher education programs often direct content to their White student base. Building on a CRT perspective, I ask how I keep the voices of racialized students central in my practice. How do I work within this White, neoliberal context and effectively help Black and racialized students address the racism they face in placements, life and inevitably in schools (James, 2021)?

I have written about the challenges racialized students can experience in classes where white students are struggling to understand their privilege. Various racialized students have "spoke[n] emotionally of how personally challenging it was during the course to 'sit back and listen' as their White classmates attempted (or not) to work through the theoretical concepts of racial identity and racial privilege" (Taylor & Tilley, 2013, p. 77; see also Taylor, 2021). In these contexts, White students often benefit from their racialized peers who become spokespeople for their race.

In a context where racialized students of color have traditionally been schooled through largely White ways of knowing, we must consider how we attend to and prepare teachers of color in university-based teacher education programs. Research finds that racialized teacher candidates can face added burdens including struggles to find support, overt and subliminal forms of racism, imposter syndrome, stereotype threat and "racial battle fatigue" (Cheruvu et al., 2015, p. 239).

Over the years, I have met with various racialized teacher candidates who come to my office to visit and to share their experiences in the program. In a recent group discussion, several racialized teacher candidates shared their views, aspirations, and teaching goals with me and with each other. They spoke passionately and with candor about their experiences navigating the pervasive Whiteness of the program and expressed concerns being among the few racialized teachers in their schools. I remember coming away from that discussion feeling energized:

> There was something dynamic about these conversations today. When was the last time I had a conversation about equity, teaching and identity

in a completely racialized space? This means something. I didn't realize how much I had been longing for it. Several TCs seemed to feel this too. Some have already emailed me to tell me that they valued that opportunity to share their views. Others are thanking me for creating the safe space. I am suddenly reminded of how that type of experience is rare in my role/work as an educator. I'm reminded again how my class is predominantly white, middle class, and straight. I am also reminded today of how the conversations in class never resemble the conversations I just had with these students. (Reflection, October 14, 2020)

For those teacher candidates of color who do enter teacher education programs, they can bring "layered experiences with marginality" and may "possess a unique and powerful capacity to reimagine boundaries strategically constructed by those in power" (Kohli, 2019, p. 25). For some, they bring a set of "knowledges and skills fostered through oppositional behavior that challenges inequality" (Yosso, 2005, p. 80). However, they enter into programs that are not only dominated by Whiteness, but where social justice education can also be directed to transforming the needs and consciousness of White students. Students share with me the reality that "despite efforts to diversify the teaching force" many can feel "silenced and marginalized in their professional training and, at times, pushed out of the profession" (Kohli, 2019, p. 25).

In these conversations, I always wonder if I am doing enough to support them. I must also take note of my privileged position and authority as a professor operating within a university structure. Do I unwittingly engage in practices that privilege White student interests despite my efforts to do otherwise? Such reflection, while unsettling, reflects "the invisible shackles of neoliberal education that I carried with me into the classroom" (Dutta et al., 2016, p. 350). These shackles include pressures to make my teaching relevant to all students in the class, create a comfortable and safe environment, including a pressure to "use more humor" and "make classes fun" (Dutta et al., 2016, p. 350).

I am also aware that my racialized experiences do not automatically align with my racialized students. "Rather, racialized students may view other racialized teachers as 'culturally suspect' (or inauthentic) and thus question their identities and performance in the classroom" (Tilley & Taylor, 2013, p. 10). I may never know how students might resist engaging in discussion or how they might respond to my perspectives. In the end, if we are to support future teachers of color professionally, culturally, emotionally and academically, then teacher educators must "be prepared in a space that actively seeks to name, interrogate, and disrupt this hegemony of Whiteness" (Cheruvu et al., 2015, p. 261).

6.1   My Approach

Building on a CRT perspective, I ask deep questions about how I keep the voices of racialized students central in my practice while upholding a critical dialogue and productive experience that will support all students to come into their consciousness. To do this, I include personal stories and counterstories (my own and those of racialized teachers and scholars) and try to create an environment where racialized students feel comfortable engaging on their own terms, not as racial spokespersons. Keeping a critical edge in the classroom helps me step in and protect the space in ways that ensure racialized students know they are seen and supported.

This practice has not always been easy and can come with consequences. For example, I recall three racialized students in a graduate education class informing me that a White student had been complaining to them and to other students about me as an instructor. She had told her classmates she wanted to file a formal complaint to the department chair because she thought I was being racist toward her. The racialized students came to me with this information because they were concerned about my well-being. They told me in no uncertain terms how much they valued my critical work in the classroom and said they appreciated my efforts to facilitate discussions and challenge problematic comments and microaggressions in a way that meant I was the one taking the heat in class. They told me this created better dialogue and subsequently promoted a safer space for them in the class. The White student never did, to my knowledge, file the complaint, but the experience reminded me of the important role teacher educators have in the classroom to ensure students are safe and engaged.

I devised the following list as a reminder of my role and purpose as a critical anti-racist educator. I refer to this list often, and add new points as relevant as I reflect on my teaching.

Keeping My Critical Edge – Some Reminders (Revised February 28, 2021)
– Address microaggressions and misunderstandings as they arise in the class. It is useful to do this by "calling in" students when possible, rather than "calling out."
– When I name my racial identity and include personal experiences openly in the class, I make myself vulnerable, but I also open the door for various students to come talk to me who might not otherwise.
– Do not assume all students in the class are new to the ideas you are introducing. There will be many racialized students who have not only lived, but

who have also studied, these issues already. But be mindful of the different starting points.
- Include material (readings/videos/supplemental resources) from racialized authors/scholars.
- Be as available and accessible as possible – both inside and outside of class. Remember that learning does not only happen during class-time.
- Be flexible in assignment options for all students and allow students opportunities to explore topics they are passionate about (e.g., racism).
- Remember the value of personal responses and reflections – they are spaces to critically examine one's experiences, but they are also opportunities for many racialized students to engage in dialogue with me one-on-one. Keep in mind that this may be the only place I get to communicate with some students.
- Develop a support system. Draw on your list of colleagues and critical friends from whom you can seek support.
- Encourage open conversations with students and check in on how they are doing in the class. In the past, these check-ins have led to rich and valuable conversations about the course that helped students appreciate why the course is structured in a particular way. It also helps me learn what might not be working and why.
- Create opportunities for students to provide anonymous feedback.
- Include examples of interrupting comments that are not just meant to support White students as they develop their skills in calling out racism. Ensure you are supporting racialized students and helping them develop strategies to address, combat and process the racism they may be experiencing.
- Keep equity literacy and structural concepts central.

7   Conclusion

Teaching for social justice demands flexibility, patience, critical reflexivity, and a willingness to adapt to shifting tensions in our classrooms. When engaging in critical and anti-racist teaching, how we negotiate teacher candidates' resistance to difficult knowledge, manage the inevitable emotional intensity that can arise, and meet the needs of racialized and other marginalized students in our classrooms requires understanding the power of epistemological and institutional racism. I hope this self-study offers insight into some of the tensions that can arise and the possible practices that can address them.

References

Adams, M., & Bell, L. (2016). *Teaching for diversity and social justice* (3rd ed.). Routledge.

Ahmed, S. (2004). *The cultural politics of emotion*. Routledge.

Ahmed, S. (2012). *On being included: Racism and diversity in institutional life*. Duke University Press.

Ahmed, S. (2017). *Living a feminist life*. Duke University Press.

Bell, L., Goodman, D., & Varghese, R. (2016). Critical self-knowledge for social justice educators. In M. Adams & L. Bell (Eds.), *Teaching for diversity and social justice* (3rd ed., pp. 397–418). Routledge.

Blake, F., & Ioanide, P. (2019). Antiracism incorporated. In R. Blake, P. Ioanide, & A. Reed (Eds.), *Antiracism Inc: Why the way we talk about racial justice matters* (pp. 17–40). Punctum Books.

Brown, E. (2004). The significance of race and social class for self-study and the professional knowledge base of teacher education. In J. J. Loughran, M. L. Hamilton, V. K. LaBoskey, & T. Russell (Eds.), *International handbook of self-study of teaching and teacher education practices* (pp. 517–574). Springer. https://doi.org/10.1007/978-1-4020-6545-3_14

Brown, K. (2013). Trouble on my mind: Toward a framework of humanizing critical sociocultural knowledge for teaching and teacher education. *Race, Ethnicity and Education, 16*(3), 316–338. https://doi.org/10.1080/13613324.2012.725039

Cheruvu, R., Souto-Manning, M., Lencl, T., & Chin-Calubaquib, M. (2015). Race, isolation and exclusion: What early childhood teacher educators need to know about the experiences of pre-service teachers of color. *Urban Review, 47*, 237–265.

Chubbuck, S., & Zembylas, M. (2008). The emotional ambivalence of socially just teaching: A case study of a novice urban schoolteacher. *American Educational Research Association, 45*(2), 274–318.

Cochrane-Smith, M., & Villegas, A. M. (2015). Framing teacher preparation research: An overview of the field. *Journal of Teacher Education, 66*(7). https://doi.org/20.10.1177/0022487114549072

Connelly, F. M., & Clandinin, D. J. (1990). Stories of experience and narrative inquiry. *Educational Researcher, 19*(5), 2–14.

Dinkelman, T. (2000). An inquiry into the development of critical reflection in secondary student teachers. *Teaching and Teacher Education, 16*, 195–222.

Dion, S. (2007). Disrupting molded images: Identities, responsibilities and relationships – teachers and Indigenous subject material. *Teaching Education, 18*(4), 329–342.

Dlamini, N. (2002). From the other side of the desk: Notes on teaching about race when racialized. *Race, Ethnicity and Education, 5*(1), 41–66.

Dutta, U., Shroll, T., Engelsen, J., Prickett, S., Hajjar, L., & Green, J. (2016). The 'messiness' of teaching/learning social (in)justice: Performing a pedagogy of discomfort. *Qualitative Inquiry, 22*(5), 345–352.

Giroux, H. A. (1983). *Theory and resistance in education: A pedagogy for the opposition*. Bergin & Garvey Publishers.

Gorski, P. (2009). Cognitive dissonance as a strategy in social justice teaching. *Multicultural Education, 7*(1), 54–57. Retrieved June 14, 2021, from https://files.eric.ed.gov/fulltext/EJ871366.pdf

Gorski, P., & Pothini, S. (2018). *Case studies on diversity and social justice education* (2nd ed.). Routledge.

Gorski, P., & Swalwell, K. (2015). Equity literacy for all. *Educational Leadership, 72*(6), 34–40.

Gorski, P., Zenkov, K., Osei-Kofi, N., & Sapp, J. (Eds.). (2013). *Cultivating social justice teachers: How teacher educators have helped students overcome cognitive bottlenecks and learn critical social justice concepts*. Stylus.

Hallander, M. (2019). On the verge of tears: The ambivalent spaces of emotions and testimonies. *Studies in Philosophy and Education, 38*, 467–480.

Han, K. (2013). 'These things do not ring true to me': Pre-service teacher dispositions to social justice literature in a remote state teacher education program. *The Urban Review, 45*(2), 143–166.

Hannon, L. (2020). Engaging my whole self in learning to teach for social justice: Where my loyalties lay. In J. Kitchen, A. Berry, S. M. Bullock, A. R. Crowe, M. Taylor, H. Gudjonsdottir, & L. Thomas (Eds.), *International handbook of self-study of teaching and teacher education practices* (2nd ed.). Springer.

Henry, F., Dua, E., James, C. E., Kobayashi, A., Li, P., Ramos, H., & Smith, M. (2017). *The equity myth: Racialization and Indigeneity at Canadian universities*. UBC Press.

Henry, F., & Tator, C. (Eds.). (2009). *Racism in the Canadian university: Demanding social justice, inclusion, and equity*. University of Toronto Press.

hooks, b. (1989). *Talking back: Thinking feminist, thinking Black*. South End Press.

James, C. (2012). Students "at risk": Stereotypes and the schooling of black boys. *Urban Education, 47*, 464–494.

James, C. (2021). *Colour matters: Essays on the experiences, education, and pursuits of black youth*. University of Toronto Press.

Kitchen, J., & Taylor, L. (2020). Preparing preservice teachers for social justice teaching: Designing and implementing effective interventions in teacher education. In C. Mullen (Ed.), *Handbook of social justice interventions in education*. Springer. https://doi.org/10.1007/978-3-030-29553-0_70-1

Kohli, R., Lin, Y., Ha, N., Jose, A., & Shini, C. (2019). A way of being: Women of color educators and their ongoing commitments to critical consciousness. *Teaching and Teacher Education, 82*, 24–32.

Ladson-Billings, G., & Tate, W., IV. (1995). Toward a critical race theory of education. *Teachers College Record, 97*(1), 47–68.

Lee, Y. A. (2011). What does teaching for social justice mean to teacher candidates? *The Professional Educator, 35*(2), 1–20.

Lipsitz, G. (2019). The logic of 'illogical' opposition: Tools and tactics for tough times. In R. Blake, P. Ioanide, & A. Reed (Eds.), *Antiracism Inc: Why the way we talk about racial justice matters*. Punctum Books.

Mahtani, M. (2014). *Mixed race amnesia: Resisting the romanticization of multiraciality*. UBC Press.

Maloney, T. (2017). Black teacher educator, White teacher interns: How I learned to bring my whole self to my work. In B. Picower & R. Kohli (Eds.), *Confronting racism in teacher education: Counternarratives of critical practice*. Routledge.

Marom, L. (2017). "We have to be really careful with what we say" Critical discourses across difference in pre-service teacher education. *Review of Education, Pedagogy, and Cultural Studies, 39*(2), 161–189.

McEvoy, J. (2020). Sales of 'White Fragility' – and other anti-racism books – jumped over 2000% after protests began. *Forbes*. Retrieved June 14, 2021, from https://www.forbes.com/sites/jemimamcevoy/2020/07/22/sales-of-white-fragility-and-other-anti-racism-books-jumped-over-2000-after-protests-began/?sh=68c2925d303d

Milner, R. (2007). Race, narrative inquiry and self-study in curriculum and teacher education. *Education and Urban Society, 39*(4), 584–609.

Milner, R. H., & Laughter, J. C. (2015). But good intentions are not enough: Preparing teachers to center race and poverty. *Urban Review, 47*(2), 341–363.

Ohito, E. (2019). Mapping women's knowledges of antiracist teaching in the United States: A feminist phenomenological study of three antiracist women teacher educators. *Teaching and Teacher Education, 86*, 1–11.

Picower, B. (2009). The unexamined Whiteness of teaching: How White teachers maintain and enact dominant racial ideologies. *Race Ethnicity and Education, 12*(2), 197–215. https://doi.org/10.1080/13613320902995475

Reed, A. (2019). Gentrifying disciplines: The institutional management of trauma and creative dissent. In R. Blake, P. Ioanide, & A. Reed (Eds.), *Antiracism Inc: Why the way we talk about racial justice matters* (pp.). Punctum Books.

Sanson, M., Strange, D., & Gary, M. (2019). Trigger Warners are trivially helpful at reducing negative affect, intrusive thoughts, and avoidance. *Clinical Psychological Science, 7*(4), 778–793.

Sensoy, O., & DiAngelo, R. (2017). *Is everyone really equal? An introduction to key concepts in social justice education* (2nd ed.). Teachers College Press.

Sleeter, C. E. (2018). Multicultural education past, present, and future: Struggles for dialog and power-sharing. *International Journal of Multicultural Education, 20*(1), 5–20.

Solorzano, D., & Yosso, T. (2001). From racial stereotyping and deficit discourse toward a critical race theory in teacher education. *Multicultural Education, 9*(1), 2–8.

Taylor, L. (2000). Black, White, beige, other? Memories of growing up different. In C. E. James (Ed.), *Experiencing difference* (pp. 59–70). Fernwood.

Taylor, L. (2017). Race, color and family: Exploring possibilities of school engagement. In C. Monroe (Ed.), *Race and colorism in education* (pp. 181–192). Routledge.

Taylor, L. (2021). 'I will treat all my students with respect': The limits to good intentions. In C. James (Ed.), *Colour matters: The experiences, education and aspirations of black youth*. University of Toronto Press.

Taylor, L., & Tilley, S. (2013). Happiness: At what cost? *Journal of the International Society for Teacher Education*, 17(1), 72–84.

Taylor, M., & Diamond, M. (2020). The role of self-study in teaching and teacher education for social justice. In J. Kitchen, A. Berry, S. M. Bullock, A. R. Crowe, M. Taylor, H. Gudjonsdottir, & L. Thomas (Eds.), *International handbook of self-study of teaching and teacher education* (2nd ed.). Springer. https://doi.org/10.1007/978-981-13-1710-1_16-1

Tilley, S., & Taylor, L. (2013). Understanding curriculum as lived: Teaching for social justice and equity goals. *Race, Ethnicity and Education*, 16(3), 406–429.

Umangay, U. (2019) Self-study of an indigenous settler in Ontario schooling: An exploration of living theory. In F. Villegas & J. Brady (Eds.), *Critical schooling* (pp. 269–298). Palgrave Macmillan. https://doi.org/10.1007/978-3-030-00716-4_12

Webb, T. (2001). Reflection and reflective teaching: Ways to improve pedagogy or ways to remain racist? *Race, Ethnicity and Education*, 4(3), 245–252.

Wing-Sue, D. (2010). *Microaggressions in everyday life: Race, gender, and sexual orientation*. Wiley.

Yosso, T. (2005). Whose culture has capital? A critical race theory discussion of community cultural wealth. *Race, Ethnicity and Education*, 8(1), 69–91.

Index

ability   29, 49, 81, 87, 208, 222
African storytelling   44, 46
anti-racism   6, 213–215, 226
apartheid   10, 44–53, 55–58
arts-based methods   12, 80, 85, 166, 169, 175

barriers that often hinder students' knowledge acquisition   79
Black   2, 9, 10, 12, 23, 24, 31, 34, 35, 45, 47–53, 55–58, 80, 85, 122–134, 136, 137, 139, 141, 142, 210, 212–214, 216, 218, 224, 228
Black culture   122, 123, 125–127, 131, 132, 136
Black music   12, 123, 125, 128, 141

caste   51
collaboration   1, 5, 11, 84, 94, 129, 130, 133, 135, 140, 142, 170–172, 176, 191
coolie   51
cooperative self-study   165
counterstory   211–213
counter-storytelling   12, 62, 63, 70, 213
critical
    dialogue   47, 170, 177, 230
    friend   10, 20, 23, 24, 38, 47, 85, 86, 91, 96, 148, 150, 161, 186, 191, 199, 201, 227, 231
    humility   8, 13, 20–24, 39
    multicultural teacher education   165, 167
    pedagogy   189
    race theory   10, 211, 213
    theory   216, 221
cultural artifacts   79, 80, 82, 85–87, 91, 93–97
culturally responsive assessment   64, 67, 70–72
curriculum   3, 12, 22, 27, 33–35, 39, 51, 53, 67, 79, 82, 84, 94, 114, 143, 153, 165, 186, 203, 211, 213, 218

decolonization of curriculum   84
deficit   11, 34, 62, 73, 109, 134, 169, 212
depersonalized history   227
dialogic space   165, 166, 168, 169
dialogue   12, 22, 26, 37, 46, 47, 54, 57, 85, 103, 106, 117, 146, 153, 165, 167, 168, 170, 176, 177, 181, 182, 195, 198, 203, 219, 221, 227, 230, 231

diversity   1–7, 9, 10, 12, 13, 17, 27, 28, 31–33, 39, 44, 46, 57, 58, 96, 107, 130, 160, 165–167, 170, 172, 186–189, 201, 203, 206, 214, 216

elementary   62, 68, 105, 147, 152, 186, 191
emotional intensity   215, 225, 231
English language learners   61–63, 65, 67–73
equity   1, 13, 16, 17, 19, 22, 26–28, 32, 33, 35, 39, 45, 70, 72, 165, 166, 171, 176, 178, 198, 200, 201, 206–208, 210, 219, 220, 222, 227, 228, 231
ethical   10, 24, 70, 85, 103, 114, 116, 117, 188, 201, 202, 206
evolving identities   46, 48

feminist   49, 224
funds of knowledge   145, 156–158, 160, 161

gay   21, 24, 25, 28, 29, 34, 36, 38, 39, 199
gender   3, 10, 11, 16, 17, 21, 24–26, 29, 31, 57, 113, 147, 151, 153, 176, 201, 210, 211
gender identity   210

heritage language   62, 65, 66, 69, 72
higher education   12, 49–53, 57, 71, 81, 84, 127, 214, 219, 224, 225
hip hop
    culture   122–125, 127, 128, 135–137, 140, 142
    literacy literature   124, 125, 132–142
    music   125, 127, 128, 130–137
homophobia   219

identity   8–12, 16, 17, 19, 21, 24, 25, 28–30, 39, 44, 46, 48, 50–59, 65, 103, 104, 106, 111, 124, 129, 130, 141, 145, 146, 149, 160, 177, 179–181, 196, 197, 199, 210, 213, 221, 228, 230
immigrant educator   145, 146, 150, 161
immigrant mother   145, 146, 150, 161
immigration   188, 189, 198, 200, 207
inclusion   1, 161, 171
inclusive education   152, 178

Indigenous
  education   10, 25, 103–106, 108, 110, 113, 114, 116, 117
  games   79, 80, 83, 85, 89, 91, 93–97
integration   79, 81–83, 86, 93, 125, 127, 130, 139
intersectionality   9, 11, 221

LGBTQ (lesbian, gay, trans, queer)   30, 31
literacy   9, 12, 63–65, 73, 122–125, 128, 131–143, 156, 172, 179, 222, 231

metaphor   12, 27, 145–150, 152, 157, 160, 161
methodology   1, 19, 62–64, 80, 84, 105, 147, 166, 186, 190, 198
Métis   103, 104, 106–108, 112
minoritized   8, 10, 16, 17, 20, 22–24, 26, 27, 30, 31, 34, 36, 201, 219
multi-cultural education   7, 8, 11, 12, 165, 166, 169–178, 181, 182, 186, 187
multiculturalism   10, 174, 186, 188–191, 193, 194, 198, 202–205, 214, 216

narrative   12, 19, 46–48, 109, 115, 117, 124, 142, 145–149, 152, 160, 198, 201, 208, 212, 213, 215, 219

pedagogy   3, 10–12, 21, 27, 32, 34, 35, 38, 62, 63, 67, 79–83, 93, 96, 97, 110, 114, 124, 127, 135, 138, 147, 153, 166, 189, 190, 199, 200, 204, 210–214, 219, 220, 223, 226
People of Color   9, 32, 112, 212
personal history   49
playful pedagogy   11, 12, 79–81, 83, 93, 97
politicizing the university   50
portraiture   109, 192
positionality   8, 18–22, 26, 28, 29, 32, 33, 38, 50, 186, 190–192, 198–200, 202, 205–208, 214, 221, 222
post-apartheid   10, 44, 45, 47, 50, 56–58
power   7, 12, 16, 25, 27, 30, 31, 33, 34, 36, 68, 109, 126, 127, 131, 132, 149, 177–179, 182, 190, 200, 207, 211, 215, 216–218, 226, 229, 231
preschool   11, 12, 65, 66, 73, 145–147, 150–154, 157–161, 172
privilege   1, 6, 8, 9, 16–22, 24, 26–34, 38, 39, 177, 181, 195, 198, 199, 210, 211, 213, 217, 220, 228, 229

race   6, 7, 10, 11, 19, 21, 22, 25, 29, 45, 46, 48–50, 57, 115, 171, 192, 196, 197, 211–213, 215, 216, 221, 224, 228
racialized   5, 9, 10, 13, 23, 38, 186, 187, 190, 191, 197–199, 205, 207, 211–217, 221, 226, 228–231
racialized positionality   186, 190–192
racialized students   9, 214, 215, 221, 228–231
racism   6, 7, 10, 24, 31, 47, 49, 58, 109, 112, 113, 117, 186, 210–219, 221, 223–225, 227, 228, 231
reconciliation   8, 10, 44, 45, 79, 81, 82, 104, 116, 218
reflective dialogue   54, 57, 148
resistance   10, 16, 17, 21, 22, 27, 29, 112, 113, 194, 195, 206, 211–213, 215, 216, 218–220, 226, 231

secondary   16, 17, 153, 187, 202, 208
self-study (S-STEP)   1–5, 8, 9, 11–13, 19, 24, 46, 47, 55, 58, 62–64, 71–73, 79, 80, 84–86, 96, 97, 103–106, 114, 116, 117, 122, 124, 125, 129, 141, 142, 145–149, 152, 155, 156, 160, 161, 165–167, 171, 173–175, 178, 182, 186, 188, 190, 191, 198, 207, 211–215, 231
sex   6, 7, 31, 34, 212, 213, 219
sexual   17, 27, 111, 219
slavery   6, 11, 123
social justice   1–4, 6–13, 16, 17, 19–22, 24, 26–29, 32, 33, 37–39, 45, 72, 73, 79, 84, 94, 96, 97, 103, 106, 178, 186–188, 191, 194, 195, 200, 201, 203, 205, 210, 211, 214–220, 222–227, 229, 231
social justice education   22, 210, 224, 229
sociocultural   79, 81, 83, 89, 93, 94, 96, 97, 172, 179, 215
socioeconomic   19, 80
storywork   12, 44, 46
systemic racism   24, 109, 112, 113, 117, 216

teacher education   1–5, 8, 11, 12, 17–20, 22, 24, 25, 27, 32–34, 38, 39, 45, 52, 53, 58, 62, 63, 70, 71, 73, 79, 81, 82, 97, 103–105, 116, 117, 132, 142, 147, 165–174, 178, 181, 182, 191, 206, 210–215, 220, 221, 225, 228, 229

teacher educator   5, 8, 10, 11, 16–25, 28, 32, 33, 38, 44–47, 49, 50, 53–59, 61–64, 70–73, 79–82, 84, 85, 94, 103, 105, 165–169, 173–176, 180, 182, 198, 199, 210–213, 215, 224, 226, 229, 230
transnational teacher educator   61–64, 70–73
truth and reconciliation   10, 44, 104

Ubuntu   84, 94, 96

vulnerability   10, 24, 29, 38, 39, 64, 70–73, 196

White privilege   6, 16, 18, 19, 30, 195, 198, 211, 229
Whiteness   217, 224, 228, 229